Justice
in the
Back Room

Justice in the Back Room

by

Selwyn Raab

The World Publishing Company
Cleveland and New York

Published by The World Publishing Company
2231 West 110th Street, Cleveland, Ohio 44102

Published simultaneously in Canada by
Nelson, Foster & Scott Ltd.

First Printing 1967

Library of Congress Catalog Card Number: 67–20806

Printed in the United States of America

Acknowledgments

My sincerest thanks to Joseph Alvarez and Lester Carson, of the defunct New York *World-Telegram and The Sun,* who copiously devoted their time, energy, and skills to the interests of justice; to Manon Tingue, Grace Shaw, Gerald Gottlieb, and Shirley Fisher, for their editorial advice and acumen; to Tom Collins and Edward Edelson, for their reportorial suggestions; to Sylvan Davis, for his technical help; and to Guenther Reinhardt, for his invaluable investigative assistance.

To Helene
for her inspiration and tolerance

Contents

Justice
in the
Back Room

It is far pleasanter to sit comfortably
in the shade rubbing pepper into a poor devil's eyes
than to go about in the sun hunting up evidence.
—The authors of the 1872 India Evidence Act.

1. *The First Victims*

The victims were Janice Wylie and Emily Hoffert. On the pleasant summer day of August 28, 1963, they were murdered in their apartment on Manhattan's fashionable East Side.

In a corner of a bedroom, wedged between a bed and a wall, their bodies lay tangled together, their faces frozen in final grimaces of agony. They were bound in death by bloodied strips of bedsheets and bedspreads which had been twisted around their bodies. Both young women were coated with their own blood, both had been stabbed repeatedly. Janice Wylie died nude, plastic curlers dangling incongruously from her blonde hair. She had been disemboweled. Her body also bore marks of sexual abuse: Noxzema had been smeared over the pubic area. Emily Hoffert met

1

death fully clothed. Her throat was sliced from ear to ear. The apparent murder tools were near by: two broken kitchen knives lay on a blood-soaked floor, and a third weapon, a carving knife, was on the washbasin in the bathroom across the foyer from the bedroom.

The savagery of the crime horrified even normally impervious police officers. Signs of violence were everywhere in the bedroom. Blood, skin, and intestines bespattered the white sheet of the bed, the beige walls behind the bed, and a white window shade a few feet above the corpses. Fragments of glass from broken soft drink bottles shone against the bloodied floor like imitation diamonds. The second bed in the room was piled with clothing, suitcases, wire hangers, and boxes, all apparently flung from a closet and a bureau. One detective, not the flinching type, turned pale after examining the mutilated bodies. "This is the bloodiest mess I have ever seen," he whispered to a colleague as he hurried out of the room.

The police would consider any double murder of women an important case. Yet there were additional reasons to put the Wylie-Hoffert slayings in a special category. Both Janice Wylie and Emily Hoffert came from fairly prominent families. Janice's father, Max Wylie, was a writer and advertising executive, and her uncle was the author Philip Wylie. Emily Hoffert's father, a surgeon, and her mother were influential figures in Minneapolis society. Janice, who was twenty-one, worked as a researcher at *Newsweek* magazine, but dreamed of a career as an actress. Twenty-three-year-old Emily Hoffert had an impressive academic record, and was about to start her first teaching job. Neither of the women could be described as an ordinary working girl. More important, the murders carried the trademark of an insane killer, a madman who had slipped into a well-guarded apartment building on a posh street off Park Avenue. Widespread publicity and a wave of public fear immediately combined to generate immense pressure on the police for a quick solution.

On the night of August 28, the police began by scrutinizing the apartment for possible clues and questioning the friends, neighbors, and immediate relatives of the victims. Patricia Tolles, the third roommate in the $208-a-month apartment, had arrived home early that Wednesday evening to find the apartment in disarray. After seeing a knife and blood-streaked strips of bedsheet in a bathroom, she was too frightened to inspect the rest of the apartment by herself. Instead, she got help by telephoning Janice Wylie's parents, who lived near by. Max Wylie was the first to enter the bedroom.

Before the night was over, the police knew they had a major crime confronting them, a mystery they wanted to solve swiftly. The city's Chief of Detectives was assigned to the inquiry, along with some of the best investigators on the police force. Within hours, they had put in motion the largest manhunt in New York City's history, a manhunt that would produce repercussions for years to come.

2. *The Court and Confessions*

Three years after Janice Wylie and Emily Hoffert were slain a decision would be shaped—in another city, on another summery day—that would cast a critical retrospective light on police conduct in the case. On August 28, 1963, no one could foresee the strange course the investigation would take, or the overwhelming significance confessions would have in the search for the killer.

By 1966, police methods of obtaining confessions had become the most thorny issue of law enforcement in the United States. Until that time, the police were virtually unhindered in their tactics for securing confessions. Except for being barred from beating a confession out of a prisoner, or from "unduly" delaying a court appearance where a suspect would be

5

apprised of his rights, most police interrogators suffered no serious restrictions. On June 13, 1966, however, a Supreme Court ruling in Washington sent forth a legal thunderbolt that rattled the rafters in every police station in the country. By a five-to-four margin, the Court laid down revolutionary guidelines for establishing the legality of confessions.

In four simultaneous decisions, commonly known as the Miranda Ruling, the justices specified that confessions would be considered admissible courtroom evidence only if a defendant had first been informed of his constitutional rights. Before any questions could be asked, a suspect had to be informed of his right to remain silent, told that anything he said might be used as evidence against him, and advised of his privilege to consult counsel, even if the police had to obtain a lawyer for him. One more safeguard was added to insure that a confession was given voluntarily and without coercion. The Court stressed that if a suspect confessed after all of these warnings, and his lawyer was not present, then the prosecution must bear the full burden of proving that the defendant had "knowingly and intelligently" waived his constitutional guarantees against self-incrimination.

The justices were, in effect, revising the contemporary legal code. They were well aware of the historical use and misuse of the confession. They knew that an area was set aside in every station house for questioning purposes, an area described by the police as the "interrogation room" but dubbed the "squeal room" by suspects and the "back room" by most criminal lawyers. This room had a history much older than the Constitution of the United States.

In another era, the interrogation room contained unmistakable signs of its purpose. Usually it was a sunless, entombed compartment with iron manacles hanging from stone walls and a rack or wheel waiting for employment. By the 1960's, the room had changed its appearance; it now had institutional green walls, a desk, several chairs, and perhaps a window.

The torture chamber of the Middle Ages and the twentieth-century interrogation room in a United States police station bore no resemblance to each other, but their purposes were the same—to obtain confessions of guilt. A confession was just as important in 1966 to a detective as it had been centuries before to a king's minister, and changes in technique had not diminished the value of incriminating words from the mouth of a suspect. Throughout history, the confession has been a major instrument in judicial proceedings, cherished by authorities in absolute monarchies, modern dictatorships, and democracies. A confession helped to ignite the pyre at the execution of Joan of Arc, while her questioners stood by

Pawle, Kathleen
—— We in Captivity

congratulating themselves for ridding France of a dangerous heretic. A confession justified severing the head of the Earl of Essex, an errant courtier of Elizabeth I. Confessions were used to send victims of the Spanish Inquisition to their deaths. And a confession was put forth as the invincible point by the Soviet State in each of the major Moscow treason trials of the 1930's, when courtroom denunciations were devised to strengthen Stalin's political position. Invariably, the confession—whether a signed document or an oral admission—has been displayed as the most useful single piece of evidence any prosecutor or judge could produce, a talisman capable of magically dispelling any public doubts about the guilt of the accused, and also of eradicating any private misgivings held by the authorities responsible for arrest and punishment.

The problem of confessions in a free society has troubled the United States from almost the first year of its existence. At the close of the eighteenth century, when the Constitution was being cast as the foundation of our government, the rack and the screw were still handy instruments for maintaining order and suppressing dissent in the Western world. Repugnance at tyrannical police powers undoubtedly influenced the framers of the Constitution to include two provisions regarding confessions. With the memory of persecutions of British sympathizers at the end of the Revolutionary War still fresh in their minds, they erected a barrier against extortion of treason admissions by the Federal government. Article III of the Constitution specifically defines treason, and then it rules out the use of involuntary confessions in such trials by declaring: "No person shall be convicted of treason unless on the testimony of two witnesses to the same overt act, or on confession in open court." Two years later, in 1791, when the first ten amendments (The Bill of Rights) were adopted, the privilege against self-incrimination was included for all criminal trials through a clause in the Fifth Amendment: ". . . nor shall [any person] be compelled in any criminal case to be a witness against himself."

For two centuries, however, these fourteen words generated more confusion than agreement. The legal minds that shaped the Constitution were devising protective clauses for a generally rural society that had no vast police forces and that relied basically on local constabularies to investigate crimes and apprehend criminals. They could not foresee the rise of big cities in the late nineteenth and early twentieth centuries, the development of large police forces, and the widespread use of the confession in criminal proceedings. By the 1960's, the confession had evolved into the most effective device for solving crime in the United States. Although no exact data were available, prosecutors in major cities like Los

Angeles, Chicago, New York, Boston, Detroit, and Philadelphia estimated that sixty to eighty per cent of the major crimes in these cities were solved substantially through confessions, not through testimony from witnesses or through the discovery of material evidence. To buttress the indispensability of confessions in American justice, the police and prosecutors could cite two centuries of Supreme Court rulings that upheld, for the most part, the use of confessions as long as there was no evidence of coercion. Until 1966, the major Court decisions stated, in effect: A defendant has the right to remain silent at his trial and not take the witness stand, but it is not incumbent upon the police to inform him of his right to remain silent or his right of counsel at the time of his arrest or during interrogation, and whatever he may say during this period of questioning can be used as courtroom evidence against him.

The 1966 Miranda Ruling was an order for an immediate change in interrogation practices. It was not retroactive. The Court ruled that only trials beginning after June 13, 1966, would be affected by the decision. The Wylie-Hoffert case, which had already altered interrogation-room activities in New York City and indirectly influenced the Miranda Ruling, was therefore outside the scope of the ruling—even though the double murder had been solved not once but twice by confessions.

3. *"I Want to Report a Double Murder"*

Murder or homicide is a commonplace statistic to the New York City Police Department. With mathematical certainty, police officials can anticipate more than six hundred murders every year. But a murderer's chances of escaping are slim. Ninety per cent of all homicide cases in the city are solved, and usually in less than two weeks. On a statistical basis, finding a murderer is easier for the police than finding a burglar or a holdup man. Whereas clues may be difficult to gather in most crimes, in murder cases the evidence seems to be self-collecting, and the police have devised routine but effective measures for uncovering it. After most murders, some solid clue will appear: a weapon, a fingerprint, an article of clothing, an eye-

9

witness, a motive. Usually, a sign will turn up to lead the police toward a suspect.

On Thursday, August 29, 1963, the day after the Wylie-Hoffert murders, the police had no reason to believe this crime would be different. The hub of the search was a half-mile from the murder scene, in the squad room or offices of the 23rd Precinct detective bureau. The precinct house on East 104th Street was in the middle of an East Harlem slum neighborhood, but its patrol boundaries covered a fringe of the East Side's expensive "Gold Coast," including 57 East 88th Street, the Wylie-Hoffert apartment building. The second-floor squad room in East Harlem therefore became headquarters for detectives assigned to track down the Wylie-Hoffert killer.

Before the day was over, these detectives had assembled a sizable dossier. One of their first tasks was to interview relatives and friends of Janice Wylie and Emily Hoffert, to dig into the backgrounds of the women, to find out how they had become roommates, and to determine where they had been and what they had done on Wednesday, August 28.

Because it was Wednesday, a work day, the three young women in apartment 3C awoke before nine o'clock. Two of them were in a hurry to begin the day. Twenty-three-year-old Patricia Tolles had less than an hour for a hasty breakfast and a trip downtown to her job. Emily Hoffert also had a busy day ahead of her; she was moving out of the apartment, and she had promised to return a friend's car she had borrowed for transferring luggage.

The only one of the three women with time for leisure on that cool morning was Janice Wylie. Originally, it was to have been an important day for her. She had arranged to participate in the first civil rights march in Washington, but she had canceled her plans because of last-minute urgings from her father. As an English teacher in India during the early 1930's, Max Wylie had seen mass meetings turn into ugly riots. Remembering those Indian incidents, Wylie had pleaded with his daughter to avoid the risk of getting trapped in a potentially violent demonstration. Finally, on Tuesday, his argument had prevailed. Janice changed her mind about traveling to Washington and assured her father she would remain in New York on Wednesday.

About nine o'clock that morning, Janice received a telephone call from *Newsweek* magazine, where she worked as a researcher. A co-worker asked if she would like to revise her schedule for the day and report to work at

11:00 A.M. instead of her assigned hour of 10:00 A.M. Janice complied with the last-minute change, and presumably she returned to bed.

Although three women were living in the five-room apartment, it retained a masculine atmosphere from its former occupants. The women had been there for only three weeks, and they had not found the time to redecorate. The two bedrooms held little furniture other than beds and bureaus. The closets were jammed with luggage and unpacked boxes of clothing. The living room, with a green sofa, two upholstered chairs, several small tables, two television sets, and a beige area-rug, resembled a modest theater lobby. Three weeks earlier, the apartment had been turned over to Patricia Tolles by her brother, Theodore, who had been sharing it with other young lawyers. A large apartment in a fashionable section of Manhattan's East Side was too valuable a prize not to pass on to a relative or friend. Besides having a prestige address between Park Avenue and Madison Avenue, it had two bathrooms. And, more important for single women, the flat was in a "luxury" neighborhood, generally considered to be a low-crime area. To provide security against intruders, a doorman and an operator for the service or freight elevator were on duty in the ten-story building during most of the day.

A skein of school ties had brought the three women together. Janice Wylie and Patricia Tolles knew each other through their fathers, who had been classmates at Hamilton College in upstate New York. The girls had agreed to share the apartment with a third roommate, who was temporarily in California. Meanwhile Emily Hoffert, Patricia's former roommate at Smith College, had been invited to stay in apartment 3C until her own apartment on Park Avenue became available at the end of August. Of the three, only Janice Wylie was familiar with that part of the East Side. She had grown up in the neighborhood, and her parents lived two blocks away on East 86th Street. Patricia was from upstate New York, and Emily, who was getting ready for her first grade-school teaching job, came from Minneapolis.

Janice and Patricia envisioned the apartment as more than a utilitarian place to sleep, eat, and store belongings. It was to provide an adventure for them, granting them independence from family chaperons and giving them a place to hold their own parties and dinners. Coming from financially secure families, and having allowances from home, the girls would hardly find the rent burdensome. The apartment was of special importance to Janice Wylie, a blonde girl who, though not overwhelmingly pretty, had a hoydenish charm. Through amateur theatricals she had acquired an assortment of show-business and café-society friends. Now, for the first time in her life, she could invite these interesting people to a home of her own.

Together that morning, Emily and Patricia had light breakfasts of sliced oranges and coffee in the tiny narrow kitchen. Before finishing her breakfast, Patricia took care of the refuse chore by placing a pail of garbage in the hallway outside the kitchen door. Because there was no incinerator in the building, a porter disposed of the tenants' trash twice a day. As she removed the pail from the kitchen, Patricia made a mental note about returning to the grocer's for deposit money a six-pack carton of empty soft-drink bottles which was on the floor. Stepping back into the kitchen, the tall, attractive girl closed the door on its automatic snap lock and then manually bolted a second lock on the door.

Emily had dressed before breakfast in the bedroom she used by herself. She was wearing a print blouse, a dark green skirt, and sandals, and she also wore eyeglasses. Quickly finishing her breakfast, she told Patricia she was driving to The Bronx on an errand, but might meet her for lunch at 1:00 P.M. in Manhattan. With a cheerful good-bye, Emily left the apartment through the front door.

Ten minutes after Emily had departed, Patricia completed dressing in the bedroom she and Janice were sharing. She put on a gay rose-colored summer dress with gold buttons and a plaid cummerbund. Before leaving, she noticed that Janice was sleeping in the nude under a sheet. A few days earlier, Janice had suffered a mild sunburn, and she felt more comfortable without night clothes. At 9:30 A.M., Patricia went out the front entrance, locking the door from the outside with her latchkey.

On that last Wednesday in August, Patricia Tolles remained downtown all day at her job in the Time-Life Building, where she worked as a researcher in the book division. That same morning, after leaving the apartment, Emily Hoffert entered a white Dodge parked near 88th Street and drove ten miles to the Riverdale section of The Bronx. The Dodge belonged to Mrs. Ann Belle Rosenberg, the sister of the friend Emily was soon going to share an apartment with. Emily owned a small Italian Fiat, and she had borrowed the larger car to move her belongings. At 10:00 A.M., the doorbell rang in the Rosenbergs' Riverdale apartment. Mrs. Rosenberg, a housewife in her mid-twenties, was friendly with Emily and was delighted to see her. The two women sat down to coffee, and Mrs. Rosenberg invited Emily to spend the day with her. Emily was too busy to remain in The Bronx; she had too many tasks waiting for her in Manhattan that afternoon. But after picking up her Fiat, which was parked near the Rosenbergs' apartment, she did stay long enough to chauffeur Mrs. Rosenberg and her infant daughter on a brief shopping trip, driving them to a Bronx bank and then back to the apartment building. Before saying good-bye, Mrs. Rosenberg repeated her invitation to spend the day in The Bronx. Again Emily declined good-naturedly. Mrs. Rosenberg and her daughter alighted from the car, and Emily, with a smile, drove off. The time was 10:45 A.M.

The long summer twilight was vanishing from the city streets when Patricia Tolles returned home. She walked slightly faster than usual toward the red-brick building on 88th Street because of an undercurrent of concern about Janice. During the afternoon Janice's mother, uncertain where Janice was spending the day, had telephoned Patricia at her office. *Newsweek* magazine had called Mrs. Wylie to inquire about Janice's failure to report to work as scheduled. Mrs. Wylie had telephoned her daughter's apartment but no one answered. Patricia told Mrs. Wylie she had no idea where Janice might be, and both women assumed she had suddenly switched plans and gone to Washington for the Freedom March. Now Patricia was anxious to reach home to see if Janice was there, or if she had left an explanatory note.

About fifteen minutes before seven o'clock, Patricia entered the building and rode the self-service passenger elevator two stories to her landing. As soon as she opened the front door of the apartment with her key, she sensed that something was wrong. In the entrance foyer, a closet door was open and a woman's tan coat lay on the floor. To get to the bathroom, Patricia had to pass through the dinette. As she did so, she glanced to the left and saw that the kitchen door leading to the service stairway, which as a rule was kept closed, was ajar about two feet. In the rear of the apartment, toward the two bedrooms, the hallway lights were on. She walked past the almost-closed door of Emily Hoffert's bedroom, and opened the door of the bedroom she and Janice shared.

The room was a shambles. Dresser drawers were pulled out, clothing was strewn over the beds and floors. Her immediate thought was of a burglary. When she turned from the bedroom to a bathroom on the opposite side of the hallway, her fear became more ominous. She saw a knife glinting on the rim of the washbasin and strips of blood-splotched sheets on the floor.

Remembering the open kitchen door, Patricia retraced her steps through the apartment to the kitchen. She opened the rear door, walked onto the service stairway, and peered down the concrete stairwell. Nothing seemed out of order here. Closing the kitchen door behind her, she went to

the living room and, without any further search of the apartment, telephoned Janice's parents. The Wylies were within minutes of leaving their
apartment for dinner when Patricia's call came through. Max Wylie
thought the young woman's voice sounded strained as she rushed out her
words:

"I wanted to speak to you so as not to alarm Mrs. Wylie, but our
apartment has been entered. It's in terrible disorder. Some thief or prowler
has torn up our room. It's in an indescribable mess."

In a few sentences Wylie did his best to calm Patricia and advised her
to call the police. Before hanging up he promised he and his wife would
hurry over.

Patricia next called the local police precinct and nervously told a desk
officer: "My apartment is a mess and there's a knife in the bathroom." The
police officer took the address and said a patrol car would be dispatched.

Feeling uneasy in the apartment, Patricia took the elevator downstairs.
In the lobby, she asked one of the building employees: "Have you seen my
blonde friend today?" He shook his head. Still reluctant to return to the
apartment, she walked out to the street and looked east and west for Janice,
Emily, or the Wylies. Finally, she returned to the silent apartment and
waited for somebody to come.

Almost running, Max and Isobel Wylie covered the two blocks between
their apartment and their daughter's in minutes. Relieved that she was no
longer alone, Patricia tried to contain her fear as she showed the Wylies the
disarray in her bedroom and the huge knife in the bathroom. Wylie, who
could see bloodstains on the knife handle, took command. Without mentioning the blood to the women, he ordered them into the living room so
that he could search the other bedroom, Emily's room. Fearful of smudging
possible fingerprints on the doorknob, he pushed open the door of the room
with his foot. It was dark inside, but he could see that this bedroom also
had the appearance of having been ransacked, with drawers askew,
clothing scattered about, and luggage heaped in disorder on the twin bed
nearer the door.

Inside, Wylie noticed that the bed farther from the door was smeared
with blood. Peering between the beds, he saw nothing. Then, moving
around the foot of the bed nearer the window, he discovered what he had
been dreading intuitively. On the floor, between the bed and a window,
were Janice and another woman. Leaning over, Wylie saw that the women
had been hideously slashed. His daughter's stomach was ripped open.
Having met Emily Hoffert only once, Wylie could not be sure she was the
clothed victim lying beside his daughter. He tried to keep a clear head,

knowing it was important not to destroy any possible clues before the police arrived, but he also wanted to spare his wife the sight. He picked up a blue blanket lying at the feet of the dead women and gently covered them.

"Sit down," he said to his wife and Patricia in the living room. "Both girls are dead. They have been murdered."

Retaining control of himself, he went to the telephone, dialed the police, and said: "I want to report a double murder."

As the police pieced together the events of that day, the macabre coincidences preceding the murders were obvious. Max and Isobel Wylie were aware of them. They had permitted their daughter to leave home only because she was moving a mere two blocks away, close enough for parental protection. They had tried to watch over Janice by keeping her away from the civil rights march. Washington would be dangerous that day, the Wylies thought; New York would be safe. A few days before the murder, Janice had optimistically reassured a girl friend who lived alone in a nearby building: "Don't worry. This is a very safe neighborhood. Nothing ever happens here." And perhaps Janice Wylie would have escaped death that day if not for a last-minute change in her work schedule.

Unmistakable ironies were also apparent to Emily Hoffert's relatives and friends. They knew apartment 3C had been a transient arrangement for her, a temporary stopover until she settled into her own apartment. Most of her suitcases were already out of the apartment. The next day she would have been living elsewhere. These were the first ironies of the Wylie-Hoffert case; more were to come.

4. *The Manhunt*

By the third day of the investigation, police officials and detectives were working round the clock to close in on the Wylie-Hoffert killer. The first days of a murder inquiry can be decisive. Time offers a growing margin of safety for the killer; every hour provides him with more time to dispose of incriminating evidence, or to get farther away from the scene. In the first two days, detectives had compiled a thick file about the killer's methods and, possibly, his motive from the autopsies, medical reports, photographs of every corner of the apartment, fingerprint tests, interviews with people who knew the victims, and their own observations.

At the start, the police leaned toward the assumption that the murderer was a sex pervert. Although autopsy reports indicated neither of the women had been raped, clues pointed to sexual aberrations. The pubic area and rectum of Janice Wylie's body had been daubed with a skin ointment apparently taken from a jar of Noxzema found near her feet. The peculiar position of the bodies and the manner in which they had been tied together gave further hints of perversion. The killer had linked the women by winding strips of bedding around their waists and forearms. The bodies seemed to have been purposely placed on their sides, almost face to face.

The autopsy reports catalogued in technical medical terms the savagery all too visible to the detectives who had seen the dead women. Both bodies had so many gashes it was impossible for the medical examiners to make a precise count. Janice Wylie had been slashed at least four times in the abdominal region, seven times in the heart, once in the lung, and once in the right side of the neck. There was no way of determining which wound had been fatal. Under "cause of death," the medical examiner listed: "Stab wounds of chest, neck, heart, abdomen." At least nine separate wounds were visible on Emily Hoffert's body, and her cause of death was described as "multiple stab wounds of the neck, trachea and jugular vein."

The many knife wounds intimated that the murderer was a sex maniac. He had not stabbed once or twice with any professional cunning. Instead, he had slashed the trussed bodies so viciously—as though in an insane rage—that two kitchen knives, with eight-inch and nine-inch blades, had snapped.

The autopsies produced two surprises. Janice Wylie had suffered a fractured skull from a blow on the left side of the head and had probably been unconscious at the time of death. And there were numerous stab wounds on Emily Hoffert's hands, palms, and wrists, as if she had raised her hands in self-defense or had tried to resist the killer as he came at her with knife or bottle. This was the only indication that either of the victims had fought for her life.

Finally, the autopsies provided police with the approximate time of the murders—noon.

Coordinating the information in the autopsy reports with the facts they had obtained from interviews and observations, the police reconstructed the events in apartment 3C. Their first premise was that Janice Wylie was alone when the murderer appeared. After getting into the apartment, the killer picked up one or two empty soft-drink bottles from the carton on the kitchen floor which Patricia Tolles had intended to return to the grocer's. One of these bottles was used to knock out Janice. Fragments from the bottle had been found on the floor near the bodies and on the bloodsoaked bed. The murderer must have been alone with Janice long enough to tie her up, because it was doubtful that an unarmed assailant would have been able to overcome and bind the two women simultaneously.

A double-edged razor blade found at the feet of the bodies indicated the method the murderer used to cut the sheets into thin strips for tying up the women. The blade probably came from a dispenser package the police discovered in a dresser in the bedroom.

There was no way to determine exactly when Emily Hoffert had returned. She left the apartment before 9:30 A.M., drove to Riverdale, returned Mrs. Rosenberg's car, picked up her own, and motored back to Manhattan. Some time between 11:15 and 11:30, she must have entered the front door of apartment 3C. Her sudden appearance undoubtedly surprised the murderer, but apparently he managed to grab another soft-drink bottle, club her over the head, drag her into her bedroom, and drop her alongside Janice. The same type of bedsheet strips as those used to tie Janice were used to bind Emily's wrists and feet.

The police assumed that both women had been stabbed while lying defenseless on the bed near the window. The bed was covered with blood, and the wall, floor, and window shade alongside were splashed with blood. No other bloodstains were visible in the apartment. Possibly the oddest detail was the way the murderer had placed the bleeding bodies on the floor afterward, as though meticulously arranging a stage set.

A disconnected electric clock-radio found on a table near the bodies offered no real clue. The cord was looped around Emily's throat and mouth. The clock had stopped at 10:37, but that was not necessarily the time of either of the murders. Janice might have been slain then, but the police knew Emily Hoffert had been in The Bronx with Mrs. Rosenberg at that exact time. The killer might have altered the position of the clock hands in an attempt to mislead the police. Or the clock might have been disconnected at 10:37 the night before, as part of Emily Hoffert's preparations for moving out of the apartment.

The police theorists saw the murderer as a burglar who went berserk; a man who knew one of the girls, probably Janice; or a homosexual woman.

Five factors supported the burglar-killer theory. The ransacked condition of the bedrooms showed that the murderer had been searching for something. The open kitchen door indicated that his escape route from the building had been through the rear service stairway—the type of pathway familiar to all apartment house thieves. A crumpled coat found on the floor of the foyer and the empty hanger by its side suggested that the murderer might have taken a topcoat left in the apartment by one of the former male tenants; unprepared for violence, the killer might have had to find a garment at the last minute to cover his bloodstained clothing. The fact that four physicians had offices on the ground floor of the building, with patients entering and leaving all day, simplified a thief's problem of walking in and out of the lobby unchallenged. Finally, since Patricia Tolles identified the murder weapons as kitchen knives from the apartment, the murders seemingly were unpremeditated; an intruder bent on murder would not depend upon conveniently finding a knife in the apartment.

Nevertheless, the police had misgivings about the burglar hypothesis. If discovered, most burglars run; few, even narcotics addicts, resort to brutality. The violence here had been of such a frenzied nature that it seemed to stem from a personal hatred of one of the women. And, though both bedrooms appeared to have been ransacked, a search by Patricia Tolles found nothing of any value missing; her jewelry had been left untouched in a bureau drawer of her bedroom. One vague sign pointed—possibly—to theft. On the bureau in the murder bedroom the police found the black handbag Emily Hoffert had carried that day. It was unclasped and empty of cash, although her identification papers, library card, and auto registration were in it. At best, the absence of money provided thin circumstantial evidence that any money that might have been in the bag had been stolen by a killer whose original purpose in the apartment was burglary.

The most puzzling knot to unravel in the burglar theory was the way in which he could have slipped unseen during daylight into the building and the apartment. Besides the doorman and two building employees on duty from 7:00 A.M. to 4:00 P.M., the building had built-in obstacles for thieves. There was no way of climbing onto the tenth-story roof from an adjoining building. Inside, two service stairways were the only footroutes connecting the upper floors with the lobby. The lobby doors to both stairways locked automatically and could not be opened from the lobby side except with keys given to building employees. Two elevators, the manually operated freight elevator used by a porter to collect garbage and the self-service passenger elevator, ran from the top floor to the basement.

A burglar could have entered the building only two ways: through the lobby on East 88th Street or through a separate basement passageway twenty feet from the main entrance. The burglar-killer would have needed extremely good luck to enter the building undetected by either method. The doorman assigned to the lobby entrance from 7:00 A.M. to 4:00 P.M. rarely left his post unattended, and then only for a few moments. The killer could have walked into the lobby during one of those brief periods but, once he was inside, his troubles would not then be over. The chances were remote, if not impossible, that the service-stairway doors would have been left open. The remaining, and the most practical, way upstairs was via the self-service elevator, but the killer could have been seen waiting for it by the returning doorman, two other building employees, or a tenant.

The second way into the building was through the basement. Here, too, a burglar would have required a measure of fortune or inside knowledge of the building to succeed. He would have had to know the layout of the passageway and the location of either the self-service or freight elevator, the only two means of getting upstairs. In the basement, the killer would have exposed himself to a meeting with the building custodian, whose apartment was in the basement, or with the two other employees who frequently went there. These were the minimum difficulties a burglar would have encountered just getting into the building.

The next puzzle was the way a burglar managed to enter the Wylie-Hoffert apartment. Since no fire escape led to the apartment or any of its windows, the only possible method of entry was through the front door, where a new lock had been installed when the women moved in, or the rear kitchen door. The police could find no evidence of picked locks or of the doors having been forced.

With all these doubts, the police could not positively accept the burglar-killer theory.

The second theory depicted the killer as someone who knew at least one of the victims—most likely Janice Wylie—who had unsuspectingly allowed him to walk in through the front door. He might even have had a key to the apartment. Once inside, being familiar with the layout of the apartment, he knew just where to find the knives. He was either preparing to kill, or had just killed, Janice when Emily returned to become the second victim. The ransacking of the bedrooms was a clumsy attempt to convince the police that a burglar was responsible for the double murder.

If this second theory was correct, the police might be after a woman. The apparent homosexual signs—the ointment on Janice Wylie's body and the almost ritualistic manner in which the bodies were tied together and laid side-to-side—compelled detectives to consider the Lesbian-killer theory. It was a farfetched surmise, however, because neither of the victims was known to have had any Lesbian friends, and the physical strength required to break the knives is rarely possessed by a woman.

Questioning of tenants and employees in the Wylie-Hoffert building during the first two days of the investigation had failed to produce a wisp of a clue. No one had been aware of any suspicious person; no one had heard screams or sounds of struggle. Chief of Detectives Lawrence J. Mc-

Kearney, Assistant Chief Inspector Joseph L. Coyle, and Captain Frank E. Weldon, the officers planning the manhunt strategy, ordered new steps taken. A door-to-door survey was devised in which anyone possibly having information about the crime was sought out. Fifty detectives were sent to interview all of Janice's and Emily's relatives, friends, and co-workers in the city, and to question hundreds of other persons who might have information. It would be the task of the detectives to search the neighborhood for possible witnesses: tenants and employees of other buildings, delivery boys, bus drivers, shopkeepers. No one was to be ignored. A doorman might have spotted a loiterer. A bus- or taxi-driver might have picked up a passenger with a bloodstained shirt. A bartender might recall a significant remark made by a customer. A delivery boy might have made a mental note of someone acting strangely. And anyone dressed in a raincoat or topcoat in order to hide telltale bloodstains might have appeared conspicuous to one of the hundreds of passers-by on 88th Street during that mild afternoon, when the temperature was about eighty degrees.

One other routine but important procedure was ordered. Detectives attached to the 23rd Precinct began sifting through files for known sex criminals or burglars whose M.O. (*modus operandi*) was similar in any way to that of the Wylie-Hoffert murderer. They were to be picked up for questioning.

Assistant Chief Inspector Coyle, as supervisor of all detectives in the north of Manhattan, was in day-to-day control of the investigation. His next in command was Captain Weldon, who was in charge of the detective district that encompassed the 23rd Precinct. With the survey and the search of the rogues'-gallery files under way, the commanding officers were confident they would soon have clues and their man.

5. *To Some, an Obsession*

A basic belief held by most high-ranking officials of the New York City police force is that all tough cases can eventually be solved if sufficient manpower is committed. Despite the publicity given to scientific criminology, the men who ran New York's Police Department in 1963 had been taught by their elders, and had learned through their own experience, to rely on legwork and tips. In the Wylie-Hoffert case, this approach was adopted fully.

The fifty detectives originally assigned to the case were a large number for even an important inquiry. When after one week they seemed stymied, police headquarters doubled the detective staff to one hundred, bringing in homicide-squad experts from other precincts in the city. This was the

23

largest contingent to work full-time on a single case in the history of New York. Even the most ordinary tasks of the investigation were carried out with unusual thoroughness and intensity. But nothing the police did, whether it was accepted or unorthodox procedure, brought them closer to a solution. And they tried every conceivable method of investigation.

Through hundreds of interviews, the police compiled comprehensive biographies of Janice Wylie and Emily Hoffert, in the hope that somewhere in their backgrounds there would be a reason for murder.

In Emily Hoffert's past, not a single person could be found who had the slightest motive for harming her. The daughter of a successful Minneapolis surgeon, she had been reared in the Midwest, coming East in 1958 to attend college. After graduation from Smith College in Northampton, Massachusetts, she earned a master's degree in English at Tufts University, near Boston, in the spring of 1963. Emily had spent July—the month before the murders—with her family in Minneapolis, returning to New York in early August to prepare for her first elementary-school teaching job, in Valley Stream, Long Island. The police profile of Emily Hoffert showed a quiet, bookish, unpretentious young woman, a woman who had dated little and was well acquainted with perhaps twenty-five people in New York City.

Janice Wylie's history gave police innumerable avenues to explore. Having lived most of her life in Manhattan, Janice knew hundreds of people in New York. Her address book was crammed with the names of men and women in the city and suburbs. Most of her schooling had been in New York, in the same neighborhood where she had lived and died. She had attended the exclusive Nightingale-Bamford School for Girls on 92nd Street and Fifth Avenue. In her late teens she began thinking of a stage career, and her hopes had led her to a year of acting school and to a few seasons in summer stock companies before she decided to take a researcher's job. While at *Newsweek,* she still talked vaguely of another try at the theater, and she had retained her show-business friends.

Among the hundreds of DD5's or detective's reports on Assistant Chief Inspector Coyle's desk, one could be labeled important. Janice's relatives and co-workers said she had received threatening and obscene telephone calls shortly before the murders, including one ten days before she was killed. The calls apparently had all been from the same man. Once he had said: "Your father will get it. Your father hasn't got long to go." Janice reported the threats to the police but, with thousands of women getting such anonymous crank messages, the police merely gave her standard advice to try to arrange a date with the caller if he bothered her again. The

CHAPTER FIVE • 25

police would try to trap him if he agreed to a rendezvous. Nothing more was done about the complaint. The caller, who identified himself as "Joe Hunter," would not be lured into a meeting with Janice. The police believed that the name "Joe Hunter" was fictitious, but nevertheless they searched their files for that name and for known telephone "Peeping Toms."

The mysterious "Joe Hunter" seemed to have roots at *Newsweek* magazine. He telephoned Janice there, and at least one other researcher had received obscene telephone calls at work. Although they knew their chances of locating any telephone "Peeping Tom" were slim, the police gave "Joe Hunter" special attention. The other researcher was asked to try to arrange a date with her caller if he bothered her again. All precincts were ordered to pick up every known telephone "Peeping Tom" for questioning, and to prepare elaborate traps for any nuisance caller willing to come into the open.

After the original inspection of the Wylie-Hoffert apartment, no further clues were found there, although every piece of furniture, every corner, every inch of the apartment was examined and re-examined by technicians and fingerprint experts. The crews found bloodstains only in Emily Hoffert's room. The search for fingerprints was equally disappointing. The bloodstained handles of the two knives with broken blades were found on a radiator cover near the bodies. The third knife lay intact on a bathroom washbasin, where the killer obviously had washed it. There were no fingerprints on any of the knives. In the kitchen, the fingerprint crews removed three sets of prints from a whisky bottle; in the murder bedroom, a print was spotted on the inside of a bureau drawer.

Fingerprints are not so easy to trace as the public generally believes. A print is easily matched only if the police have the right suspect for comparison; otherwise, the task is almost impossible. There is no mechanical system to pluck out a corresponding print from the five million on file in police headquarters. Fingerprint experts must compare the suspicious print with every category of prints on file, one at a time. Because it would have taken years to examine the active file thoroughly, fingerprint specialists were ordered to concentrate on the prints of forty thousand known sex criminals and burglars in the city. This category alone would take months to explore, but it seemed to be the most logical place to start looking.

The major investigative disappointment came from the fruitlessness of the house-to-house, apartment-to-apartment survey of the neighborhood. Detectives questioned more than a hundred persons without turning up a fresh clue. At least two other techniques remained to be used, and they were put into operation. All detectives on the East Side were told to seek out their underworld contacts. If the murderer was a burglar or a narcotics addict, he might have asked an underworld relative or friend for help, bragged about the crime to a colleague, or made some slip that aroused suspicion. Informants had been given an unusual incentive in this case: *Newsweek* magazine was offering a $10,000 reward for the capture of the killer.

The second new technique involved the establishment of a special telephone number at the 23rd Precinct, for the public to use in secretly giving information. Many persons fearful of direct confrontation with the police will contact them when assured of anonymity. Everyone involved in the manhunt could forecast that most of the callers would be crackpots; yet, out of a thousand messages, one useful piece of information might be supplied.

When no solid suspects were found, the standard survey was gradually widened to include more than one thousand people, ranging from influential magazine executives to petty thieves. Hundreds of known sex criminals, burglars, and narcotics addicts found themselves in the 23rd Precinct, answering questions about how and where they had spent August 28. Every suspect arrested in other New York murder cases involving women was carefully interrogated about the Wylie-Hoffert slayings.

Scores of persons who had worked with Janice Wylie at *Newsweek* magazine were questioned just as minutely as known criminals, but more politely and not in the restrictive atmosphere of a police station. Thirty-eight executives of the magazine, most of whom had never met Janice, were sought out by the police. They had been at a party in a German restaurant which Janice had also attended the night before she was killed. Each of them was asked to account for his movements on the day of the murders.

The survey was re-examined and double-checked for oversights and slips. A second round of questioning was ordered for all employees, former employees, and the thirty-seven tenants of the Wylie-Hoffert apartment building.

Everyone listed in Janice's address book was visited by a detective. Particular attention was given to three men she knew, whom Max Wylie believed had violent tendencies. As tactfully as possible, the same questions were asked them: Where were you on August 28? Do you know anyone who might have had a reason to harm Janice?

Telephone tipsters provided the police with more than one hundred possible suspects. A landlord on the West Side was suspicious of a roomer who had acted strangely on the day of the murders. A young woman remembered that a boy friend had boasted of knowing inside details of the crime. A woman on 95th Street said her next-door neighbor once threatened her with a knife. Each of the reports had to be investigated, even if the caller sounded incoherent or naive. Through discreet inquiries, detectives were usually able to discredit the telephone tips without embarrassing innocent persons by questioning them; most of these innocent persons never knew they had been cited as potential suspects in one of the city's most sensational murder mysteries.

The police had expected that the information supplied by outsiders would be valueless. But in this case the steps they took on their own initiative proved as unrewarding as the leads volunteered by the public. Every tangible clue the police discovered turned out to be misleading. When the search through the fingerprint files of burglars and sex criminals failed to unveil the murderer, the fingerprint experts were faced with the mammoth task of a card-by-card search of five million prints.

The search for "Joe Hunter" was as frustrating as every other phase of the inquiry. A snare was prepared for one telephone "Peeping Tom" who seemed to have a direct relationship to the Wylie-Hoffert case. A week after the double murder, Cynthia Cramer, the twenty-year-old daughter of the president of the P. Lorillard Tobacco Company, began receiving obscene calls at her family's Sutton Place apartment. Miss Cramer worked in the same advertising agency as Max Wylie, and she lived only a mile from the Wylie-Hoffert apartment. Working with private investigators employed by the Cramers, detectives captured their man three days after his first call. A woman investigator posed as Miss Cramer on the telephone and enticed the caller into a street meeting on elegant Sutton Place, where he was seized by six waiting detectives. After a thorough questioning, this "Peeping Tom"— a New Jersey truck driver with three children—was cleared of any implication in the Wylie-Hoffert case.

The first months after the murders were difficult times for other telephone "Peeping Toms." At least a dozen of them were arrested as police assiduously carried out their orders to trap any who could be brought into the open. Eventually, they were all absolved of involvement in the Wylie-Hoffert murders.

Another false trail led to Cambridge, Massachusetts. Tracing Emily Hoffert's movements in the months before the murders, a detective with a prodigious memory noted that she had been living in Cambridge in May 1963, when a woman was murdered there. Checking further, he discovered that the murder had been committed a few blocks from where Emily lived while she attended classes at Tufts University, and that there were similarities between the Cambridge and East 88th Street murders. In both cases the murderer had tied up his victims and stabbed them repeatedly but had not raped them. This led police to speculate for the first time that Emily Hoffert might have been the main target of the murderer. Could she have known the murderer in Cambridge? Could he have followed her to New York? Or was the Cambridge incident one of the endless coincidences that plagued police working on the case? Detectives sought the answers for weeks during talks with Emily's parents and friends. But except for Emily Hoffert's proximity to the murder in Cambridge, no other link between the crimes could be found.

One month after the murders on 88th Street, a former New York City policeman briefly became the chief suspect. During questioning after his arrest for having sent obscene letters to a Manhattan secretary, the ex-cop made oblique remarks about the Wylie-Hoffert case. The police then spent two days convincing themselves he had had no part in the murders.

In October, when the investigation seemed to be bogged down, it suddenly veered in another direction—toward the notorious Boston Strangler. A Boston police official belatedly remembered that a woman identifying herself as Janice Wylie had once telephoned the Boston Police Commissioner's office, asking for information about the ten Boston strangulation murders believed to have been committed by the same man. The call had been made three days before the murders in New York. The woman claimed she was interested in writing a story about the Boston Strangler for *Newsweek* magazine. *Newsweek* editors, however, said Janice had never been authorized to inquire into the Boston Strangler case or to make the telephone call. Since Janice's job at the magazine was to clip and file reference materials, not to report or write, the question of what had prompted her inquiry created another theory about the murders. Detectives pondered the possibility that Janice thought she knew the identity of the Boston Strangler, and the person she suspected had killed her and Emily Hoffert. Because the Strangler's methods were completely different from the New York murderer's, the police doubted that the Boston killer had any connection with the Wylie-Hoffert murders. They wanted to determine why Janice made the call, and if she had feared anyone. Again, their efforts were in vain. After two weeks of inquiries, they pigeonholed the incident as one more oddity in the case.

Almost every week, the investigation turned down another pathway, toward another suspect. At one point Scotland Yard was called in, when the police became suspicious of a free-lance British writer who had shown up at the apartment with other newspapermen on the night of the murders. The trenchant questions he asked about the case aroused the curiosity of a detective, who politely asked the writer to describe his own movements that day. When the police got around to verifying his alibi, they discovered that his story of being at a diplomatic party was untrue; and what was even more suspicious was that he had returned to London shortly after the murders. After a few days of transatlantic telephone calls, the confusion was cleared up and the writer's alibi established beyond doubt.

For one day, a twenty-two-year-old Bronx stock clerk found himself being questioned by the city's best detectives about the murders. The clerk had got into trouble by threatening to harm a girl unless she went out with him. When the police arrested the youth, they found a razor blade in his jacket pocket. The stock clerk remained a prime suspect until his alibi was corroborated.

During September, October, November, and December, the investigation dragged on and twisted through a thousand lives. In a city where, on the average, three murders occur every two days, news editors rarely get agitated by a murder story. But the Wylie-Hoffert murder story was exceptional. It immediately landed in the category of "sensational" news. In police and press slang, the murder of Janice Wylie and Emily Hoffert had "class," a combination of intrigue and glamour which, for editors, elevates a handful of murder stories above the ordinary horror of violent death. There was no doubt at any of the seven daily newspapers then in existence in New York, or at the city's ten major television and radio news departments, that this was a big story that required extraordinary coverage.

Probably the main reason the Wylie-Hoffert case evoked widespread interest was that the murders threatened a chic, almost adventurous, way of life in New York for thousands of young women who are either strangers in the city or who are living away from their parents. New York is a magnet each year for a multitude of young women. They are students at the colleges and universities, actresses, artists, unmarried women seeking better jobs or romance. How many of them could feel safe after the murder of Janice Wylie and Emily Hoffert?

There were other factors, too, that the police knew would contribute to public concern about the case: A double murder is rare, and it creates the apprehension that a mass murderer or a psychopathic killer is loose; a sexual motif existed in this murder of two young, attractive women, one of whom was found nude; both women had above-average backgrounds, coming from prominent, financially well-off families; and the murder occurred in a well-guarded building in a "luxury" neighborhood, thereby igniting fears that no place in the city was safe.

When the details of the murders were announced several hours after the bodies were discovered, most newspapers hauled out their largest headlines for the story. Even the New York *Times*, which rarely stresses crime news, gave the murders page-one prominence. The television and radio stations not only featured the story on their regular news programs but frequently interrupted broadcasts for bulletins. Crime reporters and headline writers quickly labeled the affair "The Career Girl Murders," an epithet the case never shook off.

The double murder had clearly frightened New Yorkers, especially women, more than any crime in decades. Locksmiths in the vicinity of the Wylie-Hoffert apartment were deluged with orders for new apartment-door locks. AIR OF FEAR GRIPS SEDATE EAST SIDE, announced one headline in the New York *Times*. And the fear was not confined to one neighborhood. Police in all five boroughs reported an inordinate number of requests for advice on protecting apartments and homes from intruders.

In the first two weeks after the murders, the telephone switchboard at police headquarters in Manhattan was almost overwhelmed by the hundreds of calls daily from frightened women. Two additional extensions, with policewomen answering the telephones twenty-four hours a day, had to be established to deal with the emergency. Policewomen were assigned to answer the calls on the theory that alarmed women callers would be more reassured by a woman's voice than a man's. The policewomen were on telephone duty to receive possible information about the Wylie-Hoffert case as well as to convince the callers that the police were available and were capable of protecting them.

A policewoman who answered hundreds of calls during the first month of the investigation observed a remarkable similarity in many of the calls. Women would state simply: "I don't have anything to report. I live alone, and I just wanted to talk to someone about this case."

Neither the press nor the public wanted to forget about the murders. During the first hectic days of the investigation, page-one stories constantly seeped out of police headquarters or the 23rd Precinct. When the "hard," or actual, news slackened the newspapers presented speculative stories, such as VIOLENCE AND BRUTALITY . . . WHY SO "AMERICAN"?, or SLAIN GIRL'S FATHER: "FORGETTING IS HARD." The newspapers did not manufacture the news, however; there was no need. Information flowed constantly from police officials or persons affected by the crime. Chief of Detectives McKearney frequently summed up the police position by cautioning that the killer was "not normal" and asking for public help in capturing him.

At Janice Wylie's funeral her uncle, Philip Wylie, expressed his horror and indignation. He urged Janice's parents to speak out "because if there is any helpful value to be gained from this atrocity it will come through the means of reporters and editors and television and communications." And, he added, it was the responsibility of the press "to make people angry, to show that we don't like what happened and that we are going to try to prevent this thing from happening again."

A warning came from Janice Wylie's father, who predicted the "killer will repeat" his murders. In addition, Max Wylie announced he was writing a book, *Career Girl, Watch Your Step*, which would advise single women living in large cities about protecting themselves.

Persistent pressure from the press and the public undoubtedly forced the police to treat the Wylie-Hoffert case differently from a less-publicized murder. The mystery was one of the biggest ever to baffle the New York City Police Department, and there was never a routine phase to its investigation. Even after seven months of dogged work had failed, twenty-five detectives were still assigned to the search. All they could do was re-examine the thousand reports already filed, question everyone arrested for murdering a woman or for a sex crime—and hope for a surprise development.

A police lieutenant who was familiar with all the segments of the investigation explained the unique pressure:

"No one got called into the Commissioner's office, no one got an ultimatum, no one ever told you this is a hot case that we have to break. But, just the same, you know this is one job they're watching downtown [police headquarters]. You also know that City Hall is watching, the newspapers are breathing down your back, and everybody in the city is waiting for something to happen, and they expect the police to make it happen.

"I don't think I ever saw so many cops try so hard to solve a case as this one. Not only was the prestige of the department on the line, but anyone who came up with the right guy knew he was going to have a promotion waiting for him. The public doesn't care if you work a month or two months to get someone for a job they never heard about, but everybody knew about the Wylie-Hoffert case. You can't let this one ride and hope for the best. You've got to keep at it every day, checking out every ex-con who has the right M.O. You've got to keep tabs on arrests all over the country. This is one guy you can't let slip away. After a few weeks, it becomes an obsession."

The police were not alone in their vigil. In March of 1964, seven months after the murders, the New York *Herald Tribune* published a thousand-word story: OUR CITY'S NUMBER ONE UNSOLVED MURDER: WHO KILLED THE CAREER GIRLS? No one had to remind the police. They had no suspects or new clues, but the possibility still existed that the killer would make a mistake, and all three thousand detectives in the city were waiting for that slip.

6. *Post Sixteen*

One place the Wylie-Hoffert investigation never meandered toward was a slum section of Brooklyn called Brownsville. Almost in the center of Brooklyn, ten miles from Manhattan's East 88th Street, Brownsville seemingly had no connection with either of the victims. There was no reason for any detective to believe a clue to the crime might be hidden somewhere in that drab neighborhood. Yet a peculiar axis was being welded to join the Wylie-Hoffert case with Brownsville. The unexpected was about to happen: the mystery was going to be solved in Brownsville.

The policemen, detectives, and prosecution officials personally involved in ending the first manhunt testified at a half-dozen trials and court hearings. Their words are now immutable parts of the courtroom record,

33

and through this combined testimony one version of the original arrest and confession of the killer unfolds. In this official police account, the end of the search began just after midnight of April 22, 1964, eight months after the double murder.

In the first minutes of Thursday, April 23, Patrolman Frank C. Isola began walking his beat in Brownsville. Twenty-seven years old, five feet nine inches tall, Isola presented the ideal public-relations image of a young, vigilant police officer. He had had three years' experience as a cop, most of it in Brownsville. His midnight-to-8:00 A.M. shift was an unenviable one. He had Post 16, a patrol through some of the most crime-troubled streets in the city.

Armed with a .38-caliber service revolver, the standard weapon for New York patrolmen, and with a lead-tipped night stick, Isola walked warily across the scarred sidewalks and past the endless rows of garbage cans lined up outside apartment buildings. He knew routine was an important part of any foot patrol. A small mistake could be fatal for a patrolman on a solitary beat in a tough neighborhood; whatever he was assigned to do, Isola did thoroughly. He dutifully tried the doors of every tiny store to make sure none of them had been forced open. Just as diligently, he scrutinized every hallway and alleyway he passed.

The weather was unpleasant. A steady downpour had stopped shortly before midnight, but a mist drove a winter chill through Isola's blue woolen uniform and black slicker raincoat. The streets were silent, almost bare of people and automobiles. The few passers-by Isola encountered scampered home, anxious for warmth and safety. It was the kind of night on which a patrolman was certain to see more stray cats than people.

At 1:10 A.M., Isola stopped in front of Junior High School 263, on Sutter Avenue, and used a green police telephone callbox to talk to the 73rd Precinct, his home base. It was Isola's second report to the station house desk that night, and again he had no news to pass on. All was quiet on Post 16. Once more Isola began trudging past the tenements, now blurred in mist.

He was fifty feet beyond the callbox when a loud scream, clearly a woman's cry, stopped him. Scanning the streets, he saw a man and a woman, about seventy-five feet away, vanish into an alleyway on Bristol Street. As the couple entered the alley, he noticed that the man had an arm around the woman's shoulders, as if embracing her. Isola did not run toward the alley. An occasional nighttime scream or shout arising from an argument in the street or inside a tenement was not unusual, and Isola had become conditioned to remaining calm in such circumstances. He walked slowly toward the alley, not certain that the scream had come from that direction. The alley descended five feet below street level between two buildings. As Isola reached the first step leading down into the alley, he aimed his flashlight into the darkness.

As soon as the light clicked on, a woman began shrieking. Isola saw her backed against a wall, about fifteen feet away from him, with a man facing her, holding a pocketbook in his hands. The man gasped: "Oh, my God," and staggered away from the beam of the flashlight. Unholstering his gun, Isola shouted the customary "Stop, or I'll shoot!" By the time the warning echoed off the stone walls, the man had bolted out of the alley through a side door leading to the vestibule of an apartment building. The patrolman brushed past the woman. Inside the hallway, he got off one shot as the fleeing man ran out the front door into the street. The bullet shattered a glass door. In the street, Isola saw the man pull farther and farther ahead of him. When Isola fell a hundred feet behind, he fired three times. His quarry faltered once, almost stumbling onto the pavement, and Isola thought a bullet had found its target. But the man righted himself, swerved into Amboy Street, and had disappeared by the time Isola reached the intersection.

The brief chase had covered three blocks. Using his flashlight, Isola probed the sidewalks for bloodspots that might lead him to the man's hiding place. He saw none. The 73rd Precinct, alerted by telephone calls from residents, had sent two prowl cars to Isola's aid. With the help of two other officers, Isola inspected all the hallways, but they found no clue.

Still not knowing why the man had fled, Isola returned to the alley. On the sidewalk in front of the buildings where the pursuit had begun, a dozen Puerto Rican tenants, many in their night clothes, were chattering excitedly in Spanish and English. They told Isola that the woman in the alley, Mrs. Elba Borrero, lived in the building, and that she had been helped upstairs to her apartment by her husband and neighbors. He found her in the third-floor apartment where she lived with her husband and six-week-old daughter. She was a short, stout, twenty-year-old practical nurse from Puerto Rico. Despite the nervous rush of her words and her slight Spanish accent, Isola quickly learned what had happened. She had been on her way home from work in a downtown Brooklyn hospital when a man grabbed her from behind as she approached the building. It was then that she let out the scream that had alerted Isola.

"He put something sharp against my throat and said he would kill me if I screamed," she continued. After seizing her by the throat, the attacker had wrenched away her pocketbook and forced her into the alley. Pressing her against a wall, he fumbled with her clothing and whispered that he intended to rape her. In desperation, she screamed again, and at that moment Isola turned on his flashlight.

Mrs. Borrero was positive the assailant was a light-skinned Negro with pockmarks or pimples on his face. She believed he was about five feet seven or eight, weighing between one hundred fifty and one hundred sixty-five pounds. He was wearing a three-quarter-length tan coat and a green hat. Listening to her, Isola made a mental note that the man he had chased was hatless.

After the attack, Mrs. Borrero's husband, Juan, and several neighbors had rushed downstairs. Mr. Borrero found his wife sitting in front of the building, crying and screaming. After taking her to their apartment, he borrowed a flashlight from a neighbor to search for her pocketbook and eyeglasses, which had fallen off when she struggled with the attacker. He found everything in the alley.

Mrs. Borrero had torn off a button from her assailant's coat as he pulled away in panic. She had also snatched a mechanical pencil from his hand. Isola took the button, which he considered a potential clue. He left the pencil with Mrs. Borrero.

Except for an understandable spasm of nerves, Mrs. Borrero was unhurt. After getting all the information he could from the victim and her neighbors, but without recording any of these interviews in his memorandum pad, Isola left the building. A patrol car gave him a lift to the precinct house, where he reported orally to his desk officer and to Detective John Grace, who was on night duty in the detective bureau at the precinct. He also gave Grace the button Mrs. Borrero had obtained. There was no need for Isola to write a report on the incident; he could relay his information to a "124 man," a patrolman assigned to clerical duties, who would type out a summary on a UF 61, an official report of the crime. Isola's only other obligation was to write an abbreviated version of the incident in his memorandum pad. He returned to his beat at 1:45 A.M. Thirty minutes had elapsed since the moment he heard the first scream.

At 2:42 A.M. the first teletype alarm about the case was sent out by the 73rd Precinct to the eighty other precincts in the city. It read: "Unknown-Male-Negro. Arrest for Attempted Grand Larceny. Pocketbook Snatch. Male, Negro 20–25. 5–9. 165 pounds, ¾ tan coat. No further description. May have a gunshot wound." There was no reference to attempted rape, or any mention that the assailant was pockmarked and wore a green hat.

The UF 61 report typed out that morning also omitted any reference to attempted rape. It read: "Complainant reports that she was approached by a male Negro, 20 to 25 years, 5 foot 9 inches, 163 pounds, who attempted to take her pocketbook at time and place of occurrence. Patrolman Isola, No. 5385, arrived on scene and pursued the perpetrator into the building and fired one shot at him, the perpetrator fled on foot on Sutter Avenue and Patrolman fired three other shots at the perpetrator, who fled north on Amboy St. and was not apprehended. Sgt. Cates, No 209, searched the area and found no damage to persons or property in the area except the door in hallway." Under the column "Crimes if Any," the UF 61 report specified: "Attempted Grand Larceny."

At the precinct, none of the officers was overly concerned about the attack, and no other steps were taken that morning. Police experts considered the 73rd a "combat precinct," a station house that had to contend with a high rate of crime and a steady flow of trouble. For minor crimes, the overworked detectives found it difficult to do more than file a report and issue the standard teletype alarm. In police jargon, the thwarted rape and purse-snatching was a "two-bit squawk," a relatively unimportant complaint similar to thousands received daily in the city.

Isola's beat was quiet again, and at 3:30 A.M. he was glad to take an hour off for a meal. At 6:00 A.M., as he was making his final rounds, daylight began cracking through the overcast skies. Isola decided to make another search for clues in the Borrero attack. He hurried to the block on Amboy Street where the chase had ended, and he examined the sour-smelling hallways for bloodstains. Again, his search was in vain. He resumed his foot patrol. At 7:00 A.M., with an hour of his tour left, Isola was at Sutter and Hopkinson Avenues, a major intersection two blocks from the scene of the attack. As he walked past the Oasis Launderette he noticed a young Negro standing in the doorway, apparently seeking shelter from the morning cold. Isola was certain he had seen him standing in the same spot an hour earlier. Suspicious, he approached him and asked:

"What are you doing here?"

"I'm waiting for my brother to go to work with him," replied the youth.

The laundry seemed a curious place to meet, and Isola asked for identification. The youth said he lived two blocks away, on Amboy Street, and showed the officer letters addressed to him. Then he offered Isola an unexpected piece of information.

"I know why you're asking me all these questions," he said. "I saw the cops chasing a man down Sutter Avenue and they were shooting at him and he went into a building on Amboy Street."

Isola was surprised and interested. Without any hesitation, the youth said he had been walking home from his girl friend's apartment when he heard shots. Seconds later, a man ran up to him and pleaded for help.

"I told him there was nothing I could do for him and he ran away, into a building on Amboy Street."

The patrolman believed he had a possible witness to the incident involving Mrs. Borrero. Uncertain about what to do, he had the youth walk with him to a nearby callbox, where he telephoned the 73rd Precinct and requested that a sergeant be sent to the laundry to question a possible witness in the Borrero matter. Isola and the youth then chatted casually for the five minutes it took a patrol car to reach them. Isola noted mentally that the young Negro was dressed in a tan coat and a green hat.

When the sergeant arrived, the youth repeated his story. The two policemen took a cursory look inside the vestibule of the Amboy Street building. Finding no bloodstains, they walked back to the police car with the young Negro. Outside the laundry, three other Negroes had arrived, and one said he was the older brother of the youth. Neither Isola nor the sergeant detained them when they walked away. Isola did scribble in his memorandum pad the youth's name and "Schoenberg Salt Company," where he had said he worked. The name Isola jotted down was "George Whitman." The sergeant drove off in the car, and Isola headed for a nearby school, where he spent the final half-hour of his duty directing traffic.

At 8:00 A.M., his tour completed, Isola returned to the 73rd Precinct. He told Detective Grace about his conversation with the young Negro. Grace took the youth's name and the other information, but saw no reason for Isola to work overtime. The day-shift detectives at the precinct could question the Negro youth again if it were necessary. Isola washed up and left the station house.

That day, April 23, none of the city's daily newspapers carried a line about the early-morning chase and shots in Brownsville. Reporters, accustomed to seeing police blotters crowded with mugging cases, quickly glossed over the attack. Two detectives, however, immediately developed a deep interest in the incident. Detective Richard Aidala, to whom Grace had passed on his reports on the Borrero case, thought the attack merited more investigation. Only nine days earlier, Mrs. Minnie Edmonds, a forty-six-year-old Negro cleaning woman, had been knifed to death in an alley one block from where Mrs. Borrero was assaulted. The murderer was still free. Aidala was working on the Edmonds case, and he wondered if there might be a connection between the two crimes. Mrs. Edmonds and Mrs. Borrero had been assaulted in alleys in the same vicinity, and both times a sex attack appeared to have been the motive.

Aidala telephoned Joseph DiPrima, a detective who had also been assigned to the Edmonds inquiry. DiPrima was attached to Brooklyn North Homicide Bureau, a regional detective unit. Detective DiPrima agreed with Aidala; he, too, wanted to know more about the attempted rape. Before the day was over, Aidala and DiPrima visited the salt-packaging plant, looking for "George Whitman." No one of that name was employed there. Mrs. Borrero was brought to the precinct, where she was interviewed and asked to examine the rogues'-gallery file of known sex criminals in the area. None of the photographs resembled her attacker. At Aidala's request, she gave him the pencil she had taken from the man during the struggle in the alley. He thought it might be useful in the investigation.

At the precinct that night, the two detectives reviewed the Edmonds and Borrero cases. If a connection existed between the two crimes, then "George Whitman" might be important. The problem was to find him. Aidala had an idea of how it might be done. He telephoned Patrolman Isola at his home, and Isola agreed to meet him the next morning in the precinct house.

Even though the next day was his day off, Isola promised to be at the precinct house early. He was certain he would recognize "Whitman" if he saw him again.

At 5:30 A.M., on Friday, April 24, Aidala and Isola met in the 73rd Precinct. Neither was in uniform for the assignment. Patrolman Isola chose to wear civilian clothes on this volunteer assignment and, as a detective, Aidala never wore a uniform on duty. The forty-year-old Aidala had been a policeman sixteen years, and his record was better than average, with six citations for meritorious work. He was a powerfully built man, five feet ten inches tall, weighing two hundred ten pounds, with the thick shoulders of the semiprofessional football player he had once been.

The two officers played a long-shot hunch that the young Negro they sought would appear again in front of the laundry. Shortly before 6:00 A.M., they staked out in Aidala's station wagon across the street from the laundry. Aidala sat behind the wheel, smoking, and Isola kept a lookout. An hour went by without a sign of the youth. It was 7:00 A.M., and the street sparkled with sunlight, when Isola spotted the person they were looking for walking toward the laundry.

"That's the fellow I spoke to," Isola said, pointing him out to Aidala.

Aidala started the car and moved slowly toward the young Negro, who wore a three-quarter-length tan coat and a green hat. About a half-block from the laundry, Aidala halted. He and Isola got out of the car, walked across the street, and intercepted the youth. After showing his gold detective's shield and identifying himself as a police officer, Aidala asked: "Are you the fellow who spoke to this police officer yesterday and told him you heard shots and saw a man running into Amboy Street?"

The young Negro nodded. Aidala asked him for identification, and the youth took out his wallet and produced a New Jersey driver's license. The name on the license was George Whitmore Jr. His home address was listed as Wildwood, New Jersey. Aidala asked if Whitmore had any objection to accompanying him to the precinct to answer some questions. Whitmore quite willingly followed Aidala and Isola to the station wagon.

Five minutes later the slender Whitmore, who looked more like sixteen than the nineteen he was, walked into the 73rd Precinct with Aidala and Isola on either side of him. The two officers led Whitmore past an American flag pinned to the wall of the lobby, toward the rear of the ground floor, and up one flight of metal steps. On the second floor, they turned right and entered the squad room, an area reserved for the use of detectives at the precinct.

Aidala told Whitmore to remove his coat and to sit down at a desk near the window. While Isola remained with Whitmore, Aidala went into an adjacent room and telephoned Mrs. Borrero. "We have someone we want you to look at," he told her. "I'm sending Patrolman Isola over to drive you to the precinct."

Out of Whitmore's range of hearing, Aidala ordered Isola to bring Mrs. Borrero to the station house in a police car. Aidala would be waiting with Whitmore in the interrogation room, so Mrs. Borrero would not see him when she entered the squad room. Isola was to take her into the squad commander's office, which would be empty at that time, from where she could observe Whitmore through a peephole in the door.

Before questioning Whitmore as a possible witness in the street attack, Aidala decided to eliminate him as a possible suspect. The quickest way of doing so was to have Mrs. Borrero look at him. As Isola left, the detective cautioned him:

"Don't speak to her about the case."

Alone now with Whitmore, Aidala sat down beside him and asked him where he worked. Whitmore said he did not have a steady job in New York, but he had had experience helping his father in an auto junkyard in his home town of Wildwood. He had been living with cousins in Brownsville for several months. The only jobs he had been able to obtain were temporary ones as a laborer with a furniture-moving company and in a salt-packaging plant.

Whitmore was a light-skinned Negro, about five feet six inches tall, weighing not more than one hundred fifty pounds. His face was blemished by pimples and deep acne pits; the merest shadow of eyebrows arched over his somber brown eyes. He was dressed like a ragamuffin. His splotched, threadbare tan coat was trimmed with an imitation leather collar; ragged tufts of thread sprouted in place of missing buttons. Under the coat he wore a frayed white cardigan sweater with blue and black stripes, and a checked gray shirt. He wore tight-fitting blue-green sharkskin trousers and black shoes that were weathered from overuse.

Whitmore gave slow, measured answers to Aidala's questions. He seemed neither brash nor afraid as he talked with the detective in the pale green room, which was about seventy feet wide and thirty feet deep. Like any squad room in the city, it was cluttered with chipped desks, uncomfortable wooden chairs, and typewriters. There were two large windows, but natural light was impeded by partly drawn black shades and wire-mesh screens. Even on the sunniest day, the electric lights were used all the time. There was one obvious sign that the room was used by police. In a corner, a cell had been erected, with wire-mesh fence on three sides from floor to ceiling. The chairless cell, which had room for only one person, was used to detain a prisoner temporarily. The police called it "The Cage."

After a few minutes of questioning, Aidala rose and asked Whitmore to step inside the interrogation room, which was a small room about twelve feet square, with a desk, three chairs, and a window covered by wire-mesh screen. By then Mrs. Borrero was in the squad room, and the police officers were ready for her to view Whitmore. Isola took her into the squad commander's office, the door of which had a peephole. She was going to look at Whitmore standing in the squad room with only a detective beside him. He was not in a line-up. While Mrs. Borrero and Isola were in the squad commander's office, Aidala brought Whitmore out of the interrogation room and told him to stand beside him in the center of the squad room. Whitmore placed himself next to the white detective, about five feet from the peephole.

Mrs. Borrero, barely five feet tall, was unable to reach the peephole even on tiptoe. To overcome the difficulty, Isola placed two telephone directories on the floor as a makeshift stool. Standing on them, she was able to put her eyes level with the peephole. She appraised Whitmore carefully through her horn-rimmed spectacles for thirty seconds before turning to Isola.

"This is the man," she said.

Nevertheless, to solidify her identification, she wanted to hear him speak. The lilt and soft intonations of the attacker's voice were still sharply defined in her memory. Isola left her, went to Whitmore, and instructed him to repeat: "Lady, I'm going to rape you. Lady, I'm going to kill you."

Aidala looked at Whitmore, who shrugged and said in a clear tone: "Lady, I'm going to rape you. Lady, I'm going to kill you."

Mrs. Borrero began to tremble. "This is the man," she told Isola, back in the squad commander's office. "This is the man."

The patrolman stepped into the squad room and nodded to Aidala. Aidala knew what the signal meant. He turned to Whitmore and said: "I'm placing you under arrest. A woman has identified you as the man who tried to rape her."

For the first time, Whitmore looked perplexed. "You're making a mistake. I didn't do anything," he mumbled.

Aidala ordered him to empty his pockets and place all his belongings on a desk. Whitmore complied by digging into his trouser pockets and pulling out a wallet stuffed with photographs and papers, a handkerchief, a black pocket comb, and a pink-handled jackknife labeled "Fish Knife." From his coat pockets Whitmore produced a fifty-cent paperbound murder mystery entitled *The Tall Dark Man*. That was all he had in his pockets. He had no money, not a penny.

Aidala told him to lift his hands in the traditional surrender pose, and the detective quickly searched him. Finding nothing else, Aidala led Whitmore back to the interrogation room, seated him at the desk, and warned him not to move. Whitmore remained there alone while Aidala and Isola calmed Mrs. Borrero. She was visibly distressed; her body quivered as she wept. The policemen assured her she had nothing more to fear. All she had to do was make one more identification, this time face-to-face, but she could do it when she felt sufficiently composed. Twenty minutes later, Aidala brought Whitmore into the squad commander's office. When Whitmore entered, Mrs. Borrero trembled again.

"You're the man who tried to rape me," she said angrily.

"You're making a mistake, ma'am," Whitmore answered.

After Mrs. Borrero's second identification, the time had come for the police to question Whitmore. Aidala asked Mrs. Borrero to wait outside in the main squad room until the police were ready to take a complete statement from her.

Before any questions were put to Whitmore, Aidala telephoned Detective DiPrima, who was waiting for the call at home. Aidala gave him a quick review of the arrest and identification.

"I'm coming right over," said DiPrima.

Until DiPrima arrived there was nothing for Aidala and Isola to do. DiPrima was known as an "old pro" in the department, and Aidala wanted him present for the questioning.

Shortly after 8:00 A.M., DiPrima walked into the squad room. The fifty-three-year-old detective looked more like a grandfatherly schoolteacher than a man who had spent twenty-seven years on the police force, eighteen of them as a detective. His gray hair, mellow brown eyes, and ready smile tended to conceal the fact that he was an alert, acute policeman. Those who met him outside of work saw a gentle-voiced, friendly man who dressed neatly. He was all these things—but he was also a detective with an exemplary record, a member of the police honor league who had been cited nineteen times for bravery and excellent police work.

DiPrima had questioned thousands of persons, and when he walked into the precinct that cool April morning, he had no reason to suspect he was entering into the most important case of his career.

The first person DiPrima saw in the squad room was Mrs. Borrero, who was seated at a desk. He had spoken to her the day before, and they nodded in recognition now. Aidala came out of the squad commander's office and briefed DiPrima about Whitmore's arrest. Stepping into the small room, DiPrima got his first look at Whitmore. To DiPrima he looked composed and relaxed.

DiPrima had come to the precinct without having had breakfast, and he was hungry. "How about something to eat?" he asked. Isola and Aidala also were hungry, and DiPrima specifically asked Whitmore if he would like to eat with them. The youth said he wanted rolls and coffee. Volunteering to buy everybody breakfast, Aidala handed two dollars to Isola and asked him to bring rolls and coffee from a delicatessen next door to the precinct.

Introducing himself, DiPrima pulled up a chair and sat next to the youth. He said he wanted Whitmore to understand that he had been placed under arrest for the attempted rape of Mrs. Borrero. "It's your privilege not to talk to us," he added. Whitmore was silent, but he seemed to comprehend the detective's words. With Aidala sitting by quietly, DiPrima began talking.

"Where are you from, George?" he asked.

Whitmore said he was nineteen years old and had been born in Philadelphia. His family had moved to New Jersey when he was a child, and they now lived in Wildwood, an Atlantic resort about one hundred twenty miles from New York City. Whitmore replied readily to DiPrima's questions about his past. He told the detective he had had little schooling. With less than a dozen questions, the detective learned that Whitmore had come to Brownsville after a long series of quarrels with his father, who owned an auto-dismantling shop. Whitmore said he had no interest in becoming an auto mechanic, but his father seemed determined to make him one. Their quarrels had prompted him to come to Brownsville and live with relatives. He complained about his mother, too: "She picks on me. She calls me crazy because I laugh at nothing, and she says I belong in a nut house."

Isola returned with breakfast while Whitmore was talking about his home life. The delicatessen was out of rolls, so he had brought slices of buttered Italian bread. No one objected. The three policemen and Whitmore spread the bread and containers of coffee on the desk and began to eat, while DiPrima continued with his questions. He next asked how Whitmore earned a living. Whitmore replied that he had trouble keeping jobs. "I have too many fights with the boss and other workers," he remarked.

When the meal was finished, Aidala offered Whitmore a cigarette. The youth seemed anxious to have one. DiPrima was now ready to question Whitmore about the Borrero case. He asked Whitmore if he wanted to describe how he had attacked Mrs. Borrero.

"I didn't do it," was the answer.

"George, Mrs. Borrero identified you as the man," DiPrima said.

Whitmore inhaled on the cigarette and reflected. The room was silent except for the street sounds that penetrated the screened window. Finally, Whitmore said:

"You're speaking better to me than anyone else ever spoke to me in my life." He paused, and then he asked: "How much time would I have to do?"

"That would be up to the judge. I can't make any promises. But the best thing to do is tell the truth," DiPrima said.

Aidala took out a yellow writing tablet, and DiPrima put his hard-covered writing pad on the desk. DiPrima said: "Start from the beginning, George. Tell us what you were doing and how it happened."

It took Whitmore about an hour to relate what had happened. The sole question asked by the detectives was: "What happened next, George?" and that was asked only when Whitmore stopped his narrative. Whitmore recalled having left his girl friend's house the night of the attack. It was late in the evening, and he was without a place to sleep. He was wandering in the streets near the elevated subway line when he saw a woman walking and he followed her. After several blocks of slow pursuit, he caught up to her and grabbed her from behind in a stranglehold. Jabbing a pencil against her throat to simulate a knife, he forced her into the alley and put his hand under her dress.

"I wanted to feel her pussy, and I told her I wanted to fuck her," he said.

At this moment the flashlight had burst upon him. He heard three shots as he raced through the streets; after eluding the policeman he hid on the roof of a building on Amboy Street, spending the rest of the night sleeping in a hallway.

"What were you wearing that night, George?" Aidala asked.

"The same clothes," he said, pointing to his tan coat and green hat.

Aidala showed him the brown leather button Mrs. Borrero had ripped from her assailant's coat. "Is this your button?" he asked.

"I don't know, it might be. I lost the top button from my coat. I don't know where."

"What about this pencil, is this yours?" Aidala showed him the mechanical pencil Mrs. Borrero had found clutched in her fist after the attack.

Whitmore nodded.

In describing his pursuit of Mrs. Borrero, Whitmore had rattled off the names of New Lots Avenue, Dumont Avenue, Rockaway Avenue, and Bristol Street, the route Mrs. Borrero had taken. He had also mentioned Chester Street, which was unrelated to the Borrero case but was the street where Mrs. Edmonds had been found slain ten days earlier.

As soon as Whitmore finished his account of the attack on Mrs. Borrero, DiPrima brought the conversation back to Chester Street.

"What about Chester Street, George? Why'd you mention it?"

"Oh, that's the street where the fellows do a lot of bebopping."

DiPrima continued: "We know all about gangs fighting in the neighborhood. Is there anything else you want to tell us about Chester Street? You don't have to say anything, but if you do tell us the whole truth, no one is going to yell at you."

Whitmore was silent for several seconds before answering:

"I heard a woman was hurt on Chester Street."

"What about the woman, George?"

"I was the one who hurt the woman."

The murder had taken place early on April 14, 1964. Whitmore said he remembered a morning when he had been out roaming the streets in the rain. About 3:00 A.M., the rain stopped. He was standing in the doorway of a store across the street from Junior High School 263 on Sutter Avenue when he saw a woman walking on Chester Street.

As he crossed the street, the woman spotted him and quickened her pace. By running, Whitmore was able to close in on her. He used a stranglehold, looping his right arm around her neck, at the same time opening with his left hand the pocketbook that dangled from her left arm. Stunned momentarily, the woman started to struggle; in restraining her, Whitmore dropped the pocketbook. All the time he kept his right arm wound around her neck.

DiPrima interrupted to ask Whitmore to demonstrate on Aidala how he had attacked the woman. Standing behind the detective, who was about three inches taller, Whitmore demonstrated the stranglehold.

"Okay, George, now sit down again and tell us what happened," DiPrima said.

Whitmore continued: "She started yelling, 'Keep your fucking hands off me, you son of a bitch.' I pushed her into the alley but she got away."

Struggling furiously, the woman managed to break loose by slipping completely out of her coat, Whitmore said. Once free of him, she ran toward the rear of the alley and into a back yard.

"What happened then, George?" DiPrima asked.

As the detectives knew, the back yard was a dead end, blocked by a ten-foot-high fence. Whitmore said he had no difficulty catching up to the woman. But she continued to squirm and struggle, even though he again tried to quiet her by choking her with his arm.

"I reached into my pants pocket and took out a knife. I had it oiled so it would open easily. All I had to do was flip it with my thumbnail. It was a black knife. I cut her several times, first in the face and then in the chest, and then she fell down."

"Go on, George."

After she sagged to the ground, Whitmore closed the knife. Not sure whether she was dead or alive, he lifted her dress, pulled off her panties, and was about to rape her when he heard a noise. Now frightened, he ran through another alley leading into the street, and walked three blocks to a building on Amboy Street, where he slept for several hours underneath the stairwell. He left his hideout after daybreak, first concealing the knife under the stairwell on the ground floor. For several hours he wandered calmly around Brownsville, speaking to no one. At 11:00 A.M., he went to the home of Beverly Payne, his fiancée, who lived with her mother and a younger sister two blocks from the scene of the murder. He walked up three flights of stairs in the dilapidated building and pounded on the door of Beverly's apartment. He woke her up, and she let him in.

While walking the streets, Whitmore had noticed blood on his shirt and trousers; now he wanted to eradicate this evidence. Fortunately for him, Beverly was alone in the apartment and she quickly returned to her bedroom. Once Beverly was out of the way he washed his black trousers in the bathtub, soaking them in cold water because he had heard it was more effective than hot water in removing bloodstains. Then, to make sure he had removed all the spots, he soaked the trousers in chlorine bleach. His bloody shirt had been torn in the struggle. He had other clothes in the apartment, and he changed into another pair of trousers and a fresh shirt. Downstairs, he stuffed the torn shirt into a garbage can. His shoes were also stained with blood, and two days later he discarded them.

"They were worn anyway, and I needed a new pair," he told the detectives.

"Do you have any more bloodspots?" asked DiPrima.

"There's still blood on my coat and my undershirt. The blood soaked through my shirt."

"The knife you have on you, the pink one, you're sure that's not the knife you used to stab the woman?"

"No, I used a black knife. It had a picture of a panther on the handle. That's the one I hid in the hallway."

Patrolman Isola, who had been in and out of the interrogation room during Whitmore's confession, heard Whitmore describe the knife used in the murder. He realized that he himself owned a similar knife. A friend had given it to him a year ago. Isola usually carried it in a pistol belt as part of his equipment.

"Is this what your knife looked like?" DiPrima asked, showing Whitmore Isola's knife.

The youth picked up the knife and opened its single blade.

"Identical," he answered.

It took Whitmore little more than an hour to relate the details of the Edmonds murder. Aidala and DiPrima, who heard the two confessions, were struck by the similarities between the attempted rape and the murder. Both M.O.'s had been the same. Whitmore each time used a mugging hold around the neck and dragged the victim into an alley.

The details of Whitmore's confession to the Edmonds murder dovetailed with all the known facts about the homicide. Mrs. Edmonds's body had been found early in the morning. The detectives knew she had left a neighborhood tavern about 2:00 A.M. and had been slain about 3:00 A.M.

The murderer had stabbed her several times in the face and chest and had removed her panties. Her coat and shoes were found fifty feet from the body, where they apparently slipped off during the struggle.

The two detectives had taken all the notes they wanted, but there was still much work ahead of them in closing out the Edmonds case. The murder weapon was missing, and they had no witnesses.

During the morning, the squad room gradually became more crowded as detectives arrived for work. A message about Whitmore's confessions had gone out to Brooklyn North Homicide, and two more detectives from the regional bureau were sent to the precinct to help out. These detectives, Edward Bulger and Charles Fazio, usually worked as a team, and they reached the squad room shortly after 10:00 A.M., along with Lieutenant John E. Currie, commander of the homicide unit. Whitmore was in the midst of his confession to the Edmonds murder when they walked in, and Currie, after hearing how smoothly the two crimes were being solved, left the interrogation room. According to later police testimony, Currie told Bulger and Fazio: "They got it all wrapped up. They don't need us." Nevertheless, Currie ordered Bulger and Fazio to stand by, in case they could be of help later.

Although, ten days had passed since Whitmore had hidden the Edmonds murder knife, DiPrima and Aidala were hopeful of finding the weapon under the stairway. Fazio, who had an unmarked police car, volunteered to drive them there, and the four police officers and Whitmore squeezed into the detective's car. Bulger remained at the precinct.

Aidala decided against handcuffing Whitmore. Handcuffs were certain to attract attention, and possibly trouble, in the slum neighborhood. The sight of handcuffed Negro prisoners on the streets of Brownsville had provoked people into taunting and interfering with the police. With four police officers surrounding him, there was no chance of Whitmore's escaping, with or without restraints.

Fazio, who had had no part in the questioning, asked Whitmore for driving directions. From the back seat, Whitmore directed him to Amboy Street. He had forgotten the address, but he assured the detectives he would recognize the building where he had hidden the knife. On Amboy Street, he told Fazio where to park, and everyone got out. With the four policemen following, Whitmore entered a typically run-down Brownsville tenement.

"I put the knife there," he said, pointing to the space underneath the first step of the stairway.

Aidala got down on his hands and knees, probing with his right hand into mounds of dirt and dust. All he swept out was a brass key.

"Are you sure you put it there, George?" DiPrima asked.

"The knife has to be there. I left it with the key."

The key, he said, was for an apartment on the fourth floor of that building, where he had once lived. It had been occupied by one of his girl friends, who had moved out shortly before the Edmonds murder. On the day of the murder, Whitmore had impulsively tossed the key under the stairs along with the knife.

At DiPrima's request, Fazio questioned the Negro custodian of the building and his son. They said they had cleaned underneath the stairwell at least once since the murder, ten days before, but neither of them had found a knife.

"Maybe I left it at Beverly's," Whitmore suggested. "It might be at her place. I store a lot of my belongings there."

Beverly Payne's apartment was a two-block drive from Amboy Street. Beverly seemed frightened by the cluster of men gathered in the hallway. "I can't let you in, my mother's not here," she said.

"It'll be all right; they're with me," Whitmore said.

Inside, Whitmore showed the detectives the living-room couch where he had often slept, and a closet where he kept his belongings. But no jackknife with a panther emblem could be found. He gave the police the trousers he had worn the morning of the murder.

Beverly and Whitmore were asked to sit at a kitchen table where the detectives could talk with them about the morning of Tuesday, April 14, when Whitmore came to the apartment and woke Beverly. Although only ten days had passed, Beverly could not recall the morning. Whitmore tried to jog her memory:

"Sure, you do. Don't you remember you were in your pajamas? You opened the door and ran right back to the bedroom."

Beverly was still unable to bring that morning into focus. It seemed useless to remain in the apartment, and DiPrima rose, motioning to the others to follow. Beverly asked if she could accompany them to the precinct. She was worried that George might be in trouble.

"I'm sorry, there's no room for you in the car," Aidala told her. "But you can come over by yourself, if you want to."

Back at the precinct, Aidala asked Whitmore to remove his undershirt, which Whitmore said had been soaked with Mrs. Edmonds's blood. The undershirt and trousers would be sent to the police laboratory for analysis.

It was noon now and everyone was hungry again. The detectives agreed to send out for lunch, because they still had questions to ask. Whitmore wanted a ham, cheese, and tomato sandwich on Italian bread.

"You're lucky," DiPrima told him. "You can eat meat on Friday. All of us are Catholics, and we're having cheese or egg sandwiches."

DiPrima continued sounding out Whitmore about his home life and his problems. At times during his confessions to the Borrero attack and the Edmonds murder, Whitmore had broken into smiles. He had seemed relieved at the unburdening of his guilt, and DiPrima believed he wanted to talk freely about himself, wanted someone with a sympathetic ear to listen to his frustrations and problems. DiPrima was not surprised at Whitmore's eagerness to talk. He had seen other prisoners become chatterboxes once they had revealed the worst about themselves.

"Why do you stay out at night?" the detective asked.

"I like to be by myself, and I have trouble sleeping. Sometimes, I go on the roofs to look in other people's apartments."

Whitmore said he sometimes stayed with relatives, sometimes stayed at Beverly Payne's, and sometimes slept in hallways. He had no home of his own in the city.

"I know I need help. Can you help me?" he asked DiPrima.

"You'll have to ask your lawyer or a judge for that kind of help," replied the detective.

DiPrima did ask Whitmore if he wanted to notify any of his relatives about his arrest. "They'll have to learn about it some time, George."

The suggestion distressed Whitmore. "No, I don't want anyone to know about it."

While DiPrima talked with Whitmore, Aidala made a more careful examination of the youth's possessions. Sifting through the papers in Whitmore's wallet, he came across two photographs, both of white girls. In one, two girls in their late teens were in an open convertible parked near a wooded area. One girl, a blonde, was perched on the rear seat of the car, while the other sat in the front passenger's seat. In the other snapshot, two other girls in white dresses, both dark-haired and appearing to be about fourteen years old, were standing on a stairway leading to a building. They seemed to be posing for a school graduation photograph.

"Where'd you get these pictures, George?" Aidala asked.

"A girl in New Jersey gave them to me."

Satisfied, Aidala put the photographs back on the desk. They did not seem to have any relation to the Edmonds or Borrero cases.

After lunch, Aidala and DiPrima agreed it was time to alert the District Attorney's office. In New York City, the five borough District Attorneys or prosecutors have assistants available at all times to record the official confession known as the "Q and A," a statement in question-and-answer form. It is the investigating detectives who determine when a suspect is ready to see the D.A.'s man. At 12:45 P.M., Aidala telephoned the Brooklyn District Attorney's office and was told an Assistant District Attorney would be dispatched to the 73rd Precinct.

The detectives knew it would take the A.D.A. at least thirty minutes to reach the precinct, time enough for Whitmore to re-enact the murder. Again using Fazio's unmarked car, they drove Whitmore to the street where he said he had first seen Mrs. Edmonds. Whitmore told Fazio to halt the car on Sutter Avenue, a busy Brownsville thoroughfare between Bristol and Chester streets.

"Show us exactly how you committed the crime," Aidala said. "You're on your own."

Whitmore, unhandcuffed, walked into the entranceway of a store in the middle of the block which was used as a lawyer's office. It was opposite Junior High School 263 and the police callbox Isola had used the night of the Borrero attack, and it was a half-block from both the Edmonds murder site and the alley where Mrs. Borrero had been terrorized.

"I was standing here when I saw her on the left walking up Chester Street. That's when I started out after her."

Whitmore, with the police at his side, walked diagonally across the street. "I wanted to head her off," he said. "She must have been scared because she started to walk fast."

He walked to the entrance of the alley where he said he had grabbed Mrs. Edmonds and the struggle began. Finally, he led the officers through the alley and into the garbage-littered rear yard.

"I caught up with her here," he said, stopping near a stone wall. It was the exact spot where Aidala and DiPrima had seen Mrs. Edmonds's body lying in the rain.

The detectives were satisfied. Essentially, all that remained was the "Q and A." In the squad room, Detective Fazio examined Whitmore's possessions, which were spread out on a desk. The two photographs caught his attention, especially the one of the two young women sitting in the convertible. The blonde in the rear seat looked about twenty years old. Fazio showed the photograph to Bulger.

"Did you see this?" he asked.

Bulger scrutinized the snapshot for a long minute. "This girl resembles Janice Wylie," he said, pointing to the blonde.

If anyone in that squad room knew what Janice Wylie looked like, it was Bulger. He had been assigned to the Wylie-Hoffert investigation for four months. Like hundreds of other detectives, he had been relieved of his other duties and sent to Manhattan during the height of the double-murder inquiry. In January, only three months earlier, when all leads in the case had been exhausted, he had returned to Brooklyn North Homicide.

"Are you going to talk to him about it?" asked Fazio.

"I'd sure like to."

Bulger did not wait. He asked DiPrima to step outside the squad commander's office and showed him the snapshot.

"Joe," Bulger said, "the girl in this picture bears an awful resemblance to Janice Wylie. I'd like to talk to him about it. I could swear this is a photo of Janice Wylie."

The Assistant District Attorney had not arrived, and DiPrima saw no reason why Bulger should not question Whitmore about the photograph. The Wylie-Hoffert murder was still the biggest case in the city, and Bulger had a reputation for not making mistakes. The forty-five-year-old detective was lean and forceful-looking, with an athlete's carriage, shoulders arched back, jaw set rigidly, eyes piercingly bright. He was difficult to deceive, and his colleagues knew he would strive equally hard to prove or disprove a man's guilt. Three years earlier, Bulger had developed doubts about the guilt of a man arrested for two murders. Working on his own time, he established the suspect's innocence.

Bulger's first questions to Whitmore were explicit.

"Where did you get this picture?"

"I found it in a junkyard in Wildwood, where I used to work."

"Are you sure that's where you got it?"

Whitmore remained silent, and Bulger repeated: "Are you sure that's where you got it?"

After another pause, Whitmore murmured: "I'm not sure."

"Where'd you get it, George?"

"A girl I know in Jersey gave it to me."

"What's her name?"

"Carol, I think."

"Remember, George, tell us the truth. We can always check," DiPrima interjected. "You've been truthful all day. Are you sure you're telling the truth?"

"This girl who gave it to me, her father had a riding academy and he'd let me ride the horses. That's how I knew her."

"Come on, George, tell us where you really got the photo. Did the girl really give it to you?" Bulger said.

Now Whitmore offered another explanation:

"I was in the girl's house once, and I took it from a drawer."

"We'll have to call the girl," Bulger said.

Once more, Whitmore said the photograph came from a house in Wildwood. But Bulger countered by reminding him this was his third version:

"Which one is true? Did you find it in a junkyard? Did a girl give it to you? Or did you steal it?"

"I stole it from a house in New York," Whitmore said, eyes cast down.

"Do you remember where in New York you got the photograph? What street?"

"It was 88th Street. I took it from a drawer."

7. *"... Only the Killer Could Know"*

On the witness stand at one of Whitmore's subsequent hearings, the detectives would recall that Whitmore's first confession to the Wylie-Hoffert murders was slow-paced. He frequently halted, as if searching for words. But as soon as one of the detectives asked a question, he was spurred into resuming his chronicle.

"When did you go to New York, George?"

"About the end of August 1963, it was a weekday."

"How'd you go?"

"I was in Brooklyn and I felt like going for a train ride. It was about ten in the morning. I took the 'A' train and rode to the 42nd Street station near the Port Authority building."

"What'd you do next, George?"

"I came to the street and did some window-shopping. I walked uptown, just looking around. At 88th Street, near Park Avenue, I saw a building with a canvas canopy out to the street; it looked like wealthy people lived there."

"What happened next, George?"

"I went into the building to go to the roof to look around. I went through the lobby past the elevator and then an exit door to the left. There were concrete steps leading upstairs. I went up and I don't remember if it was three or four flights of stairs and I saw a door open on a crack on the second or third floor landing leading to the kitchen of the apartment. I pushed open the door and stuck my head in and looked around."

Whitmore stopped abruptly as Aidala came into the room. Aidala had to interrupt the questioning because he was ready to "book" Whitmore— officially accuse him of murder and attempted rape and robbery. Bulger raised no objection. Whitmore was Aidala's prisoner, and it was Aidala's prerogative to decide how he was to be handled. At 3:30 P.M., Aidala led Whitmore down to the precinct lobby. A desk lieutenant pulled out a thick ledger and entered Whitmore's name. His was the 1,557th arrest at the precinct in 1964. Asked by the lieutenant if he was a narcotics addict, Whitmore whispered: "No, sir." Aidala informed the desk officer that Whitmore was accused of the murder of Mrs. Minnie Edmonds and the attempted rape and assault of Mrs. Elba Borrero. The booking took ten minutes, and then Aidala, holding Whitmore by the arm, guided him up the flight of stairs into the squad room.

DiPrima and Bulger were anxious to resume questioning. Bulger, who was familiar with many of the circumstances of the double murder and the police theories about the killer, was ready to ask most of the questions. He thought it would be advantageous if DiPrima aided in the interrogation, since Whitmore apparently trusted him.

The squad commander's office was bustling with people and was needed for the normal work of the day. Bulger and DiPrima took Whitmore into the interrogation room, where they would be assured of privacy. But there was one more problem before they could resume. After almost three hours of delay, Assistant District Attorney Edward Alfano had arrived to take the question-and-answer confessions from Whitmore for the Edmonds and Borrero cases. DiPrima and Isola explained that they were obtaining a confession to a serious crime in Manhattan from the prisoner, and they believed an interruption would be unwise. Alfano had other confessions to obtain at different precincts, and he agreed. He told the detectives to call

the District Attorney's office whenever they were ready, and he or another
A.D.A. would be sent over. Alfano did not even see Whitmore.

In the next two hours, most of the questions put to Whitmore came
from Bulger, with an occasional query thrown in by DiPrima. Bulger
thought Whitmore remarkably calm and friendly. He was convinced, as
Aidala and DiPrima had been earlier, that Whitmore's cooperation indicated he was troubled by his own evil violence, and confession was a
mental purgative, a "getting it off his chest."

Whitmore repeated that he had traveled to Times Square on the
subway, aimlessly wandered the streets, then entered a building and walked
toward the roof.

"After I saw the door to the apartment open, I walked in."

"What did you see inside?"

"I looked around and saw a carton with all the soda bottles in it."

"Do you remember what kind of soda bottles, George?"

"They were Coca-Cola bottles, I think, and they were empty. I took
three bottles from the carton in case somebody walked in and caught me.
Then I would use the bottles to protect myself."

"Go on, George, what happened next?"

"I walked through the dining room from the kitchen."

"Which way did you go?"

"I went to the right and into the front room and looked around. Then I
picked up a picture off the end table in the front room parlor."

"What kind of table, do you remember?"

"I think the table is mahogany, and I think there was a lamp on it."

"What picture did you take from the table, George?"

"The picture of the blonde girl," Whitmore said, pointing to the
photograph on the table.

"What happened after you took the photograph?"

"Well, before I went into the front room, I set the bottles on the floor of
the hall so I could get to them in case I needed them. I picked up quite a
few things and looked at them. I needed my hands free."

"Okay, then what?"

"When I was leaving the parlor I picked up the bottles and walked
through the hall and looked in the first bathroom and no one was there. I
looked in the bedroom and walked in and looked around."

"When did you see someone?"

"As I was coming out of the bedroom, I saw a girl with blonde hair
coming out of the bathroom in the back."

"How was she dressed?"

"She was naked but she was holding a sheet around her hips and she was naked from the waist up."

"Did she say anything?"

"She got hysterical when she saw me and started to scream and I tried to stop her from screaming."

"How'd you try to stop her?"

"I set the bottles on the floor and grabbed her around the neck and with my left hand I pulled her left arm behind her back. I told her to shut up, 'I don't want to hurt you.' "

"Did she fight back?"

"She kept screaming. I dragged her into the bedroom, pushed her between the beds, but she wouldn't stop screaming. So I pushed her head towards the window and ran back, grabbed a bottle, and hit her on the head with the bottle. I hit her once and she just laid there. I think the bottle broke."

He recalled tearing sheeting into strips with his hands and using them to bind her hands and feet. As he was leaving the bedroom, a second woman appeared. He had not heard her enter the apartment. Because she looked older than the blonde girl and wore eyeglasses, he referred to her as "the mother."

"She said, 'Who the hell are you? What are you doing in my house?' " Whitmore continued. "I ran towards her and told her to be quiet and she kept on screaming for help. She kept on making a lot of noise. I grabbed another bottle that was lying on the floor and hit her on the head."

He remembered dragging her into the bedroom, placing her on the bed, and binding her hands and ankles, too. He was committing cunnilingus on "the mother" when she awoke and screamed. Panicking, Whitmore ran into the kitchen, brought back three knives, and plunged one of them into "the mother." When she was quiet, he stabbed the blonde girl, even though she had not cried out.

"What happened next, George?"

"I washed up and left the apartment."

Apparently no one saw him leave through the service stairway. Once outside, he walked forty blocks to Times Square and rode the subway back to Brownsville.

As Whitmore confessed to the double murder, the telephones in the squad room were busy. Calls were going out to police officials in Manhattan and Brooklyn, the big brass of the police department. Inspector William E. Coleman, commander of the 13th Police District in Brooklyn, was one of the first to reach the 73rd Precinct for a briefing on the Edmonds and

Borrero cases. But these crimes were now overshadowed by Whitmore's confession to the Wylie-Hoffert murders, and the news could be contained no longer within the precinct's walls. In Manhattan, Chief of Detectives McKearney was among the first to be notified. The startling news was rushed to Police Commissioner Michael J. Murphy and other high-ranking officers. Before starting for Brooklyn, McKearney alerted Inspector Coyle and Captain Weldon, who were still in control of the Wylie-Hoffert investigation.

By 5:00 P.M., after ninety minutes with Whitmore, Bulger and DiPrima believed they had obtained the essential facts. Bulger was familiar with the file on the case, but he had not been privy to all the minutiae. DiPrima had no inside knowledge of the case at all. Until the brass and the Manhattan detectives arrived, they had run out of questions. DiPrima had one other idea. Whitmore had mentioned he was fond of drawing, and so DiPrima said: "George, you were in the apartment. Draw us a diagram."

The detectives supplied Whitmore with a pencil and several sheets of yellow paper with blue lines. Bulger helped him by drawing the kitchen and other rooms as Whitmore described them. Together they produced a rough drawing of the murder scene. Bulger asked Whitmore to use the first sketch as a model for drawing an accurate layout of the apartment.

Shortly before 6:00 P.M., as dusk was falling on Brownsville, the police brass arrived. They examined carefully the two photographs Whitmore had been carrying. An inscription on the back of the snapshot of the girl who appeared to be Janice Wylie read: "To George from Louise." A telephone number was scrawled beneath the inscription. The other photograph was inscribed: "Janice and Katy M." The police were interested solely in the blonde girl sitting in the convertible, even though the name Janice was written on the other photograph.

Detective John Lynch of the 23rd Precinct in Manhattan, still the headquarters for the Wylie-Hoffert inquiry, arrived with the brass. One of the first detectives at the murder scene, he had been assigned to the case from its beginning and was an expert on every detail of it. After he had been filled in by Bulger and DiPrima, Lynch agreed that more precise details were needed from Whitmore. Several aspects of the confession needed clarification. How had he tied up the women? What had he seen in the apartment? Why had he not raped Janice Wylie? Bulger and DiPrima were sent back to put the new questions to Whitmore, since he appeared willing to talk freely to them.

McKearney and the other officials were not so certain as Bulger that the blonde girl in the photograph really was Janice Wylie. Yet, even if she was not, the photograph could have been stolen from the apartment, just as Whitmore said, and it was a vital piece of evidence. In the hope of resolving all doubts, McKearney ordered Lynch and Andrew Dunleavy, another detective, to drive back to Manhattan and show the snapshot to Janice Wylie's relatives and friends.

Although it was night, the squad room throbbed with more activity than during the day. Five top-ranking officers and a dozen detectives nervously waited for final word on the photograph and the concluding parts of Whitmore's confession. Mrs. Borrero was there, too. The police had asked her to wait until an Assistant District Attorney could take her statement.

Before Bulger and DiPrima posed their final questions, each police official was introduced to Whitmore by Deputy Chief Inspector Edward Carey, commander of Brooklyn North Detectives, who served as unofficial host. Carey had instructed Whitmore to mark the location of the kitchen table and other furniture on his diagram of the Wylie-Hoffert apartment, and also the spots where he encountered the women. Carey thought Whitmore's diagram comprehensive; it included small pictures of the bathroom plumbing fixtures and x's to designate where a tennis ball, a clock, and a soda bottle had stood on a night table in the murder bedroom.

McKearney, the highest-ranking officer there, exchanged no words with Whitmore. He looked in as the questioning was going on. Inspector Coyle, who had worked so long and hard on the seemingly unsolvable murders, turned up just as Whitmore was describing the knives he had taken from the kitchen. Coyle had brought colored photographs of the bodies and the bedroom with him. All the officials thought Whitmore remarkably serene. But if they had learned one thing in their long police careers, it was never to be surprised by a murderer's behavior.

In thirty minutes, Bulger and DiPrima had Whitmore's explanation for the unclarified aspects of the crime. Whitmore said he had found a razor blade in the bathroom and had used it to cut thin strips of bedding with which he gagged the women. He said he had tied them together to make escape more difficult should one of them regain consciousness while he was still in the apartment.

After knocking out Janice Wylie, he had discovered she was menstruating. He removed her sanitary napkin and tossed it under a bed. The police had found it there. He had noticed a bottle of skin cream in a drawer, and he dabbed the ointment on her legs and pubic area. She was unconscious at the time. All this occurred before Emily Hoffert returned to surprise him.

Whitmore said that once he had killed, an uncontrollable rage seized him. To relieve the fury within him, he placed two of the knives under his shoe and snapped off the blades by bending the handles.

At 7:30 P.M., everyone took a break for sandwiches. When the brief respite was over, Bulger and DiPrima reviewed the confession with Whitmore to make sure it was complete. At the conclusion, Bulger read back five pages of notes he had taken.

"Any changes you want to make, make them now," said Bulger.

Whitmore wanted none. He initialed the first four pages and signed his name at the bottom of the last page.

It was 9:00 P.M. The questioning was over. The time had come for an Assistant District Attorney to record the official confessions. Before the A.D.A. arrived, detectives again took time out for snacks. Two hamburgers were brought for Whitmore—his fourth meal of the day. He ate one but rejected the second, making his first complaint in police custody:

"You're giving me too much food. I can't eat so much."

Saul Postal, a Brooklyn Assistant District Attorney, walked into the crowded squad room. A small, thin man in his forties, Postal knew his business. During ten years as an aide to various Brooklyn District Attorneys, he had conducted more than a thousand interrogations. When he entered a precinct, he took charge or, as he put it, "was the boss." A stenographer, Raymond Linkletter, had come with him.

Before Aidala and DiPrima finished briefing Postal about the backgrounds of the Edmonds murder and the Borrero attempted rape, an Assistant District Attorney from Manhattan arrived. He was Peter J. Koste, assigned that night to taking official question-and-answer confessions for crimes committed in Manhattan or New York County. The two A.D.A.'s agreed that Postal should interrogate Whitmore first. When Postal had finished with his two cases, Koste would question Whitmore on the double murder in Manhattan.

Before interrogating Whitmore, Postal wanted a separate statement from Mrs. Borrero. With the stenotypist recording the conversation, Postal questioned her about the attack and her identification of Whitmore. Mrs. Borrero was finally free to go home, and the A.D.A. was ready for Whitmore.

Whitmore was sitting at the desk in the interrogation room, with Detectives Aidala and DiPrima standing near by. Postal introduced himself to Whitmore, and the monotonous clicking of the stenotype machine began. In question-and-answer form, Postal obtained a statement from Whitmore on the Borrero case, a statement later used as court evidence against Whitmore.

Q: What is your name?

A: George Whitmore.

Q: Where do you live?

A: 191, apartment 17.

Q: What street?

A: Amboy.

Q: How old are you?

A: Nineteen.

Q: When were you born?

A: May 26, 1944.

Q: Do you know the lady who was here just a moment ago when you came into the room?

A: Yes.

Q: Did you ever see her before today?

A: Yes.

Q: When did you see her?

A: At night.

Q: What night?

A: That night I started following her.

Q: How long ago was that?

A: The night before last.

Q: This is Friday night. Was that Wednesday night?

A: Yes.

Q: Where did you see her when you followed her?

A: On Sutter.

Q: And what other street?

A: She was coming down towards Sutter.

Q: And what other street?

A: She was on Rockaway.

Q: Did you see her come off the train station?

A: No.

Q: Was she coming from that general direction?

A: Yes.

Q: Were you with anybody at that time?

A: No.

Q: What were you doing in the area just then, when you saw her?

A: I didn't go home that night, so I stayed out.

Q: Were you staying there for any particular reason?

A: No.

Q: When you saw this lady, did you decide to follow her?

A: Yes.

Q: For what reason?

A: I tried to have relationship.

Q: Did you follow her?

A: Yes.

Q: How many blocks?

A: Approximately two blocks.

Q: Do you remember down which streets you went?

A: She came down Rockaway and turned up Sutter.

Q: Then what?

A: That is when I started following her.

Q: Then do you know which streets, do you remember?

A: I know what street I followed her down.

Q: Do you know where you ended up? Where did she finally come to, what street?

A: Bristol.

Q: Between what other streets?

A: Between Sutter and Blake.

Q: When you said you wanted to have relationship with her, you mean sexual relationship, sexual intercourse?

A: Yes.

Q: Have you ever seen the lady before this time?

A: No.

Q: When she got to Bristol, what happened?

A: She started walking fast, and started into a run.

Q: Did you finally catch up to her?

A: Yes.

Q: And what happened when you caught up to her?

A: She put up a little fight.

Q: Did you do anything to her first?

A: I grabbed her.

Q: How?

A: From behind.

Q: Around what part of her person?

A: Around the neck.

Q: Was she carrying anything at that time?

A: She was carrying a pocketbook.

Q: Did you do anything to the pocketbook?

A: I took it.

Q: Do you remember what kind of pocketbook she was carrying?

A: No.

Q: I show you this pocketbook. Does this look like a bag she was carrying at this time?

A: Yes.

Q: Did you open up the pocketbook?

A: Yes.

Q: What did you do?

A: I looked inside.

Q: Did you find anything inside?

A: No.

Q: What was she doing?

A: She was putting up a struggle.

Q: And where did you take her?

A: Into a house.

Q: Into a what?

A: An alley.

Q: An alley or basement?

A: A basement.

Q: When you got her down, did you say anything to her?

A: Yes.

Q: What?

A: I told her I wanted to fuck, have intercourse.

Q: Did she say anything?

A: She started screaming and what not.

Q: Did you tell her to stop screaming?

A: Yes.

Q: Did you say what you would do if she didn't stop screaming?

A: Yes. I told her if she didn't shut up I'd kill her.

Q: And what did you do when she screamed?

A: I ran through the back.

Q: What happened to the bag?

A: I dropped it on the sidewalk.

Q: You went out the back entrance although you went in the front?

A: Yes.

Q: What were you wearing?

A: I was wearing black pants and that coat.

[*Mr. Postal: Indicating tan poplin coat.*]

Q: Did you have that coat on when you were apprehended by the police today?

A: Yes.

Q: I notice there is a button missing from that coat. Do you know when that button was lost?

A: She could have grabbed it and pull it off.

Q: I show you a button. [*Indicating a brown leather button.*] Is that the kind of button you had on there?

A: Yes.

Q: And did you have that button on your coat before you grabbed hold of this woman?

A: Yes.

Q: Were you armed at the time you grabbed the woman?

A: No.

Q: Did you pretend that you had some weapon?

A: No, just a pencil.

Q: Did you hold that to indicate you held a knife?

A: Yes.

Q: Do you remember saying something to her to the effect that you wanted to touch her pussy?

A: I told her I wanted relationship with her.

Q: Did you put your hands under her clothing?

A: Yes.

In twenty minutes, the sixty-five–question confession was completed. Detective Bulger then came in to be present and hear the Edmonds statement. Five minutes later, the stenotypist nodded to Postal that he was ready, and the Assistant District Attorney began his second round of questions. This time it was the Edmonds murder, and again Postal was the only one who interrogated Whitmore for an admission that one day would be marked as a courtroom document for a judge and jury to examine. After establishing Whitmore's name, address, and age, Postal began.

Q: Do you remember an incident that happened about ten days ago on Chester Avenue—an incident that happened between you and some woman that you stabbed? Do you remember this?

A: Yes.

Q: Had you ever seen this woman before?

A: No.

Q: Were you living at home on April 14?

A: Yes, sir.

Q: April 14 was a week ago Monday night, going into Tuesday morning. So that it was Tuesday morning?

A: Yes.

Q: Do you remember who you were with earlier in the evening?

A: I was by myself.

Q: All evening?

A: Yes.

Q: What time did you go to bed that morning, if you recall?

A: I didn't.

Q: At about 3:00 or shortly before, do you recall seeing a woman on Chester Avenue?

A: Yes.

Q: Where did you see her for the first time? Chester and what other street?

A: Chester and Sutter.

Q: Had you ever seen her before this time?

A: No.

Q: What were you doing on the streets at that time?

A: I didn't go home sometimes. I stay in a building.

Q: Were you looking for anything or anybody?

A: No.

Q: Did you have something in mind? Were you waiting for some woman to come along?

A: No.

Q: Did you have any weapon on you that evening?

A: Yes, I have it right there.

[*Mr. Postal: Indicates black-handled knife with the picture of a small animal on it. A blade about four inches long.*]

Q: Did the knife that you had seem to be an exact copy of this?

A: Identical.

Q: Where did you get that knife? Do you recall?

A: I think I found it down by a girl's house. Down on Hopkinson Avenue.

Q: Why were you carrying it this particular morning?

A: I usually keep it in my pocket.

Q: When you saw this woman, did anything come into your mind about her?

A: Yes.

Q: What?

A: Follow her and have intercourse with her.

Q: About how old a woman was this, do you recall?

A: She could have been about twenty-nine.

Q: And was she white or Negro?

A: She was white. I'd say she was white—more Spanish.

Q: When you say, "She was white," do you mean a white person or light-colored?

A: She was really light-skinned—could pass for Spanish.

Q: Do you know whether or not she was a Negro?

A: No.

Q: Did she seem to be Negro? Did she have Negro features?

A: I didn't notice her features.

Q: Did you start to follow her?

A: Yes.

Q: And what did she do?

A: She cut down Chester.

Q: From what other street?

A: From Sutter.

Q: She turned into Chester?

A: Yes.

Q: And how far down the street did she go before you caught up with her?

A: I'd say about the middle of the block.

Q: And when you caught up, did you do anything or say anything to her?

A: I said I wanted intercourse with her.

Q: And what did she say? Did she say anything?

A: Yes.

Q: What?

A: When I grabbed her she called me a dirty filthy scum.

Q: You say you grabbed her? How?

A: From behind.

Q: In what manner? In a mugging position?

A: Yes.

Q: Put your arms around her or what?

A: I grabbed her from behind.

Q: How? You mean a mugging position? Was she able to speak?

A: Yes.

Q: When she said those words to you, what did you do?

A: I told her to shut up.

Q: Then what did you do?

A: That is when I pulled her into the alley.

Q: And was that right near where you stopped her on Chester Street?

A: Yes.

Q: When you pulled her into the alley, was this level or steps?

A: Go down.

Q: You had to go down steps?

A: Yes.

Q: And did she walk or did you push her or carry her?

A: Pushed her down the steps.

Q: About how many steps? Do you recall?

A: Four or five steps.

Q: Did you, in the struggle with her, before you pushed her down the steps, was any article of her clothing torn?

A: Yes.

Q: What?

A: Collar. She tried to pull away; I grabbed her by the coat collar.

Q: And then what?

A: It tore.

Q: Then what?

A: She got out of her coat and ran through the alley.

Q: And when she ran through an alley, did she come out the back yard?

A: Yes.

Q: What happened in the back yard? Did you follow her there?

A: We had another struggle.

Q: What kind of a struggle?

A: Just like she's fighting to get away.

Q: When you started to struggle with her in the yard, did you have your knife in your hands at the time?

A: No, I pulled it out later.

Q: So that you had no knife?

A: No.

Q: And what did you do to her in the course of the struggle? How were you struggling?

A: Just tried to push her down—hit and keep her from hollering.

Q: And what did you have in mind?

A: I wanted intercourse.

Q: And how were you going to keep her from hollering?

A: Only way I knew was to hit her.

Q: With your fists?

A: Yes.

Q: And where was your knife at the time you were hitting her—that you were shoving her down?

A: It was in my pocket.

[*Mr. Postal: Indicating back right pocket.*]

Q: Now, at some point, did you take out the knife?

A: Yes.

Q: At what point was she thrown to the ground?

A: She was thrown to the ground and struggled.

Q: And up to this point, did you make any effort to have intercourse with her?

A: No.

Q: Had you taken off any articles of her clothing other than the coat?

A: No. That is when I pulled my knife out and started cutting her in the face.

Q: How many times did you stab her in the face?

A: Two or three times.

Q: Did you say anything?

A: No.

Q: Did you stab her any place other than the face?

A: I stabbed her in the chest or stomach some place.

Q: Do you have any idea of how many times you stabbed her?

A: Two or three times, I believe.

Q: And if you stabbed her in the face, I assume she was lying face up—

A: Yes.

Q: [*Continuing*] or on her side?

A: She was lying down on her face.

Q: How could you stab her on the face?

A: She was struggling.

Q: Did you take off any of her clothing while she was down on the ground?

A: Yes.

Q: What?

A: I took her underclothes.

Q: Panties?

A: Yes.

Q: After you got her panties off, what did you do?

A: I had intercourse with her.

Q: Did you take out your penis?

A: Yes.

Q: Did you put it into her?

A: I couldn't get a hardon.

Q: And in what position was she lying at the time you tried to put it into her?

A: I turned her over.

Q: So she was lying how?

A: Facing me.

Q: Do you mean she had been lying on her stomach or side or what?

A: She was lying on her back.

Q: And you stabbed her a few times; then turned her over on her—

A: She was in a side position when I was struggling and I cut her and when she stopped struggling that is when I turned her face up.

Q: Did you get between her legs?

A: I tried to.

Q: Did you get between her legs?

A: Yes.

Q: Her legs were spaced or were they not?

A: They weren't far apart.

Q: Then what happened? What drove you off?

A: I heard somebody coming.

Q: From where?

A: Outside the alley.

Q: The same way you had come?

A: Yes.

Q: Did anybody come there? Did anybody come into the yard?

A: That is when I took off and started running.

Q: How did you get away?

A: There was another opening.

Q: You didn't come out the same way?

A: No.

Q: Do you recall how the woman was dressed? Did you see how she was dressed?

A: She had a black coat.

Q: Did you take anything belonging to the woman before you stabbed her?

A: No. I didn't get a chance to.

Q: Did you take anything after you stabbed her?

A: No. Her pocketbook was lying outside on the sidewalk.

Q: Had you taken that away when you first mugged her?

A: Yes.

Q: And did you find anything in the bag?

A: When I opened up the bag, that is when she took off and I grabbed her by the collar.

Q: Did you find any money or any other valuables in the bag?

A: No.

Q: When you grabbed her originally, what was your intention?

A: Intercourse.

Q: What about stealing her pocketbook?

A: No.

Q: How is it that you did first look into her pocketbook?

A: Yes.

Q: Was that partly a thought to get money?

A: Yes.

Q: I show you this coat. [*Indicating a tan poplin.*] Were you wearing this coat at the time of this incident with the woman?

A: Yes.

Q: Have you had it cleaned since that time?

A: No, it's never been cleaned.

Q: What else were you wearing at that time?

A: A black pair of pants and a short-sleeve shirt and I was wearing a pair of shoes.

Q: Was there any blood on the shoes?

A: Yes.

Q: Where are the shoes now?

A: I threw them in the garbage.

Q: Is that because there was blood on them?

A: The heels were run down and—

Q: How about the shirt?

A: Yes, had blood on it.

Q: How did the shirt get torn?

A: She grabbed me here.

Q: You mean the woman you cut and tried to rape tore your shirt?

A: Yes.

Q: I show you this undershirt. Does that belong to you?

A: Yes.

Q: Were you wearing that on the night of that occurrence?

A: Yes.

Q: I see some blood on the tan coat. Do you know how that blood got there?

A: It was there that day.

Q: I show you these black pants? Were these the pants you were wearing that night?

A: Yes.

Q: Did you get any blood on the pants?

A: Yes.

Q: What did you do?

A: I washed them out.

Q: When was that? The same day?

A: The same night.

Q: How did you wash them?

A: I put them in cold water and cold water soaks out blood and bring it out; and I use Clorox at least twice and soaked them.

Q: Where did you wash these black pants to get the blood out?

A: At my girl's house in her bathroom.

Q: What is her name?

A: Beverly Payne.

Postal had put one hundred twenty questions to Whitmore who had answered everything the Assistant District Attorney asked. Together, the Borrero and Edmonds statements had taken thirty-seven minutes to record. Postal packed up his notes and, with the stenotypist, left the precinct. Now it was Assistant District Attorney Koste's turn to question Whitmore, about the Wylie-Hoffert murders.

Until the night of Friday, April 24, 1964, Peter Koste had had no association with the Wylie-Hoffert case. The vagaries of work schedules had unexpectedly flung him into the midst of it. When the police believed Whitmore had cleared up all the mysteries of the investigation, Captain Weldon telephoned the Manhattan District Attorney's office to request that an official confession be taken. Koste was not hand-picked to obtain the Wylie-Hoffert confession; the task fell to him only because he was on duty that night.

Koste was thirty-nine years old and had been with the District Attorney's office four years. Like many other young lawyers, he had been drawn to the job through the esteem and reputation District Attorney Frank S. Hogan had acquired for running a nonpolitical, crusading department. Hogan chose his men carefully; each of them was a knowledgeable lawyer and a tough prosecutor.

Before Koste saw Whitmore, he was apprised quickly of all details of the Wylie-Hoffert slayings and of exactly what Whitmore had told his police questioners in the last six hours. Koste obtained every fragment of information. The evidence seemed more than sufficient for him to question Whitmore.

A problem arose, however. Detectives Lynch and Dunleavy had shown the photograph of the girl in the convertible to Janice Wylie's parents and sister and to a close friend of Emily Hoffert, and none of them could positively identify the girl as Janice. The police told Koste that Whitmore had changed his story about finding the photograph, claiming to have picked it up in various places. They were convinced the photograph had come from the Wylie-Hoffert apartment—as Whitmore said at one point— even if the blonde in the snapshot was not Janice Wylie. Koste ordered Weldon and McKearney to continue trying to identify the photograph.

It was now early Saturday morning. Koste pored over the information he had obtained. Finally, at 1:40 A.M., he was ready. Whitmore was still seated in the interrogation room. Before asking his first official question, Koste advised Whitmore of his constitutional right to remain silent, adding that if Whitmore wanted to volunteer a statement there was a stenotypist available to record his confession. Koste noted Whitmore's remarkable composure and his precise, slow manner of speech. Whitmore hardly hesitated before assuring Koste he was willing to answer any questions. Koste summoned Dennis Sheehan, a stenotypist attached to the Manhattan District Attorney's office. Whitmore was ready for his third "Q and A" confession of the night, a confession that one day would be converted into a remarkable piece of courtroom evidence against the police. As Bulger, DiPrima, and Aidala watched and listened, Koste began. He put his first question to Whitmore at exactly 2:00 A.M.

Q: What is your full name?

A: George Whitmore Jr.

Q: How old are you?

A: Nineteen.

Q: Where do you live?

A: Here in New York.

Q: Yes?

A: 191 Amboy Street, apartment 17.

Q: With whom do you live there?

A: My brother and cousin.

Q: What is your brother's name?

A: Gerald.

Q: What is your cousin's name?

A: Lita Johnson.

Q: How long have you been living at that address, George?

A: About six months.

Q: Where were you born?

A: Philadelphia.

Q: When were you born?

A: May 26, 1944.

Q: How many brothers or sisters do you have?

A: Three brothers, one sister.

Q: How far did you go in school?

A: Eighth grade.

Q: Where did you go to school?

A: Wildwood.

Q: Where was that school located?

A: Wildwood.

Q: Yes?

A: Name of the street, I don't know.

Q: When did you come to New York?

A: First come to New York?

Q: Yes.

A: About two years ago.

Q: You have lived in New York since?

A: No. I been running back and forth from Jersey to New York, Jersey to New York.

Q: How long have you been living at 191 Amboy Street?

A: About six months now.

Q: You have been living with your brother and cousin at that address?

A: Yes.

Q: George, my name is Peter Koste. I'm an Assistant District Attorney in New York County. This gentleman that I'm pointing to is Detective Edward Bulger. You have spoken to him before, is that correct?

A: Yes.

Q: This gentleman I'm pointing to is Detective Joseph DiPrima. You have spoken to him before, have you not?

A: Yes.

Q: And this gentleman I'm pointing to is Detective Richard Aidala. Do you see him, the man I'm pointing to?

A: Yes.

Q: You have seen him before, have you not?

A: Yes.

Q: This gentleman to my left is Mr. Sheehan.

[Detective DiPrima leaves room.]

Q: He is a stenographer and the machine he has in front of him —do you see him operating it now?

A: Yes.

Q: That's a stenotype machine. Everything that I'm saying now, George, is being taken down by Mr. Sheehan, and anything you say or anybody says in this room will be taken down on the machine, do you understand that?

A: Yes.

[Detective DiPrima returns to room.]

Q: Do you understand that, George?

A: Yes.

Q: Now, George, I would like to ask you about an event that took place in a building on 88th Street located between Park and Madison Avenue in New York. Did there come a time in August when you went to that building?

A: Yes.

Q: Now, will you tell me the whole truth about everything that you know about that building and what went on in that building?

A: Yes.

Q: You will tell me the whole truth of your own free will?

A: Yes.

Q: You understand that you don't have to tell me everything and I will listen to you only if you tell me the truth, do you understand that?

A: Yes.

Q: You have a right not to say anything if you don't want to, do you understand that?

A: Yes.

Q: Do you want to tell me the whole truth about what I have spoken to you about before and anything I ask you now?

A: Yes.

Q: You are doing it of your own free will, George?

A: Yes.

Q: Now, did there come a time some time in August when you went up to that building located on 88th Street between Park and Madison Avenue?

A: Yes.

Q: Now, when in August did you go up to that building located on 88th Street?

A: About the last two weeks in August.

Q: It was during the last two weeks of August?

A: Yes.

Q: Could it have been the last week of August, some day during the last week?

A: Yes.

Q: Was it a Saturday, Sunday or week day you went up there?

A: Week day.

Q: Do you remember what day?

A: Wednesday or Thursday.

Q: Now, that building is located in New York. Where were you coming from or leaving from before you went into New York that day?

A: I come from my house.

Q: That was a Wednesday or Thursday of August 1963, is that correct?

A: Yes.

Q: That's last year?

A: Yes.

Q: What time did you leave your house, George?

A: About eight-thirty. Eight.

Q: About eight or eight-thirty in the morning?

A: Yes.

Q: Did you leave alone?

A: Yes.

Q: Where did you go after you left?

A: I went to the train station. Fulton.

Q: What train station?

A: 8th Avenue.

Q: Did you take the train?

A: Yes.

Q: Where did you take the train to?

A: 42nd Street.

Q: You took the train to 42nd Street?

A: Yes.

Q: You got off at that station?

A: Yes.

Q: How much money did you have on you?

A: About fifty cents.

Q: What happened when you got to the 42nd Street station, George?

A: I got out, got off the train. Start sightseeing.

Q: Where?

A: Sightseeing the stores.

Q: Where, on the street level?

A: I came up out of the street level.

Q: You got off onto the platform? Did you walk up the steps out into the street?

A: Yes.

Q: What did you do when you got out there?

A: Start sightseeing, looking around.

Q: Looking around where, George?

A: Sightseeing, you know, the strange sights I never seen before.

Q: What sight did you see, George?

A: Different places.

Q: Stores?

A: Yes.

Q: Did you go into the stores?

A: Looked in the windows.

Q: Window shopping?

A: Yes.

Q: What did you do while window-shopping, were you walking?

A: Yes.

Q: Toward where?

A: Toward Park Avenue.

Q: Did there come a time you got to Park Avenue?

A: Yes.

Q: Where on Park Avenue? What street? When you reached Park Avenue what street was it? Was it 42nd Street and Park Avenue?

A: [No response.]

Q: You say you went out on 42nd Street and went window-shopping, is that correct?

A: Yes.

Q: Then you came to Park Avenue?

A: Yes.

Q: Did you continue walking?

A: When I got to Park Avenue?

Q: Yes. What did you do when you got to Park Avenue?

A: Before I got to Park Avenue I made a couple of turns.

Q: Into some street?

A: Yes.

Q: What did you do, continue walking on the street?

A: Yes.

Q: Where did you walk to?

A: I end up 88th Street.

Q: 88th Street?

A: Yes.

Q: 88th Street and where?

A: I don't know the name of the street.

Q: What did you do when you got to 88th Street?

A: Park Avenue.

Q: 88th Street and Park Avenue?

A: Yes.

Q: Did you walk into 88th Street then?

A: Yes.

Q: Where did you walk to on 88th Street?

A: I was on the block.

Q: On 88th Street?

A: Yes.

Q: What did you do then when you were on the block?

A: Spotted the building.

Q: What kind of building?

A: About a four-story house.

Q: Four-story house you think it was?

A: Yes.

Q: What did you do when you spotted this four-story house? You think it was four stories?

A: Four or five stories.

[*Detective Bulger leaves room.*]

Q: You spotted a four- or five-story house. Could it have been more than four or five stories?

A: Yes, it could have been.

Q: It could have been more than that?

A: Yes.

Q: What did you do when you spotted this house?

A: It gave me the idea I could go up on the roof.

Q: Of that house that you spotted?

A: Yes.

Q: Why did you want to go up on the roof?

A: To get a better view, you know, down.

Q: So you could look down from the roof of this house?

A: Yes.

Q: Did you go into the building?

A: Yes.

Q: How did you go into the building?

A: Front entrance.

Q: Front entrance?

A: Yes. Walked around through the lobby.

Q: You went through the lobby?

A: Yes.

Q: Was that on street level?

A: Yes.

Q: What did you do after you got into the lobby?

A: There was an exit to the left. I went in the exit to go upstairs.

Q: After you went to the lobby you saw an exit?

A: Yes.

[*Detective Bulger returns to room.*]

Q: Where was this exit?

A: You go into the building it is to the left.

Q: You spotted this exit from the lobby?

A: Yes.

Q: Did you go into the exit?

A: Yes.

Q: What happened after you went into the exit?

A: I went upstairs, the third floor.

Q: What did you do after you went up the steps on to the third floor?

A: There was this door open. I saw the door cracked.

Q: The door of an apartment?

A: Yes.

Q: You mentioned that this building was about four or five stories, could it have been eight to ten stories?

A: I don't know if it's quite that high or not.

Q: Could it have been eight stories?

A: Yes.

Q: But it could have been more than four or five stories?

A: Yes.

Q: Now, you say you walked up through the exit to the third floor and what did you see on the third floor?

A: This apartment door was cracked open.

Q: How far open was it?

A: About an inch and a half.

Q: What did you do when you saw this door cracked?

A: First I listened to the door.

Q: Why did you listen to the door?

A: I don't know.

Q: But you just listened?

A: Yes.

Q: Did you want to listen to see whether you heard anyone in the apartment before you went into it?

A: Yes.

Q: Is that why you listened?

A: Yes.

Q: So what happened? Did you hear anything?

A: No.

Q: What did you do then?

A: I pushed the door open, looked in. Wasn't nobody in the kitchen.

Q: The door opens into what room?

A: The kitchen.

Q: Did you go into the kitchen?

A: Yes.

Q: What did you do in the kitchen?

A: I look around.

Q: What did you see?

A: I saw a table.

Q: What did you do then?

A: I start walking through the kitchen. I saw a case of soda bottles.

Q: What kind of soda bottles?

A: Coca-Cola bottles.

Q: Were they full or empty bottles?

A: Empty.

Q: What did you do after you saw the soda bottles?

A: Picked up three.

Q: Empty bottles?

A: Yes.

Q: What did you do with them?

A: Hold them in case somebody came in.

Q: What were you going to do in case somebody came in?

A: Protect myself.

Q: With the bottles?

A: Yes.

Q: So what did you do after you picked up the bottles?

A: Walked into the dining room.

Q: What did you see in the dining room?

A: I saw a little table.

Q: In the dining room?

A: Yes.

Q: Yes?

A: I didn't pay too much attention to the dining room. I went out to the hall.

Q: When you went into the dining room did you have the three bottles in your hand?

A: Yes.

Q: You say you looked on the table in the dining room?

A: I said there was a table in there.

Q: Was there anything on the table?

A: Not that I know of.

Q: What did you do after that?

A: Went out to the hall.

Q: The hall of the apartment itself?

A: No, the hall of the house.

Q: Which is part of the apartment?

A: Yes.

Q: You walked through the kitchen into the dining room and then you went into the hall of the same apartment, is that right?

A: Yes.

Q: Did you still have the bottles in your hand when you went out into the hall?

A: Yes.

Q: What did you do then, George?

A: I went into the bedroom. The front room.

Q: The front room. You walked down the hall?

A: Yes, made a right and a front room. Living room.

Q: You went into a living room?

A: Yes.

Q: It is off the hallway?

A: Yes.

Q: Did you go in the living room?

A: Yes.

Q: What did you do in the living room?

A: I set the bottles down at the door.

Q: Of the living room?

A: Yes.

Q: You set them down at the door there?

A: Yes.

Q: You went into the living room?

A: Yes.

Q: What did you do in the living room?

A: I looked around.

Q: What did you see in the living room?

A: There was this big couch. It had an end table.

Q: At the end of the couch?

A: Lamp table. There was this picture on it.

Q: What kind of picture?

A: Picture of a girl.

Q: Photograph?

A: Yes, on a car.

Q: It was on this table, this lamp table?

A: Yes.

Q: Was the lamp on the table?

A: Yes.

Q: Do you recall what color the material on the couch was?

A: It was a dark color.

Q: Dark material or leather?

A: Dark material.

Q: What did you do after you saw this photograph?

A: Picked it up and looked at it.

Q: It was a photograph of what?

A: A girl.

Q: One girl?

A: Yes.

Q: After you looked at it what did you do?

A: Put it in my pocket.

Q: What did you do then?

A: I start looking around the front room.

Q: Did you leave the living room then?

A: Yes.

Q: You went out where?

A: Back into the hall.

Q: The bottles were outside the doorway leading into the living room?

A: Yes. I picked them up on the way out.

Q: The bottles?

A: Yes.

Q: The three bottles?

A: Yes.

Q: What did you do then?

A: Walked toward the bedroom. There was a small bathroom. I peeked in there.

Q: In the bathroom?

A: Yes.

Q: Did you see anyone in the bathroom?

A: No.

Q: What did you do after you looked in the bathroom?

A: I went out into this bedroom next door across the hall from it.

Q: Across from the bathroom?

A: Yes.

Q: Did you go into the bedroom?

A: Yes.

Q: Did you still have the bottles in your hand then?

A: I set them down by the door.

Q: Of the bedroom?

A: Yes.

Q: Then you went into the bedroom?

A: Yes.

Q: What did you see in the bedroom?

A: The bed, bed lamp.

Q: How many beds?

A: Two beds. Twin beds.

Q: Anyone in there?

A: No.

Q: What did you do then in the bedroom?

A: I was on my way out.

Q: Of the bedroom?

A: Yes.

Q: What happened then?

A: That's when this girl came out as I was coming out. She was out in the hall. She spotted me.

Q: Where was she when she spotted you?

A: Came out of the bathroom.

Q: The same bathroom you peeked in?

A: Two bathrooms.

Q: She was coming out of another bathroom?

A: Yes.

Q: How far was she away from you at that time when you saw her? From where you're sitting to where was she?

A: That distance over to the wall.

Q: About six feet?

A: I'd say about six feet.

Q: Was she wearing anything at that time?

A: She had a white sheet covering her body.

Q: What kind of sheet?

A: Bedsheet.

Q: What part of her body was the bedsheet covering?

A: Just the bottom part.

Q: From her waist down?

A: Yes.

Q: What did she have from the waist up?

A: Nothing.

Q: She was nude?

A: Yes.

Q: Did you or she say anything then?

A: That's when she start screaming.

Q: What did you do when she started to scream?

A: I ran over to grab hold of her, told her shut up.

Q: How did you grab her?

A: Around from the back. Grabbed her by the neck.

Q: How did you grab her by the neck?

A: Caught her around like that.

Q: You put your arm around her neck?

A: Yes.

Q: You were standing behind her at that time when you put your arm around her neck?

A: I grabbed her and turn her around.

Q: Where were the bottles at this time?

A: By the door.

Q: Of the bedroom?

A: Yes.

Q: What happened after you grabbed her around the neck, still screaming?

A: Kept on screaming.

Q: What did you do then?

A: I pulled her into the room and grabbed the bottle.

Q: What room?

A: The bedroom I came out of.

Q: The same bedroom you came out of?

A: Yes.

Q: What happened in there after you dragged her into the bedroom? She still screaming?

A: Still screaming. I got excited and hit her.

Q: After you pulled her into the bedroom did you have the bottle in your hand at that time?

A: I grabbed one and shut her up.

Q: While you were holding her you grabbed the bottle also?

A: Yes.

Q: What happened in the bedroom, she still screaming?

A: Yes.

Q: What did you do then?

A: I hit her with the bottle.

Q: How many bottles did you have in your hand?

A: One.

Q: You hit her with the bottle?

A: Yes.

Q: Where did you hit her with the bottle?

A: Beside the head.

Q: Beside the head?

A: Yes.

Q: On the head?

A: Yes.

Q: Did you hit her hard on the head?

A: Yes. The bottle broke.

Q: What did you do after you hit her on the head with the bottle and the bottle broke?

A: She fell unconscious.

Q: She fell on the floor?

A: Yes.

Q: Where in the bedroom did she fall?

A: By the bed.

Q: By the bed?

A: Yes.

Q: Where was the bed located? You mentioned there were twin beds.

A: One by the door and one by the window. In between there's a lamp and table.

Q: Where did she fall?

A: Between the window and the table. The window and the bed.

Q: Between the window and the bed?

A: Yes.

Q: Is this bed the first bed that you come to when you enter the room or the furthest bed from you when you enter the room?

A: The furthest bed.

Q: She fell between the window and the bed after you hit her on the head with the bottle and the bottle broke?

A: Yes.

Q: What did you do then, George?

A: I tied her up.

Q: How did you tie her up?

A: With the sheet she had covering her body. I tore strips from it.

Q: How did you tear it?

A: With my hands.

Q: With your hands you tore strips?

A: Yes.

Q: What did you do with the strips?

A: Tied her hands.

Q: How did you tie her hands?

A: Together in front of her.

Q: Together in front of her?

A: Yes.

Q: Did you tie any other part of her body?

A: Tied up her feet.

Q: With what?

A: Same material.

Q: The strips that you ripped from the sheet?

A: Yes.

Q: Did she have anything on her other than the strips you tied her with at that time?

A: No.

Q: She was nude?

A: Yes.

Q: How was she lying on the floor then?

A: She was on her side then.

Q: What happened after you tied her up?

A: That's when I start to play with her. No, first she had the Kotex and I pulled it out.

Q: How did you know she had the Kotex on?

A: You could see it sticking out.

Q: Sticking out of where?

A: Pussy.

Q: What did you do with the Kotex?

A: Pulled it out.

Q: What did you do with it?

A: Threw it on the floor.

Q: Any particular place on the floor?

A: By the bed.

Q: What did you do then?

A: Start to play with her.

Q: How did you start to play with her?

A: Put my finger in her.

Q: In where?

A: Her pussy.

Q: What did you do?

A: I got tired. I just got up and start searching the drawers.

Q: How long did you play with your finger in her pussy?

A: Ten minutes, fifteen minutes, maybe more.

Q: Is that all you were doing at that time, playing with your finger in her pussy?

A: Yes.

Q: Did she appear unconscious then? After ten minutes did you take your finger out of her pussy?

A: Yes.

Q: What did you do?

A: Start searching the dresser.

Q: A dresser in the bedroom?

A: Yes.

Q: What did you do when you went up to the dresser?

A: I opened the dresser, looked in and found this Noxzema.

Q: Where was this Noxzema?

A: Second drawer.

Q: Of the dresser?

A: Yes.

Q: How did you know it was Noxzema?

A: It was in a Noxzema bottle. Jar.

Q: The printing read Noxzema?

A: Yes.

Q: What did you do with the Noxzema jar?

A: Come back over, start putting it in her pussy.

Q: You took Noxzema out of the jar with your finger?

A: Yes.

Q: What did you do with the Noxzema you took out of the jar?

A: Start putting it in her pussy.

Q: Why did you do that, George?

A: I don't know.

Q: You put it in her pussy?

A: Yes.

Q: What did you do after you put the Noxzema in her pussy? After you put the Noxzema in her pussy what did you do, did you start playing with her again?

A: Yes.

Q: With the Noxzema in her pussy?

A: Yes, finger in again.

Q: Did you play with her pussy some more then?

A: Yes.

Q: About how long did you play then?

A: About twenty minutes.

Q: What did you do after twenty minutes, George?

A: That's when her mother came in.

Q: Why do you say it was her mother?

A: That's what I understand, it was her mother.

Q: How was this woman dressed you say was her mother?

A: I couldn't describe how she was dressed.

Q: Was she wearing anything?

A: She had on a dress.

Q: She have any glasses on?

A: Yes.

Q: When did you first see her?

A: When she said, "Who the hell are you? What the fuck you doing in my bedroom?"

Q: What were you doing at that time when you heard her saying that?

A: Kneeling down beside the girl.

Q: Playing with her at that time?

A: Yes.

Q: You had your finger in her pussy when you saw a woman you call her mother come in?

A: Yes.

Q: What did she say?

A: "Who the hell are you? What the fuck you doing in my bedroom?"

Q: What did you do?

A: I got up, told her to be quiet. She start hollering. I ran over.

Q: Ran over to her?

A: And grabbed her, yes.

Q: Was she in the bedroom when you grabbed her?

A: No.

Q: Where was she?

A: Out in the hall.

Q: Of the bedroom?

A: Yes.

Q: You ran over and grabbed her?

A: Yes.

Q: What did you do after you grabbed her?

A: Kept telling her shut up. She wouldn't shut up.

Q: What was she doing when you say she wouldn't shut up?

A: Screaming and hollering help.

Q: You were telling her to shut up?

A: Yes.

Q: Did she shut up?

A: No.

Q: What did you do?

A: Took her in the room by the wrist.

Q: Into the bedroom?

A: Yes.

Q: What happened then?

A: Grabbed the bottle.

Q: Where did you grab the bottle from?

A: From the door.

Q: This was a Coca-Cola bottle?

A: Yes.

Q: Where was the bottle when you grabbed it?

A: By the door.

Q: What did you do with the bottle?

A: Hit her up beside the head.

Q: How many times did you hit her on the head?

A: Once.

Q: What happened after you hit her on the head with the bottle once?

A: She fell in the bed.

Q: She fell onto the bed?

A: Yes.

Q: Which bed did she fall in?

A: By the door when you walk in.

Q: The first bed when you walk in?

A: Yes.

Q: What did you do with the bottle?

A: Dropped it.

Q: What happened after she fell on the bed?

A: I tied her up.

Q: How did you tie her up?

A: Same manner as the girl on the floor. Her hands and feet.

Q: With what did you tie her up?

A: The sheet.

Q: Did you cut strips off the sheet?

A: Yes.

Q: How did you cut the strips off?

A: With my hand, tore off.

Q: What did you do with the strips from the sheet?

A: I used it to tie her up.

Q: How did you tie her up?

A: Her hands in front and legs.

Q: Strips from the bedsheet that you ripped off with your hands?

A: Yes.

Q: After you tied her up how was she lying on the bed?

A: She was laying on her back.

Q: What did you do then after you tied her up and she was laying on her back? Was she unconscious?

A: Yes.

Q: Was she saying anything?

A: No.

Q: What did you do then?

A: I start to have intercourse with her.

Q: You started to have what?

A: Start to have intercourse with her.

Q: How?

A: I said I start to.

Q: Did you take your penis out of your pants?

A: Yes.

Q: Was it hard?

A: No.

Q: You just took your penis out of your pants?

A: Yes.

Q: How did you take your penis out of your pants?

A: Pulled my zipper down, took it out.

Q: What did you do after you took it out?

A: It wasn't hard. I put my mouth down.

Q: Down where?

A: To where her pussy was.

Q: Did you do anything before you put your mouth down to where her pussy was?

A: No.

Q: Did she have pants on, bloomers?

A: Yes.

Q: Did you do anything with the bloomers?

A: Stretched the rubber down to where her pussy was.

Q: You stretched the rubber down below her pussy?

A: Yes.

Q: Didn't take her bloomers off?

A: No.

Q: What did you do, pull the front part of her bloomers down below her pussy?

A: Yes.

Q: What did you do after that?

A: I start putting my mouth down there. She came to.

Q: Did you put your mouth on her pussy?

A: That's when she came to.

Q: What happened when she came to?

A: She start screaming and hollering again.

Q: What did you do?

A: I picked the bottle up from the floor, hit her again.

Q: The Coke bottle?

A: Yes.

Q: Where did you hit her this time?

A: Beside the head again.

Q: How many times did you hit her?

A: Once.

Q: What happened after you hit her on the head?

A: I got excited. It didn't knock her out. Still screaming.

Q: After you hit her this time on the head she kept screaming?

A: Yes.

Q: Still have the bottle in your hand?

A: No.

Q: What did you do?

A: I ran to the kitchen.

Q: Why did you go to the kitchen?

A: Looking for a knife.

Q: What did you do in the kitchen?

A: Look in the sink, didn't see a knife. Happened to turn around and saw the table drawer.

Q: The kitchen table drawer?

A: Yes. There was knives in there.

Q: You opened the drawer?

A: Yes.

Q: There were knives in there?

A: Yes. I put my hand in, grabbed a handful.

Q: How many knives did you grab?

A: About three.

Q: What did you do?

A: I ran back in.

Q: Into the bedroom?

A: Yes.

Q: She still on the bed at that time?

A: Yes.

Q: What did you do?

A: Start cutting and swinging at her.

Q: With one of the knives? You say you had three knives?

A: Two in this hand, one this hand.

Q: Two in your left hand, one in your right?

A: Yes.

Q: What did you do?

A: Swinging with my right.

Q: The hand you had one knife in?

A: Yes.

Q: You started swinging at her?

A: Yes.

Q: Did you hit her with the knife?

A: Yes.

Q: Did you cut her with the knife?

A: Yes.

Q: Where did you cut her with the knife?

A: In the face.

Q: How many times?

A: About three times in the face, about two times in the body, chest.

Q: Two times in the body, in the chest?

A: Yes.

Q: You stabbed her with the knife in the body in the chest?

A: Yes.

Q: How many times?

A: Twice.

Q: Then what?

A: She stopped hollering. I was still heated when she stopped.

Q: You were still heated?

A: Excited.

Q: You say you cut her with this knife about three times on the face and you stabbed her about the chest two times?

A: Yes.

Q: Did you cut her any more with the knife after that?

A: No, because she stopped hollering.

Q: What did you do? You had one knife in the right hand, two in the other, what did you do then?

A: Before I knew it I turned around and turned on the little girl, start cutting her. Two times in the face.

Q: Which knife did you cut her with?

A: Same knife.

Q: With the one knife you had in your hand?

A: Yes.

Q: Still have the other two in the other hand?

A: Yes.

Q: Which knife did you cut her with?

A: It wasn't the big one.

Q: Which hand was the knife in that you cut her with?

A: The right hand.

Q: Which girl did you cut after you cut the girl on the bed?

A: The other girl was on the floor.

Q: She still unconscious?

A: Yes.

Q: The girl that was lying on the floor between the window and the bed?

A: Yes.

Q: How did you cut her with the knife?

A: Swinging at her face.

Q: Did you cut her face?

A: Yes.

Q: How many times?

A: Twice.

Q: What did you do then after you cut her twice?

A: Then I was still kind of angry.

Q: You cut her any more after you cut her twice on the face?

A: No.

Q: You were still angry then?

A: Yes.

Q: Did you still have one knife in one hand and the other two knives in the other hand?

A: Still had three in my hand. I took the two in my left hand and put them on the floor and put my foot on them and broke the blade.

Q: Why did you do that?

A: Satisfaction.

Q: Satisfaction for what?

A: I don't know, I was angry.

Q: You were angry?

A: Yes.

Q: Did the blades of the two knives break?

A: Yes.

Q: What did you do with the other knife?

A: I put the two handles on the radiator.

Q: Of the broken knives?

A: Yes.

Q: Did you still have the other knife in your hand?

A: Yes.

Q: Where was the radiator you put the handles on?

A: By the window.

Q: In the bedroom?

A: Yes.

Q: What happened to the broken blades of the two knives?

A: They just flew.

Q: How big were these two knives?

A: Butcher knives, about like that.

Q: Were they about ten or twelve inches long?

A: About eleven inches.

Q: What did you do with the other knife after you put the handles of the two broken knives on the radiator?

A: I ran to the bathroom.

Q: With the one knife?

A: Yes.

Q: Why did you run into the bathroom?

A: To wash it off.

Q: What did you do in the bathroom?

A: Washed the blood off. Washed my hands.

Q: Blood off the knife?

A: Yes.

Q: And washed—

A: Blood off my hands.

Q: What did you do then? Did you go back into the bedroom?

A: Before I left the bedroom I pulled the shades down.

Q: Where were the shades?

A: Over the window.

Q: The windows of the bedroom?

A: Yes.

Q: Before you left to wash the blood off the knife and your hands?

A: Yes.

Q: Why did you pull the shades down?

A: If they came to they would get up.

Q: The two girls you cut?

A: Yes, and somebody in the next apartment could see them tied up.

Q: You were afraid somebody from the outside could look into the apartment?

A: Yes.

Q: You pulled the shade down?

A: Yes.

Q: How many shades?

A: Two.

Q: What did you do after you pulled the shades down?

A: Cut some material from the spread that was on the floor.

Q: A bedspread?

A: Yes.

Q: How did it get on the floor?

A: The little girl pulled it off the bed.

Q: Which one?

A: The first one laying on the floor.

Q: The first one you cut laying on the floor between the window and the bed?

A: Yes.

Q: What did you do with the bedspread?

A: Put it in their mouths.

Q: The girl between the window and the bed?

A: Yes. Before that I took the other girl and—

Q: That was on the bed?

A: Yes.

Q: What did you do with her?

A: Put her down with the other one. Tied them together.

Q: Alongside the other one?

A: Yes.

Q: How did you tie them together?

A: Side by side.

Q: Lying alongside each other?

A: Yes.

Q: How did you tie them together?

A: With the sheet.

Q: The bedsheet?

A: Yes.

Q: The same sheet you tore strips from to tie each girl's hands and feet?

A: Yes.

Q: Did you tear more strips from the sheet?

A: I tore enough to get around the waist. Tied them up.

Q: You tied them around the waist?

A: Yes.

Q: You tied them together around their waists?

A: Yes.

Q: Where else did you tie them other than around the waist?

A: The waist was the only place I tied them together. Individually I had their hands and feet.

Q: Why did you tie them together?

A: So they couldn't get loose so easy.

Q: Did they appear to be unconscious then at that time, when you tied them together around their waists?

A: Yes.

Q: What did you do then after you tied them together around their waists?

A: I went to the bathroom.

[*Detective Bulger leaves room.*]

Q: Before you went to the bathroom you mentioned something about a bedspread. Did you do anything with the bedspread?

A: I got a razor from the bathroom.

Q: When did you go to the bathroom to get the razor?

A: In the time this girl was knocked out on the bed.

Q: Yes?

A: There was a box of razors.

Q: Where were the razors?

A: In the toilet bowl, the thing that hold the water.

Q: This was at the time one of the girls was laying on the bed?

A: Yes.

[*Detective Bulger returns to room.*]

Q: You got a razor blade from the bathroom?

A: Yes.

Q: Where did you find the blade?

A: On the thing that hold the water.

Q: The water tank?

A: Yes.

Q: What was it, a box of razor blades?

A: Yes.

Q: What did you do?

A: Took one razor blade.

Q: What kind of blade was it, double-edge or single-edge?

A: Double-edge.

Q: What did you do?

A: Took it back in, cut a piece of spread.

Q: The bedspread?

A: Yes.

Q: And the girl was still laying on the bed then?

A: Yes.

Q: What did you do? Did you cut the bedspread?

A: Yes.

Q: What did you do with the piece you cut?

A: Cut two pieces, one for each one, and put it in their mouths.

Q: Each of the girl's mouths?

A: Yes.

Q: The girl on the bed, you put a piece in her mouth and the girl on the floor you put a piece of bedspread in her mouth?

A: Yes.

Q: What did you do after you did that?

A: I went to the bathroom.

Q: Before you went to the bathroom when did you take the girl off the bed and tie her up with the piece of bedsheet stripping, tie them together on the floor?

A: That was after I got finished with everything.

Q: So then after you put a piece of bedspread in each of the girl's mouths one of the girls was still on the bed?

A: No, both tied up then. That was the last thing I did.

Q: Let's go back. After you cut the girl that was on the floor, the other girl was still on the bed, right?

A: Yes.

Q: What did you do then?

A: Right after I finished cutting that's when I dragged her on the floor.

Q: Dragged the girl that was on the bed onto the floor?

A: Yes.

Q: What did you do?

A: Tied her up along with the other one.

Q: Around the waist with the piece of bedsheet strip?

A: Yes.

Q: What did you do then?

A: I got the razor.

Q: Went to the bathroom and got the razor?

A: Yes.

Q: Came back to the bedroom?

A: Yes.

Q: What did you do in the bedroom?

A: I cut the bedspread.

Q: Yes, what did you do with it?

A: Rolled it up, put it in their mouths.

Q: In each of their mouths, after you tied them together?

A: Yes.

Q: What did you do then?

A: After I tied them together I went to the bathroom, washed my hands.

Q: Did you take the knives with you?

A: Only took one with me.

Q: The other knives, the handles were on the radiator, the broken knives, is that right?

A: Yes.

Q: You went to the bathroom with one knife?

A: Yes.

Q: What did you do with it in the bathroom?

A: Washed the blood off.

Q: The knife?

A: Yes.

Q: Did you have blood on your hands?

A: Yes. Washed the blood off my hands.

Q: What did you do then?

A: Left the knife in the bathroom.

Q: How big was the knife you left in the bathroom?

A: About like that.

Q: About ten, twelve inches long?

A: Yes.

Q: You left the knife in the bathroom?

A: Yes.

Q: Do you recall where in the bathroom you left it?

A: On the sink.

Q: Is this the knife you cut the girls with?

A: Yes.

Q: Same knife?

A: Same knife.

Q: You left the knife on the sink?

A: Yes.

Q: What did you do then? Did you leave the bathroom?

A: Yes.

Q: Where did you go?

A: The soda bottles, I had got the ones that weren't broken and put them back and tried to wipe my fingerprints off.

Q: How many of them?

A: Two I think it was.

Q: Two of them because one broke?

A: Yes.

Q: Did you wipe your fingerprints off the soda bottles?

A: Yes.

Q: What did you do with the bottles?

A: Put them back in the case.

Q: Where you originally took them out?

A: Yes.

Q: Where was this case?

A: In the kitchen by the door.

Q: Kitchen door?

A: Yes.

Q: What happened after you put the two bottles in the case?

A: I listened to the door, see anybody out in the hall.

Q: Of the apartment, the outside hall of the apartment?

A: Yes.

Q: Was that the same door you came into the apartment from?

A: Yes.

Q: What happened when you went to the door and listened?

A: I didn't hear nobody. I looked out. Didn't see nobody. That's when I took off.

Q: Where did you take off to?

A: Same entrance I took to come up. Downstairs.

Q: Through the stairs?

A: Yes.

Q: Down the stairs?

A: Yes.

Q: Where did you go when you got downstairs, the last set of steps?

A: Came back out through the front.

Q: Went into the lobby and out through the front, the same place you came into the building from?

A: Yes.

Q: You went out on the 88th Street sidewalk then?

A: Yes.

Q: Where did you go then?

A: Start walking down Park Avenue. Then I made a turn, a couple of turns. I don't know the name of the street. I got back to the subway.

Q: What subway?

A: 42nd Street.

Q: Did you walk all the way back to 42nd Street?

A: Yes. When I got there I got the "A" train and come back to Brooklyn.

Q: Now, George, you mentioned to me earlier that you left home around eight or eight-thirty in the morning, is that correct?

A: Yes.

Q: Now, what time did you go into the building at 88th Street, into the apartment where you cut these two girls as you told me, about what time did you go in there?

A: About noon.

Q: Well, you left your house about eight or eight-thirty, is that correct?

A: Yes.

Q: What time did you get to New York? Did you get to New York about nine o'clock?

A: I got there about nine-thirty.

Q: About nine-thirty?

A: Yes.

Q: So would you say you got to the building on 88th Street, the one you're telling me about, at around ten o'clock?

A: About ten or twelve because I did a lot of looking around.

Q: You say you got to New York about nine, nine-thirty, right?

A: Yes.

Q: You walked over to this building you went into where you cut these two girls, right?

A: Yes.

Q: How long did it take you to walk to the building if you got to New York between nine and nine-thirty? Did you get there around ten o'clock or around that time?

A: I say about ten.

Q: About ten o'clock?

A: Yes.

Q: Did you get into the apartment some time about ten o'clock, ten, ten-fifteen when you went into the apartment, about that time?

A: Approximately.

Q: Approximately?

A: Yes.

Q: Now, you say you went back to 42nd Street?

A: Yes.

Q: Did you take the subway at 42nd Street?

A: Yes.

Q: Where did you go?

A: I got off on Rockaway.

Q: What train did you take?

A: "A" train.

Q: You got off where?

A: Rockaway.

Q: What did you do at Rockaway?

A: Got off Rockaway, start walking down Hopkinson.

Q: Why did you get off at Rockaway?

A: That's the only street I know. If I get off Rockaway and Fulton I know how to get home.

Q: You got off at the Rockaway-Fulton station?

A: Yes.

Q: Where did you go when you got there?

A: I went back to the block, Amboy.

Q: Did you go home?

A: I didn't go in the house. I sat on the stoop.

Q: About what time was it now when you sat on the stoop?

A: In the evening.

Q: Well, early afternoon?

A: Yes.

Q: You don't know about what time you got home when you sat on the stoop outside of your house?

A: School wasn't out yet.

Q: School usually lets out about three o'clock, right?

A: Yes.

Q: So it was before three o'clock, right?

A: Yes.

Q: Still light out?

A: Yes.

Q: How long did you sit on the stoop?

A: Sit out there pretty good while. Until dark.

Q: Did there come a time you went into your apartment?

A: No. I didn't go home at all that night.

Q: Where did you go?

A: Went around my uncle's house.

Q: Where is that?

A: Hopkinson.

Q: How far is your house?

A: Next block.

Q: Did you see your uncle then?

A: Yes.

Q: What is his name?

A: Blandell.

Q: What did you talk to him about?

A: Asked him lend me a dollar.

Q: Did he lend you a dollar?

A: Yes.

Q: What did you do?

A: Bought something to eat in the delicatessen. Ten-cent franks. Next day I went to the movies.

Q: The next day you went to the movies?

A: Yes.

Q: What movie did you go to?

A: East New York.

Q: Did you read the papers the next day?

A: No, I didn't read papers at that time.

Q: Did you read the papers at any time from the time you cut these two girls some time during the last week in August— you think it was a Wednesday, is that correct?

A: Yes.

Q: August of 1963?

A: Yes.

Q: Did you read anything about the cutting of these two girls in the newspapers?

A: No.

Q: Did you hear anybody talking about it?

A: No.

Q: Did you ever hear anything about the two girls that you cut from anyone?

A: No.

Q: You never read anything about it in the newspapers?

A: I didn't start reading newspapers until recently.

Q: Recently did you ever read anything about these two girls that you cut in the newspapers?

A: No.

Q: Nothing about them?

A: No.

Q: Now everything that you have told me, George, you told me voluntarily, is that correct?

A: Yes.

Q: And everything that you told me is the whole truth and nothing but the truth?

A: Yes, sir.

Q: As best you can recall?

A: Best I know.

Q: Is there anything else you remember about these two girls and what happened that you didn't tell me?

A: No. I guess I told you about everything.

MR. KOSTE: All right, thank you, George. I have no further questions.

The Assistant District Attorney had questioned Whitmore for fifty minutes. Koste now left the interrogation room and asked Captain Weldon if the three kitchen knives used in the murders could be brought to the precinct.

Meanwhile, Chief of Detectives McKearney and one of his aides, Lieutenant Cyril R. Regan, went about the precinct collecting facts on Whitmore's arrest; they were preparing an announcement for the press. McKearney and Regan interviewed Detectives Aidala, Bulger, DiPrima, and Fazio, and Patrolman Isola, all of whom had participated in Whitmore's arrest and confession. Isola had left the precinct at 7:00 P.M., before Whitmore had confessed fully to the Wylie-Hoffert murders. Shortly before midnight, he received a telephone call at home from a friend at the precinct who told him how important a catch Whitmore had become, and that the Police Commissioner might visit the precinct that night to congratulate the men responsible for the arrest. Hearing this, Isola hurried back to the squad room.

After an hour's wait, Koste learned there was no hope of getting the knives until 8:00 A.M., when the police property clerk's office opened. He returned to the interrogation room to complete the confession.

Q: George, there are a few more questions I would like to ask you and clear up a few things, okay?

A: Yes.

Q: Now, George, I show you a photograph and ask you whether you have ever seen that photograph before?

A: Yes.

Q: Where did you see that photograph for the first time?

A: In the front room on the end table where the lamp is.

Q: In the living room?

A: Yes.

Q: This is the photograph you took off the table and put into your pocket?

A: Yes.

Q: Did there come a time when you wrote on the back of this photograph?

A: Yes.

Q: When did you write something on the back of the photograph?

A: Couple of days after I got it.

Q: What did you write on the back of it?

A: From George to—

Q: It reads To George from—

A: Louise.

Q: What are these numbers?

A: 4657180.

Q: There are initials GW, are those your initials?

A: Yes.

Q: All the handwriting on the back of the picture is in your own handwriting?

A: Yes.

Q: You say this is the photograph you took off the lamp table in the living room and put in your pocket?

A: Yes.

Q: Why did you take the photograph?

A: She took a nice picture so I took it and put it in my pocket.

Q: What did you intend to do with the picture?

A: Show it to the boys and tell them I used to go with the girl.

Q: You wanted to show off for the boys?

A: Yes.

MR. KOSTE: Let the record indicate that the identifying mark of Detective Edward Bulger appears on the back of the photograph.

Q: George, I show you another photograph and in the photograph are three knives and a ruler. Have you ever seen those knives or knives similar to them before?

A: Yes.

Q: When?

A: At that apartment.

Q: In the apartment?

A: Yes.

Q: Where did you get those knives in the apartment?

A: From the kitchen table.

Q: Is that the time you told me previously that you took them from the table drawer in the kitchen?

A: Yes.

Q: Can you pick out the knife that you cut both girls with?

A: Yes.

Q: Point to it, will you?

A: This middle one.

MR. KOSTE: Let the record indicate that George is pointing to the middle knife of the three knives in the photograph.

Q: You say the middle knife is the knife you cut both girls with?

A: Yes.

Q: What did you do with the other two knives?

A: Broke them.

Q: Where did you break them?

A: On the floor with my foot and pulled up on them.

Q: What part of each of the knives, the knives on either end of the center knife, did you break?

A: How much did I break?

Q: Yes.

A: About that much.

Q: [*Indicating about three-quarters of the way up on the knife on the bottom of the photograph.*] How about the top knife, what part of that knife did you break?

A: Say about here.

Q: Could it have been a little less?

A: Yes, it could be.

Q: [*Indicating approximately halfway up from the tip of the knife.*] Is that correct?

A: Yes.

Q: Those are the two knives you broke?

A: Yes.

Q: The center knife is the knife you cut the two girls with, is that correct?

A: Yes.

Q: The two knives that you broke, you placed the handles with the remaining part of the blade on each knife on the radiator?

A: Yes.

Q: Where was this radiator?

A: Near the window.

Q: In the same bedroom where you cut the girls?

A: Yes.

MR. KOSTE: Let the record indicate that the photograph identified by the defendant has the identifying mark of Detective Edward Bulger.

Q: Now, George, I just would like to clear one further thing up. I believe you called the first girl that you cut "the little girl," that is the girl that fell between the window and the bed.

A: Yes.

Q: Is that correct?

A: Yes.

Q: Now, you originally told me that you cut her a few times around the face.

A: Yes.

Q: Now, was that correct?

A: No.

Q: Where did you cut her?

A: In the stomach.

Q: How did you cut her around the stomach?

A: Slice.

Q: How many times did you slice her on the stomach?

A: Two or three times.

Q: Now, the other woman that you say fell on the bed after you hit her the first time with a Coca-Cola bottle, you first told me that she fell on the bed closest to the entrance into the bedroom, was that correct?

A: No.

Q: Which bed did she fall on?

A: The one by the window.

Q: The second bed further away from the entrance to the bedroom, is that correct?

A: Yes.

Q: Is that the same bed which the little girl was lying between the bed and the window?

A: Yes.

Q: Mother, as you call her, was on that bed?

A: Yes.

Q: You also mentioned, George, that when you went up to the third floor in the building on 88th Street that you saw the door cracked. It was slightly open?

A: Yes.

Q: You went over to listen to find out if anybody was in there?

A: Yes.

Q: Why did you go over and listen to find out whether anybody was in there?

A: I was curious, I guess.

Q: Why did you go into the apartment?

A: [No response.]

Q: Did you go in there to steal something?

A: No.

Q: Why did you go in there?

A: I guess I went in there to look around.

Q: Just to look around?

A: Yes.

Q: No other reason?

A: No.

Q: Now, after you washed the blood off the knife you cut both girls with did you go back to the bedroom and go to the bureau drawers and do something?

A: No.

Q: Did you look in any of the other bureau drawers other than the bureau drawer from which you took the jar of Noxzema?

A: Yes. I looked in the top drawer.

Q: Did you take anything out of the top drawer?

A: No.

Q: Did you take anything other than the Noxzema out of one of the drawers of the bureau?

A: Yes, two pictures.

Q: Two pictures?

A: Yes.

Q: What was each photograph?

A: Of the lady and another lady with her.

Q: What did you do with these photographs?

A: Destroyed them.

Q: When did you destroy them?

A: Couple of days after I had them when I cleaned out my wallet.

Q: Where did you throw the pieces?

A: In the garbage.

Q: From which drawer did you take out the Noxzema?

A: Middle drawer.

Q: Do you remember how many drawers the bureau consisted of?

A: No.

Q: But you are sure you took it out of the middle drawer?

A: Yes.

Q: You opened the top drawer and took out two photographs?

A: The photos come out of the middle drawer too.

Q: The same drawer that you took the Noxzema out of?

A: Yes.

Q: Did you look in any other place in the apartment before you left other than the bureau you just mentioned?

A: No.

MR. KOSTE: All right, thank you, George. No further questions.

At 4:12 A.M., the Wylie-Hoffert confession was completed. Koste ordered Whitmore's arrest, and the police put the youth in the cage for the first time. In the one-man cell he could be under constant surveillance by anyone in the room.

McKearney had made his last important telephone call of the night during Koste's second "Q and A" session. He awoke Deputy Police Commissioner Walter Arm at his home in Queens, to notify him of Whitmore's confession and arrest. Arm, a former newspaper reporter who was in charge of police public relations, telephoned the Associated Press in Rockefeller Center to relay the news.

When the Associated Press has a big story moving over its wires, bells on its teletype machines ring dramatically at the start of the transmission of the story. At 3:30 A.M., the A.P. machines in the city rooms of New York's daily newspapers and in the news departments of television and radio stations began to clang. The bulletin read:

> A NINETEEN-YEAR-OLD NEGRO HAS ADMITTED SLAYING JANICE WYLIE AND EMILY HOEFFERT [sic] IN THEIR EAST SIDE APARTMENT LAST AUGUST 28, DEPUTY POLICE COMMISSIONER WALTER ARM SAID EARLY TODAY.

The story added that the suspect, identified as George Whitmore Jr., was being questioned at the 73rd Precinct.

Until that bulletin was dispatched, not more than twenty police and prosecution officials knew something extraordinary was occurring in the 73rd Precinct squad room. The police wanted no premature information about Whitmore leaking out to the press or the public until they were ready.

Thirty minutes after the story broke, six reporters were pacing the musty ground floor of the 73rd Precinct. A detective told them they would shortly be summoned upstairs for a press conference. "As soon as someone from the D.A.'s office is through. It won't be long." Koste was then completing his interrogation of Whitmore.

At 4:30 A.M., minutes after Koste had the reply to his final question, the reporters were permitted upstairs. No one had to hurry them. They knew a big story was breaking, and they moved quickly. In the squad room, they saw Whitmore standing in the cage. The youth peered out at them as they walked past him. He made no attempt to speak. But as each newsman entered the room, a detective motioned toward the caged Whitmore, warning: "Don't talk to him."

"Is this the guy?" a reporter asked. A detective nodded.

More than a dozen newspaper, television, and radio reporters squeezed into the squad commander's office, which could hold about six people comfortably. Reading from notes, McKearney gave a straight narrative account.

He told the reporters the trail toward Whitmore had started with the assault on Mrs. Borrero in Brownsville. Thirty hours later, at 7:00 A.M., Friday, April 24, Patrolman Isola spotted Whitmore as the man. Isola and Detective Aidala picked him up and brought him in for questioning. After being identified by Mrs. Borrero, Whitmore blurted out confessions to other crimes. He confessed not only to the Borrero attack but also to the murder of Mrs. Minnie Edmonds and—this was what the newsmen were waiting for—to the Wylie-Hoffert murders. McKearney also added: "We got the right guy—no question about it. He gave us details only the killer could know."

In his statement, McKearney described the assault on Mrs. Borrero as a purse snatch, never mentioning the attempted rape. He also omitted Patrolman Isola's first encounter with Whitmore near the laundry, five hours after the attack on Mrs. Borrero, and he made mistakes in describing the way the police had picked up Whitmore. None of the other police officials and detectives in the hot, smoke-clouded room corrected him. The press conference was disorganized and confused, with reporters barraging McKearney and the other police officials with questions. Interested only in the big case, none of the newsmen dug deeply into the Borrero or Edmonds investigations.

McKearney revealed only parts of Whitmore's Wylie-Hoffert confession. In answering reporters' questions, sometimes with the help of a detective or another police official, he said Whitmore had told the police he had taken the subway to Manhattan and wandered haphazardly into the Wylie-Hoffert building. Once inside the apartment, he picked up an empty Coca-Cola bottle and used it as a club to subdue Janice Wylie and Emily Hoffert. Later, after Miss Hoffert began screaming, he stabbed the bound women. The Chief of Detectives mentioned that Whitmore had taken photographs from the apartment and the police had found one of them on him.

Reporters for the afternoon newspapers—the *Journal-American,* the *Post,* and the *World-Telegram and The Sun*—had heard enough. With deadlines closing in, they left the squad room, took a final look at Whitmore in the cage, and hurried into the empty streets of Brownsville to telephone their stories.

By 6:00 A.M., McKearney, Weldon, Coyle, and the other top officers were on their way home to bed. DiPrima, Aidala, and Bulger remained behind to complete the paper work. When all this work was finished, Aidala and Detective Lynch, who had returned from Manhattan, removed Whitmore from the cage. For the first time since he had been picked up by the police, Whitmore was handcuffed. The detectives led him downstairs, out the front door, and into the rear of a police van. Lynch and Aidala were the only persons with Whitmore in the van as it headed toward downtown Brooklyn.

For several minutes there was silence. Lynch and Aidala agreed later on the witness stand that Whitmore seemed absorbed in thought, and neither of them started a conversation. Finally Whitmore spoke:

"Do you think they'll give me the gas chamber for what I did to those women?"

"There's no gas chamber in New York—there's an electric chair," Lynch said.

"Will there be a lot of people in court?"

The detectives had no answer.

A stop had to be made at Brooklyn police headquarters before Whitmore was taken to court. Like all felony prisoners, he had to get his police pedigree: a full set of fingerprints and rogues'-gallery photographs. He stripped and was photographed in the nude, in accordance with a police policy of photographing murder suspects naked to provide rebuttal evidence against charges of brutality. Then Whitmore was taken to the courthouse for his hearing.

By the time Whitmore arrived in court, his name was known to millions of people in New York City. When the city awoke that Saturday morning, it heard the news that the Wylie-Hoffert killer had been captured. Lawyers and spectators in court carried newspapers with immense headlines reading: DRIFTER ADMITS WYLIE MURDER, and ACCUSED KILLER CALLED ANIMAL BY GIRL'S DAD. Newspaper and radio reports described him as a "lone-wolf burglar," a "sadistic knifer." As the police van pulled into the courthouse driveway, television cameras recorded the event.

Whitmore was brought before State Supreme Court Justice James J. Comerford for arraignment on charges of murder and attempted rape. Detectives Lynch, Aidala, and DiPrima were there to hear the judge declare:

"Without saying or implying any guilt in this matter, the people of this town are pleased with the arrest for murder in which the citizens were very concerned. The police are doing a fine job. Our citizens have a good deal more confidence than they had a few days ago."

Robert Walsh, a Brooklyn Assistant District Attorney assigned to the hearing, also joined in the praise: "I think the officers should be commended in this matter. I know this man [Whitmore] has been wanted for a long time and a lot of people will feel better that he is apprehended."

Judge Comerford asked Whitmore if he had a lawyer to represent him. When Whitmore said, "No," Comerford looked around the room. On Saturday mornings the courtroom is usually empty except for a handful of lawyers there to represent clients arrested during the night. Spotting Jerome J. Leftow, a young lawyer, Comerford asked him to represent Whitmore for his plea at the hearing.

Leftow was permitted to consult with Whitmore in the jury box at the side of the room for fifteen minutes. The lawyer returned to the defense table with Whitmore and announced Whitmore was recanting his confessions, on the grounds that the police had beaten him and forced him to admit falsely all of the crimes.

After hearing Leftow, Judge Comerford ordered Whitmore held without bail until grand juries could determine whether he should be indicted, and on what charges.

The police officers, their job done, turned Whitmore over to prison guards. All that remained for the police was to testify some day about the way Whitmore had voluntarily confessed in the back room of a Brooklyn precinct.

8. *Arrest and Awards*

While Whitmore spent his first hours inside the House of Detention for Youth in Brooklyn, the opposing sides in the coming court battles began to form. In the hearing before Judge Comerford, the Brooklyn District Attorney's office had asked the judge to jail Whitmore without bail on "short affidavits," which meant there was cause—the confessions—to detain him until formal indictments could be handed up. One complication seen immediately by the District Attorneys of Manhattan and Brooklyn was the matter of where Whitmore would be tried first. Two of the accusations had been made in Brooklyn, but the most sensational and oldest one—the Wylie-Hoffert slayings—had occurred in Manhattan. Since Whitmore's first court hearing took place on Saturday, there was no need to rush the decision as

121

to which charge would get precedence. Neither District Attorney could bring evidence to a grand jury before Monday, and after the indictments were obtained the prosecutors could decide the sequence of the trials. Meanwhile, the D.A.'s used the weekend to prepare the next step in the legal process.

That Saturday, Whitmore's defense began taking shape. Attorney Leftow drove Whitmore's aunt, his uncle, and his younger brother, Gerald, home from the courthouse after the arraignment. (Whitmore's relatives had hurried to the court after reporters notified them of his arrest.) Leftow promised them he would visit Whitmore in prison the next day. They were too distressed to think clearly about his defense. None of them knew how to obtain a lawyer; and, in any event, Whitmore's parents in Wildwood would have to make that important decision.

On Sunday, Leftow kept his promise by visiting Whitmore in jail. Later, the lawyer recalled that the conversation began with his saying to Whitmore: "Listen, anything you say to me is confidential. I'm here to make sure your rights are protected. Are any of these charges true?"

"No, I didn't do these things."

"The police say you admitted these crimes. Is that true?"

"Yes, I admitted them, but it's not true that I did these things."

"Then why did you admit them?"

"They beat me and scared me into confessing," Whitmore said. "I didn't know what they wanted from me. I didn't know I was charged with murder until I saw you in court."

"Have you spoken to anyone else about what happened to you?"

"No, I didn't have the chance to speak to anybody. Except for the cops, you're the first person I spoke to since my arrest."

For the next two hours, Whitmore did most of the talking. He described how the police had beaten and coached him into confessing to crimes he knew nothing about.

Leftow also got Whitmore to talk about himself, about his past. Whitmore recalled that his family had moved a great deal around the Philadelphia and South New Jersey areas when he was a boy, before settling in Wildwood in 1955, when he was eleven. School had never interested him, and in 1962 he dropped out after finishing only eight grades. His family had had money problems for as long as he could remember; after quitting school, he helped his father operate an auto junkyard in Wildwood. That same year, his parents temporarily separated; Mrs. Whitmore, together with George, Gerald, and Geraldine, his younger sister, moved in with relatives in Brownsville. It was the first time Whitmore had seen New York. His parents came together again in 1963, and the entire family returned to Wildwood. But it was a short-lived reunion. After frequent quarrels with their father, George, who was nineteen, and his brothers Shellie, twenty-one, and Gerald, eighteen, came separately to Brownsville to board with relatives. Whitmore lacked a trade, and he had difficulties getting a steady job in New York. Another complication developed when he lost his eyeglasses and was unable to earn enough money for a new pair.

Attorney Leftow finally asked an inevitable question, one every lawyer puts to a client: Had Whitmore been arrested or been in trouble with the police before?

"No, I swear I've never been," was the reply.

One glance at Whitmore was enough to see he had endured a wretched night. His eyes were swollen, either from lack of sleep or from crying. Leftow tried to rally his spirits by assuring him that he had no cause to worry if he was innocent. As Leftow rose to leave, Whitmore said gravely:

"I want you for my lawyer. I trust you; you got a good face. I think you've been sent by God to help me."

Leftow realized Whitmore's defense would be arduous. The police said they had admissions to each of the crimes, and there was a known witness—the victim—in the attempted-rape case. Like every criminal lawyer in New York, Leftow was aware of the importance of the Wylie-Hoffert case. It seemed likely the police must have had a mountain of damning evidence before accusing anyone of that crime, in view of the attention the trial would attract.

Despite all these obstacles, Leftow was interested in Whitmore and wanted to defend him. He decided to get in touch with the parents and let them make the decision. Before the end of that week, Leftow found himself appointed Whitmore's lawyer. Whitmore's parents had come to Brownsville, and they were grateful for Leftow's offer to defend their son without a fee, especially since George was so anxious to have him.

Leftow was soon summoned for the first indictment against his new client. A Brooklyn grand jury, having heard five police witnesses testify about Whitmore's alleged confession to the knifing of Mrs. Minnie Edmonds, indicted him for first-degree murder. At the brief hearing, Leftow entered a "not guilty" plea. He also made an unusual offer: Whitmore, he said, would be willing to take a lie-detector test if the police officers who questioned him would accept the same challenge. The Brooklyn District Attorney never replied to the proposal. There seemed no reason for the prosecutors to question the policemen responsible for Whitmore's capture and admissions. Indeed, they were receiving honors from the New York *Journal-American* for bringing him in. The newspaper's "Public Protector Awards" of April 1964 were conferred on Detectives Bulger, DiPrima, and Aidala, and Patrolman Isola, each with citations for "brilliant police work" in solving the Wylie-Hoffert case.

On Friday, May 8, exactly two weeks after his arrest, Whitmore was taken from his Brooklyn cell to a Manhattan courtroom. He had already been indicted once more, for the attempted rape of Mrs. Borrero, and the journey across the East River was to inform him that a grand jury in the County of New York had formally brought in a third indictment against him, for the murders of Janice Wylie and Emily Hoffert. His head drooping, Whitmore, still without eyeglasses, squinted as he pleaded "not guilty" before New York State Supreme Court Justice Charles Marks. The judge looked over the indictment papers before him and noted that Leftow had entered a pauper's plea in behalf of Whitmore. Judge Marks said that, because of the petition for state legal aid, he was removing Leftow from the case and assigning two lawyers with more trial experience. Under New York law, an indigent murder-defendant is given a staff of two or three counsels at the expense of the county. Whitmore was puzzled by the judge's announcement. Leftow had entered the pauper's affidavit with the expectation of being included in the defense staff. He was the only lawyer Whitmore's mother, Birdene, knew or trusted in New York, and in open court she told the judge:

"He [Leftow] knows my son. We want him."

Not wishing to influence so important a decision, Judge Marks withdrew Whitmore's affidavit of indigence. But he emphasized to Whitmore and his mother that removal of the affidavit meant the state would not provide a penny for his defense. Whitmore stuck to his decision.

The judge, alluding to the brutality of the Wylie-Hoffert murders, ordered that a psychiatric report on Whitmore be completed by June 12. Leftow raised no objection, and Whitmore was taken to the prison ward at Bellevue Hospital. For at least thirty days, until the psychiatrists were finished with George Whitmore, the District Attorneys could delay their decision on which trial to hold first.

9. *"In the Best Interests of Justice"*

May, June, July, August, and September of 1964 passed without a hint of which trial would be first for Whitmore. He faithfully followed the routine ordered for inmates of the prison psychiatric section, and he was careful not to be embroiled in any incidents. Leftow, realizing a defendant's demeanor and attitude in court can affect the verdict of a jury, did his best to boost Whitmore's spirits. The lawyer also warned him against listening to "jailhouse lawyers" full of bad advice on the way to testify and the way to behave in a courtroom; he feared Whitmore might be adversely influenced by older hands inside Bellevue.

Leftow knew the two District Attorneys were trying to uncover enough

125

evidence to send Whitmore to the electric chair, and he was troubled by the way Whitmore's stay in Bellevue was being extended. Since the psychiatrists insisted they needed more time for their examination, he was powerless to get Whitmore released. He was personally convinced that Whitmore was sane, yet there had been no legal way of preventing his commitment to Bellevue, nor was there any way to have Whitmore discharged quickly from the hospital. And he had no way of determining which of the District Attorneys would get the opening shot at Whitmore; the D.A.'s had authority to decide that question by themselves.

Trying to anticipate the most likely possibilities, Leftow prepared to defend Whitmore on either the Wylie-Hoffert homicide charge or the attempted rape. The Wylie-Hoffert case was the most important one, and obviously the police and Manhattan District Attorney Frank S. Hogan wanted it stamped with a conviction as soon as possible. If, however, there was a snag in bringing Whitmore to trial for the double murder, Leftow believed the Brooklyn prosecutor would try Whitmore for the attempted-rape charge before disposing of the Edmonds murder indictment, because the police had a witness as well as a confession in the Borrero case.

Leftow did not know whether the police had any extrinsic evidence against Whitmore for the Wylie-Hoffert murders. All he knew about the double murder and the Edmonds killing was what Whitmore claimed had happened: that he had been forced to memorize facts and to confess. Unfortunately, the youth was fuzzy about details.

Beverly Payne, his former fiancée, and her mother had corroborated part of Whitmore's alibi in the Borrero case. They told Leftow that Whitmore had spent the hours preceding the attack with them, and on that Wednesday night he had been wearing a black coat, not the tan coat Mrs. Borrero said her attacker had worn. Furthermore, Beverly said she had seen Whitmore exchange his black coat for his brother Shellie's tan coat in her apartment on the night of Thursday, April 23. Her story backed up Whitmore's story about the tan coat he wore when he was picked up by the police fifteen hours after Mrs. Borrero had been mugged. Because Beverly had witnessed the switching of the coats, her evidence was vital. But would a jury believe her? Three months after Whitmore's arrest, she had become pregnant by another youth; this fact might discredit her with some jurors. Whitmore had suspected Beverly's new romance when her letters to him stopped. But Leftow still needed her testimony at the trial.

Whitmore's long wait in Bellevue ended in October when, after an unexplained four-month delay, the psychiatrists found him sane and mentally capable of standing trial. The two psychiatrists who signed the report noted that Whitmore "steadfastly maintained his innocence," and their report concluded:

"He is not in such a state of idiocy, imbecility or insanity as to be incapable of understanding the charge, indictment, proceedings, or of making his defense."

The psychiatrists remarked at Whitmore's reluctance to talk with them. His "answers to questions were noticeably meagre and lacking in elaboration," they pointed out. "There was a striking lack of spontaneity, and it was almost impossible to get the patient to carry the ball conversationally, even in regard to neutral day-to-day events. . . ."

Without specifying sources or reasons for their opinions, they summarized Whitmore in this manner:

"Although not seclusive, he seems to have mingled with his peer group less than usual for this age. . . . His guarded and reticent manner precluded the obtaining of detailed information concerning his sexual adjustment or intimate fantasy life. His personality structure presented many passive aggressive and schizoid traits, ill adapted to the handling of sexual and aggressive impulses. Such an individual remains vulnerable to stress at which time he may react with ill conceived violence. During the rather prolonged period of hospitalization he has remained well behaved and unobtrusive. During interviews he was alert and in good contact. No overt delusions or hallucinations were elicited. The patient's affect was blunted and he seems unable to react to people in a warm, friendly manner.

"Impression: Without psychosis; Personality Pattern Disorder of the Schizoid type."

The two psychiatrists who studied Whitmore neglected to mention, in their three-page report to Judge Marks, one aspect of their examination. Courtroom testimony from Dr. Jordan Lachman later disclosed that twice during Whitmore's five months in Bellevue he was injected with a barbiturate in an effort to get him to talk more freely. The drug, sodium amytal, although not a truth serum, is a sedative and hypnotic that can induce recollection and discussion of painful incidents. The drug was infrequently used at Bellevue, but the psychiatrists believed it might help penetrate Whitmore's reticence. It was administered on their own initiative, without the knowledge of Leftow or the District Attorneys. Each time Whitmore was given the drug his conversation was recorded, and each time he repeated his innocence.

Once Whitmore's sanity had been established there could be no reason for further delay in bringing him to trial. Five days after the mental report was submitted to Judge Marks, Brooklyn District Attorney Aaron E. Koota announced his office would have the first opportunity to convict Whitmore, who would be prosecuted for attempted rape before any of the murder trials was held. Koota considered the decision "in the best interests of justice."

Leftow had two weeks notice of the trial date, enough time for an incredible rumor to reach him. He heard that another suspect was under investigation for the murders of Janice Wylie and Emily Hoffert. The rumor came from unconfirmed newspaper stories that a narcotics addict who had been arrested for murder in East Harlem had implicated a fellow junkie as the real killer of the two women.

Leftow would later remember that a week before the trial he visited the office of Assistant District Attorney Peter Koste. The lawyer wanted to know if there was any truth to the rumor. He got no answer from Koste. Instead, Koste took him to the office of another Assistant District Attorney, an older man whom Leftow did not know but who was apparently Koste's immediate superior. Again Leftow explained the reason for his visit. If the Wylie-Hoffert charge against Whitmore was being reconsidered, he thought this might be grounds for an adjournment of the attempted-rape trial.

Both A.D.A.'s remained still. Leftow squirmed in his seat, waiting for one of them to speak. After a few minutes of this queer silence, the lawyer demanded: "Either answer or I'll leave."

"Mr. Leftow, we know a great deal about this case, and we'll do what's right," replied the older A.D.A.

Leftow saw no hope of prying information from the Manhattan District Attorney's staff, and he dejectedly left. Walking out of the building on Leonard Street, in downtown Manhattan, he met two detectives whom he knew slightly, and stopped to say hello.

"You're getting lucky, counselor," one detective said. "Your client is getting out of this."

"What do you mean?"

The detectives looked perplexed, as if one of them had said too much. They refused to discuss the matter further.

"Look," Leftow pleaded, "the public is against Whitmore, and the atmosphere is against him in this trial for attempted rape. I don't want to use any clichés, but if you people have anything that shows he's innocent in the Wylie-Hoffert case, then help me get an adjournment in the attempted-rape trial. That's all I'm asking."

The detectives were unable to help Leftow. An adjournment was no business of theirs.

The final days before the trial were anxious ones for the lone defense counsel. He was having trouble with two of his most important witnesses. Shellie Whitmore was in prison in New Jersey, awaiting trial on a larceny charge, and Beverly Payne had disappeared. But his greatest disappointment was the lack of news from Manhattan. No indication came from District Attorney Hogan's office of any change in the Wylie-Hoffert indictment against Whitmore. Apparently no new suspect existed. When Whitmore entered the Brooklyn courtroom as a defendant in an attempted-rape trial, he would carry the additional burden of being the accused killer of Janice Wylie and Emily Hoffert.

10. *Nailed on the Button*

Whitmore's trial began on the morning of Monday, November 9, 1964, six months after his arrest. At 10:00 A.M., Whitmore, bundled in a sport jacket and a heavy sweater, stepped into the room in the State Criminal Court Building in downtown Brooklyn where he would be tried for attempted rape and assault. That crime had been committed in Brooklyn. The Manhattan murders could never be openly mentioned during the trial; even a whisper of the names "Janice Wylie" or "Emily Hoffert" could result in a mistrial.

Two days were required to select the jury, which comprised twelve white men of middle-class background: merchants, clerks, insurance salesmen, businessmen, and a teacher. The slowness in picking jurors was

131

normal for a controversial trial. Every prosecutor and criminal lawyer knows that as much as half of his case rests with the selecting of jurors. A prosecutor strives to eliminate anyone who might be "soft" or possessed of a "bleeding heart" when duty calls for punishing a criminal. Conversely, defense lawyers search for "Doubting Thomas" jurors who will observe the precept that a vote for conviction requires assurance "beyond a reasonable doubt." Without referring to the Wylie-Hoffert case, Leftow tried to weed out anyone who had formed an opinion of Whitmore because of the double-murder publicity.

When the full jury was seated, Sidney A. Lichtman, a ruddy-complexioned, heavy-set prosecutor wearing a suit of banker's gray, delivered his opening remarks. In a flat voice, occasionally punching the air with his left fist for emphasis, he outlined the way in which Mrs. Borrero had been followed and assaulted. The criminal, he asserted, was George Whitmore Jr.

In his first turn before the jury, Leftow gave no hint of the approach he intended to use in establishing Whitmore's innocence. A former counsel for the Legal Aid Society, an organization representing indigent defendants, Leftow had a total jury-trial experience of six minor cases. Nevertheless, the thirty-three-year-old lawyer seemed self-assured as he cautioned the jury to be impartial and fair in evaluating testimony. ". . . Keep an open mind. . . . Listen carefully, scrutinize" the evidence, he urged.

The first important witness was Mrs. Borrero. The jury and the one hundred spectators packed into the room strained to get a look at her as she settled into the witness stand. Stout, wearing a green print dress, the twenty-year-old woman looked closer to thirty. Her English, although tinged with a Spanish accent, was articulate and vivid.

Mrs. Borrero's tour of duty at Long Island College Hospital on Wednesday, April 22, had been from 3:30 P.M. to midnight. It was her second night at the hospital after a year's leave. The subway trip from the hospital in downtown Brooklyn to her station in Brownsville took forty-five minutes on the IRT Seventh Avenue Line. Close to 1:00 A.M. on Thursday, April 23, she began to descend, together with a dozen other passengers, from the elevated Rockaway Avenue station in Brownsville. She was uneasy; in later testimony she would recall that all day an inexplicable premonition had troubled her. As she walked down the station stairs, the streets below looked menacing to her. Remembering that her husband Juan, a waiter at the Copacabana nightclub in Manhattan, was home, she stopped before reaching the street to telephone him from the public booth in the station waiting room. Mr. Borrero said he was too tired to meet her at the station; couldn't she walk home without him? It was only five blocks and he was alone with their six-week-old daughter.

On the misty street, the only person she saw was a man walking in the opposite direction to her, across the street. She noticed he wore a tan coat and a hat. The swishing of her thick-soled nurse's shoes against the damp pavements was the only sound for an entire block. She forgot about the man walking in the opposite direction until "all of a sudden I heard footsteps in back of me." Glancing back, she saw a man one hundred feet behind her, walking fast; it was the same man who, a minute before, had been walking in the opposite direction. Turning a corner, she accelerated her pace, but the man came closer with every step he took.

She later testified that a self-protection lesson taught in nursing school popped into her mind at this time: a good defense against muggers at night is to walk in the roadway where a motorist may be flagged down for help. She stepped into the roadway, but no cars came. Whenever she peered back, she could see the man drawing ominously closer. Her fears intensified when the man began a strange zigzagging movement, darting from one side of the street to the other, but steadily gaining on her.

Turning into Bristol Street, her home street, Mrs. Borrero stayed in the roadway until she was in sight of her apartment building. With safety a few feet away, she ran, getting within fifteen feet of the entrance when suddenly he grabbed her.

One scream was all she could get out. A hand was on her mouth, stifling her outcries. Another hand was firmly around her neck. "Don't scream or I'll kill you," he said in a hushed tone. In one quick motion, he snatched her pocketbook with his right hand. She was shoved forward, helpless to resist or scream again. He directed her slowly across the street until he halted at a lamppost. Then he pushed her toward the other side of the street, the side on which her apartment building stood. Under a lamppost, he waited, seemingly pondering his next move.

Lichtman interrupted: "Did you see the face of the assailant?"

"Well, constantly, as we were walking back and forth; my head was turned so that I was looking at him. . . . I saw his complete face."

The man maneuvered her toward the cellarway of her own building. "Something" was pressed against her neck; she had no idea whether it was a knife, a razor blade, or a gun. Inside the dank alley, she was slammed against the wall.

Mrs. Borrero's plump cheeks glowed crimson as she continued:

"He said, 'Let me touch your pussy.' And then he put his hand under my coat and under my uniform, under the slip, and he touched my pubic area. . . . He said to me he wanted to have intercourse with me."

"What was his exact language?" Lichtman asked.

" 'I want to have intercourse with you. I want to have sexual relations. . . . I am going to rape you. Then I'm going to kill you first, and then rape you.' "

Convinced she was in a life-or-death struggle, Mrs. Borrero fought back.

"I grabbed a hold of his hands then, and of his coat, and I started screaming."

As her screams reverberated through the alley, the beam of a flashlight lit the darkness. The man, thrusting her aside, scrambled away. A policeman ran past her, chasing her assailant.

Lichtman held up the ragged coat Whitmore had worn at the time of his arrest, and he asked Mrs. Borrero if she recognized it.

"It looks like the coat the man was wearing that night; the man that was following me and attacked me."

"Now Mrs. Borrero, do you see the man who followed you, and the man who attacked you that night? Do you see him in this courtroom this morning?"

Without hesitation, she pointed a finger at Whitmore, sitting fifteen feet from her. "Yes . . . he is right there."

Leftow's cross-examination began with questions about whether it had been raining that night and, if so, whether Mrs. Borrero's glasses had been water-streaked or blurred.

"There was no moisture on my glasses. . . . My glasses were dry. . . ."

Next, the defense lawyer concentrated on her identification of Whitmore at the 73rd Precinct. The jury learned that she had viewed him through a peephole as he stood next to Aidala, not in a line-up.

And why had Mrs. Borrero requested that Whitmore speak? Was it because she was not sure of the identification? Leftow asked.

"No, because I wanted to be sure beyond any shadow of a doubt."

Leftow switched to a different topic, one that the prosecution had perhaps not anticipated.

"You have nothing to gain or lose whether this defendant is convicted or acquitted?" he asked.

"Of course not."

With her answer on the record, Leftow delivered his surprise. If she had no special interest in Whitmore's conviction, why had she consulted two lawyers about a possible $10,000 reward in connection with his arrest? The reward was the money offered by *Newsweek* magazine for the capture of the Wylie-Hoffert killer, and Leftow, as the defense lawyer, could make an oblique reference to another case, even though he could not fully explain to the jury the reason for the reward. He was content to have Mrs. Borrero confirm that she inquired about collecting the money. He thought he had softened the impact of her testimony by providing the jury with a $10,000 reason for her positive identification of Whitmore.

Patrolman Isola was next on the stand. He told of hearing a woman's scream, flashing his light into the narrow alley, vainly pursuing a man in a tan coat, and then encountering Whitmore outside the laundry.

Leftow chipped away at Isola's testimony by noting that the original police teletype described the attacker as older, taller, and heavier than Whitmore. Isola insisted Mrs. Borrero had described him as pock-marked. Since Whitmore's face was pitted with acne scars, the pockmarks were an important part of her identification. Isola could not explain why the teletype failed to mention the facial blemishes. Also, a contradiction existed between his description of the wanted man and the description Mrs. Borrero gave. She said the man wore a hat; Isola said he was bareheaded.

A potential weakness in the prosecution's framework was Isola's chat with Whitmore at the laundry five hours after the attack, at which time, Isola recalled, Whitmore wore a tan coat and a green hat. Presiding Judge David L. Malbin interrupted Leftow for a question of his own:

"The crime had taken place approximately five hours before. . . . The description of the assailant was still fresh in your mind. . . . You stopped to question this defendant [about a man fleeing the scene of the attack]. . . . At the time, you had no suspicions that this defendant might be implicated in the crime, did you?"

"That's correct," Isola answered.

On the fourth day of the trial, Lichtman called his two principal police witnesses, Detectives Aidala and DiPrima. Before Aidala could begin describing the events leading up to the confession, Leftow demanded a ruling from Judge Malbin on whether the confession had been obtained voluntarily, and whether it was admissible evidence.

Until shortly before this trial, the New York State criminal law permitted jurors to hear testimony relating to the manner in which a disputed statement or confession had been obtained by police, and to decide for themselves how much weight to give the statement. In 1964, the United States Supreme Court had declared unconstitutional this method of bringing recanted confessions into courtrooms. At the time of Whitmore's trial, New York judges were ruling in the absence of juries whether a statement was voluntary and admissible, or was inadmissible because police had used coercion.

Malbin cleared the jury from the courtroom and, as soon as the last of the twelve jurors and two alternates had filed out, he began a *voir dire* hearing on the statement Whitmore had allegedly given the detectives.

Leftow opened the hearing by calling Aidala. The detective said he had recorded Whitmore's words on a pad in the presence of DiPrima. There had been no brutality; Whitmore confessed freely and willingly.

Leftow's other witness was Whitmore himself. Speaking in almost a whisper, but in tones audible throughout the hushed courtroom, Whitmore gave his version of the confession. After the identification by Mrs. Borrero, he insisted that there had been a mistake. But Aidala and Isola ignored his protest.

". . . They stood me in front of a chair. . . . They called me a liar. . . . I told them if I said I did it, I would be lying. . . . So, every time I said I didn't know what happened, I got knocked into the chair. Then they stood me up aside this wall and I continuously got beat until I couldn't take it no more. So I just broke down and shook my head."

Under friendly questioning by Leftow, Whitmore added that he had been hit in the back, chest, and stomach, but never in the face.

When Leftow finished, Lichtman got his opportunity to cross-examine Whitmore. The Assistant District Attorney asked him for a tally of how many blows he had received from Aidala and Isola.

Many times, Whitmore said, but he was unable to recall the exact number of blows. He was positive DiPrima had not been present during the beatings.

Lichtman called Detective DiPrima and Patrolman Isola as rebuttal witnesses. They supported Aidala. There had been no threats; Whitmore had talked freely, without any coercion.

Mrs. Borrero was Lichtman's last *voir dire* witness. She said that she had sat in the main squad room from 8:30 to 10:30 A.M. while Whitmore was questioned in an adjoining office.

"Did you hear anybody yell or scream inside that room?" Lichtman asked.

"No."

Judge Malbin ruled for the prosecution: the confession made to Aidala was valid evidence.

The jury returned to hear Aidala and DiPrima testify. The detectives answered Lichtman precisely, each recounting the manner in which Whitmore had admitted the crime. Leftow did not succeed in undermining their testimony. When he asked Aidala why Whitmore had not been afforded a line-up for Mrs. Borrero's identification, the detective replied:

". . . he was brought in as a potential witness. . . . I didn't want to offer a potential witness the embarrassment of placing him in a line-up."

The prosecution rested on the fourth day, reserving the right to call rebuttal witnesses. Lichtman had called ten witnesses; collectively, they created a seemingly impregnable accusation. Mrs. Borrero had been consistent in her identification, and Aidala, DiPrima, and Isola had agreed on the most microscopic details of Whitmore's capture and confession.

Leftow planned to counter with two witnesses—Whitmore and Beverly Payne, whom he had located a few days before the trial.

Whitmore was dressed in his best clothes—a bulky yellow sweater under a sport jacket. On the witness stand, he clutched the arms of his chair, and glanced back and forth, from the judge seated above him on his left, to the jury on his right. Speaking in a whisper, he testified that on the night of the attack he had been with Beverly Payne and her mother. He left the Payne apartment about 12:30 or a little later. He was uncertain of the exact time because he did not have a wrist watch. He walked to Amboy Street, a block from the Payne apartment. There a man he had never seen before almost collided with him.

"This guy, about twenty-three, twenty-six years old, he came running up the block and he was excited and kept saying, hide him, hide him. . . . So I told him there was nothing I could do for him. So he started running again. And two officers, two or three officers, came running around the corner and they started shining flashlights and looking for him. And after that, there was squad cars all over the place and they were shining flashlights in buildings. They were looking for him. And they didn't find him."

He then went to a cousin's apartment on Amboy Street. When no one answered his knocks on the door, he slept across the street in a hallway.

Leftow asked why Whitmore had not slept at a relative's apartment.

"Well, it wouldn't be right to, you know, just up and ask somebody to spend the night. My uncle, he has a houseful of girls. I couldn't spend the night there."

Turning to another crucial subject, the tan coat, Leftow asked Whitmore what he had been wearing the morning he met Patrolman Isola outside the Oasis Launderette.

A black trenchcoat, a green hat, and a green pair of sharkskins, was the reply.

The important item was the black trenchcoat, and Whitmore repeated that it was a black, knee-length coat, not the tan, fingertip-length coat he was wearing when arrested the following day. He acquired the tan coat the evening after he first met Isola. He spent that evening in the Payne apartment with Beverly Payne and her eight-year-old sister. His brother, Shellie, arrived about 10:00 P.M. This was the evening of Thursday, April 23, almost a full day after the attack on Mrs. Borrero. Realizing the significance of the testimony he was about to give, Whitmore straightened up in his seat as he told about Shellie's offering him one dollar for the loan of his black coat just for the evening.

"He said he was going to the city."

The next morning, Whitmore said, before he could reacquire his own coat from Shellie, he was arrested.

Leftow pointed to the tan coat. "Is this the coat?"

"Yes."

Once Mrs. Borrero had identified him, Whitmore testified, the two policemen began punching him, although he insisted: "I never seen the lady before."

Leftow got into the record Whitmore's contention that the police had never asked him if he wanted to contact a lawyer or his relatives. Judge Malbin interrupted the lawyer to explain a point of New York State law to the jury. He said there was no requirement for the police to advise Whitmore of his right to counsel or that anything he said could be used against him. Only when a suspect is brought into court is it mandatory to advise him of his right to consult an attorney.

Now it was Lichtman's turn to question Whitmore. The prosecutor placed himself between Whitmore and the jury as he launched his examination. He had no intention of putting Whitmore at ease. In a mocking tone, he searched for flaws in Whitmore's story of meeting a man running away from the police on the night of the attack. Whitmore said he had seen two or three policemen chase the suspect.

"And they [the police] didn't stop and talk to you, is that right?" Lichtman asked.

"Yes."

Lichtman moved into the events inside the 73rd Precinct. Whitmore repeated his charge of police brutality. He contradicted his earlier testimony, however, about being unable to recall how many times he had been hit. Now he said he had been punched fifty times by Aidala and at least ten times by Isola. But he was unclear about when the beatings occurred, changing his statements several times. First he said the police cuffed him about before breakfast; then it was after breakfast.

"I was assulted before," Whitmore finally said. "In other words, I got beat up and then I ate."

While Whitmore was on the stand, Lichtman moved to introduce the official question-and-answer confession given to Assistant District Attorney Postal. Once more Judge Malbin removed the jury from the courtroom and held a *voir dire* hearing—this time to decide if the "Q and A" had been obtained without duress.

The hearing began with Leftow questioning Whitmore. He was "scared and frightened of beatings" by the police, Whitmore testified. At one point, Aidala had threatened: "In about five seconds if I didn't tell him what he wanted to know they were going to kick me in my balls."

Whitmore added an unexpected element to his account. He insisted he had not seen Assistant District Attorney Postal during his interrogation at the precinct.

To refute Whitmore, Lichtman called Aidala and DiPrima, who both testified they had been present when Postal obtained the "Q and A" confession.

Judge Malbin required a few minutes of deliberation to decide that the "Q and A" confession had been given voluntarily.

On the sixth day of the trial, the jury heard from Whitmore's own lips that he did not recall giving any statement to Postal. The detectives, he insisted, were the only persons who had questioned him. Picking up the twelve-page confession, Lichtman slowly read each question, and the answer Whitmore supposedly made. After every question and answer, he looked up at Whitmore and inquired: "Were you asked that question, and did you make that answer?"

Whitmore never replied affirmatively. Most of his answers were, "No," but several times he said, "I'm not sure," or "I don't recall," or "I don't know."

Leftow saw how damaging the confession was and, as soon as Lichtman completed reading it to the jury, the defense lawyer jumped up. He wanted to spotlight Whitmore's limited intelligence and his possible mental confusion during the interrogation. Leftow made a final stab at demonstrating to the jury Whitmore's retarded state. It was Tuesday, November 17, and he asked Whitmore: "What day is it today?"

"Approximately November the 15th."

"November 15th?"

"Sixteenth?" Whitmore said hesitantly.

"Do you know the day?"

"I'm not sure."

The next day, Leftow called his second and last witness. Beverly Payne walked through the courtroom, past Whitmore, and took her seat on the witness stand. She was four months pregnant. The coat-switch was the only important aspect of the case Leftow took up with her. She corroborated Whitmore's story in every detail, except for one important item: she believed George and Shellie exchanged coats at 7:00 P.M. on Thursday, April 23, the night after the attack, not 10:00 P.M. as Whitmore had testified.

Lichtman immediately picked up the difference in time. The prosecutor also noted for the jury that a week before the trial began he had questioned Miss Payne in his office and, at that time, she said Whitmore obtained the tan coat on Wednesday night, April 22, several hours before the attempted rape. Why was she changing her story now? Lichtman asked her.

"You started getting me confused so I said 'yes.' "

Lichtman called five rebuttal witnesses, and each of them punctured part of Whitmore's defense. Raymond Linkletter, the stenographic reporter, testified that Postal had been the only person to ask Whitmore questions during the "Q and A" confession. Postal took the witness stand to state flatly that he alone had interrogated Whitmore and that no one had suggested answers. Isola denied Whitmore's statement that patrol cars had taken part in the immediate chase for Mrs. Borrero's assailant. Finally, Aidala and DiPrima reiterated that Whitmore had been neither threatened nor punched during the questioning.

Each side had called all its witnesses, but Leftow had two manuevers left. He asked Judge Malbin for permission to alert the jury to something that had not been discussed at the trial: the fact that Whitmore had been subjected to continuous questioning during twenty-one hours at the 73rd Precinct. The judge ruled this information inadmissible. The jury was aware that Aidala and DiPrima had finished getting a statement from Whitmore at 10:30 A.M., and that Postal had obtained the official confession at about midnight, but the judge refused to permit any reference in the trial record to the interim period during which the police had interrogated Whitmore about the Edmonds and Wylie-Hoffert murders. Officially, the jury would have to remain ignorant of anything that had happened in the precinct house except during the hours when Whitmore was questioned about the attack on Mrs. Borrero.

Leftow's last motion was to ask Lichtman to stipulate for the record that Shellie Whitmore was in jail. Both the defense counsel and the District Attorney's office were aware that Shellie had been arrested for automobile theft shortly before the trial had begun, and that he was now in the Cape May, N.J., County Jailhouse. Lichtman consented to the motion, making it possible for Leftow to explain to the jury why he had not summoned Shellie to substantiate George's story about the coat.

The summation to the jury was Leftow's final chance to sway the twelve men. Speaking smoothly, without gesticulation, he began with a reference to the publicity Whitmore had received, without mentioning the Wylie-Hoffert case by name.

". . . jury cases are decided in a courtroom, not in newspapers," he cautioned. He urged the jury to be "free of prejudice, free of bias" in the coming deliberations. Then he ticked off the strong points of Whitmore's defense.

One: There was testimony from Patrolman Isola, "the man who was actually at the scene of the crime," that he had no reason to suspect Whitmore when he chanced to meet him five hours after the incident.

Two: Since the weather was damp, Mrs. Borrero's glasses could have been veiled with moisture, resulting in a mistaken identification.

Three: The first description of the assailant which was sent over the police teletype did not fit Whitmore, except for his being Negro; and there was no reference in the teletype to pockmarks, a conspicuous point in any description.

Four: Mrs. Borrero said her assailant wore a hat, whereas Isola said the man was hatless—an indication of how misleading eyewitness identification can be.

Five: Whitmore was not given the protection of a line-up when he was singled out by Mrs. Borrero.

Six: Whitmore was asked to repeat in Mrs. Borrero's presence the same words she had heard the morning she was attacked. "Was this a fair test?" the lawyer asked.

To strengthen Beverly Payne's testimony about the exchange of coats, Leftow entreated the jury to understand the milieu in which Whitmore lived and the scant sophistication he and Miss Payne possessed.

"He has to depend upon a girl with a tenth-grade education; a girl who could be confused, just as Whitmore could be confused because George Whitmore has only an eighth-grade education."

Nearing the end of his fifteen-minute plea for acquittal, Leftow repeated that Whitmore had no previous police record; and, with as much urgency as he could muster in his voice, he urged the jurors to consider Whitmore's educational background in arriving at a verdict.

"He is going to contradict himself. He is going to make mistakes, not because he is lying, not because he is trying to fool you; simply because he is George Whitmore, who is trying to express himself as best he can."

Lichtman began his summation standing fifteen feet from the jury, his arms folded. He then moved about, gesticulating to emphasize each point. He scornfully labeled Whitmore's testimony a "cock-and-bull story." He brushed aside the argument that Isola's failure to arrest Whitmore at the laundry proved Whitmore's innocence. The patrolman was at that time "tired and weary from an all night of activity . . . and in his relative inexperience" thought of Whitmore only as a witness.

Lichtman scoffed at Whitmore's allegation that he had been battered around and frightened. The prosecutor asserted that the police photographs of Whitmore's nude body failed to show a single bruise. He asked the jury to picture what would have happened if Aidala, the two-hundred-pound detective, had "belted this guy in the solar plexus five or six times." Certainly Whitmore would have been in "no condition to eat hero sandwiches or rolls with butter."

And why should detectives like DiPrima and Aidala "want to hang this one on him?" They were in the highest rank of detectives, with no promotions in sight. And would Assistant District Attorney Postal also lie about the confession? Lichtman asked.

There was still more evidence against Whitmore. "What more damaging proof" existed than Mrs. Borrero's positive identification, Lichtman asked, punching the air for emphasis.

Picking up the tan coat from the evidence table, he advanced toward the jury and concluded:

". . . Is it a coincidence, or is it a solidly guilty circumstance that the button and the coat match? . . . Gentlemen, Mr. Foreman, haven't we nailed George Whitmore right on the button in the truest sense of the word, in the truest sense of the term?"

The next day, the seventh day of the trial, Judge Malbin devoted the entire morning to instructing the jury about what verdicts it could reach and what evidence to consider. Shortly before noon, the jury filed out to deliberate.

Whitmore was taken to a detention cell outside the courtroom. Leftow, together with Mrs. Whitmore and her son, Gerald, spent the slow hours inside the courtroom, where Lichtman also waited. Except for reporters drifting in and out, the courtroom was almost empty. Five or six of the courtroom buffs who always sit through interesting trials gathered in the lobby outside. They were of mixed opinion about the jury's leanings.

"A fast verdict is always an acquittal," one septuagenarian offered. "If they're not in right away, then it's a guilty verdict."

"You're crazy," interrupted another in the group. "The longer they're out, the better for the defense; someone is holding out for not guilty."

At 9:25 P.M. the suspense ended. The jury, after nine hours, returned.

On both charges, the attempted rape as well as the assault, the verdict was unanimous. "Guilty," announced the foreman. The trial was over.

Handcuffed, Whitmore was led from the courtroom. Newspaper reporters gathered around Leftow for a statement, but the disappointed defense lawyer had little to say except to congratulate Lichtman for presenting "a perfect case."

Several newsmen waiting outside the courthouse intercepted jurors as they left the building. Most of the jurors refused to discuss the trial or their verdict. One stopped to talk amicably to reporters. He was certain all of the twelve men on the panel had been aware that Whitmore was under indictment for the Wylie-Hoffert and Edmonds slayings. But this juror also insisted that the foreman had excluded any discussion of the murders during deliberation. As he was about to break away from the reporters, the juror casually noted that one member of the panel had commented inside the jury room: "This is nothing to what's coming to him."

The next day, Whitmore was brought before Judge Malbin in the same courtroom. The maximum sentence for attempted rape was ten years, and for second-degree assault, five years. But before pronouncing sentence Malbin ordered Whitmore sent to the prison mental ward at Kings County Hospital. Although Whitmore had been found sane during his five-month stay in Bellevue, Malbin was following the letter of the law by having him examined a second time by city psychiatrists. New York State law required a judge to obtain a mental report on anyone convicted of a sex crime. If the psychiatrists concluded that Whitmore was a "perpetual sex menace," then the judge would be compelled to commit him to a state hospital for the criminal insane until he was psychologically sound. The commitment would be for an indeterminate term, up to life. Therefore, by having been convicted of a sex crime, Whitmore faced the possibility of lifetime imprisonment—even if he never stood trial for any of the murder charges still on the docket against him.

Before Whitmore was turned over to his guards for the trip to the mental ward, his mother was allowed to meet briefly with him. Whitmore's eyes clouded with tears.

"I may as well give up, Mom," he said. "They're going to send me to the electric chair."

Mrs. Whitmore had no reply that could alter her son's despondency, no idea of what more she could do to aid him. Nevertheless, she promised: "We'll do something for you. We won't forget you, George."

11. *The Other Story*

Kings County Hospital, in the center of Brooklyn, is a sprawling, drab, gray-brick institution with a somber Victorian architectural flavor. Whitmore was fully accustomed to the monotonous prison existence behind the padlocked doors of the hospital psychiatric ward, but his conviction for attempted rape bred one more resentment in him. He was sure that Leftow's lack of courtroom experience had been the major reason for the guilty verdict. Other prisoners at the House of Detention for Youth and at Kings County agreed about his supposed bad luck. These "jailhouse lawyers," more familiar than Whitmore with trial proceedings, convinced him that only a lawyer who received a sizable fee would properly defend him in such a complicated case. Although Whitmore recalled how kind

145

Leftow had been, he told his mother that another lawyer was needed to save him.

Mrs. Whitmore, penniless and on the welfare rolls, consulted the dozen relatives and friends she had in Brownsville for help in finding another lawyer. None of them knew any. One friend, a beautician, did have a suggestion. She urged Mrs. Whitmore to see Arthur H. Miller, an attorney practicing in the neighborhood.

Two days after her son's conviction, Mrs. Whitmore walked the four blocks from her home to Arthur Miller's office. Miller, thirty-three years old, and his partner Edwin Kaplan, thirty-two, had opened an office in Brownsville a year before. They were white and relatively inexperienced, but they had acquired a reputation among Negroes and Puerto Ricans in the area for their honesty and zeal. Also—and this was equally important in a neighborhood where every penny counted—Miller and Kaplan had the distinction of taking on unpopular cases without the prospect of payment. Their office, a ground-level store with huge plate-glass windows, was a fishbowl at a busy intersection; any passer-by could glance inside and see what was going on.

Miller and Kaplan of course knew about the Whitmore case, but for the first time they heard Mrs. Whitmore's account of her son's troubles. Uncertain what they could do, they explained to her the legal difficulties in changing lawyers, especially since Whitmore was indigent. Both of them knew Leftow and thought highly of him. Astonished that someone wanted them to take over such a complex case, and needing time to reflect, they asked Mrs. Whitmore to return the next day for their answer.

Like Leftow, the two lawyers were well aware that representing Whitmore could be significant for their futures. Any murder trial is important for a novice criminal lawyer, and Whitmore's trial promised to be one of the biggest the city would see for years. Yet Miller and Kaplan both ridiculed the thought of their jointly defending Whitmore. They knew they lacked the experience, the courtroom *savoir-faire* mandatory for a tough trial. Although eager to participate in Whitmore's defense, they were modest enough to realize that their inexperience precluded their taking it on alone.

Kaplan thought of another possibility. He had worked for Stanley J. Reiben, a criminal lawyer in Manhattan with an impressive trial record. Reiben had won acquittals or dismissal of charges for fifty-two persons accused of murder, an enviable record for any lawyer. Miller and Kaplan knew that anyone who assumed Whitmore's defense would have to be a hard-working scrapper, uninterested in a fee. They believed Reiben was that type.

That same afternoon, Kaplan telephoned Reiben and told him of Mrs. Whitmore's visit. Reiben was hesitant about committing himself; after all, he pointed out to Kaplan, every client, guilty or otherwise, blames his lawyer when the verdict is unfavorable. Reiben suggested that Kaplan and Miller bring Mrs. Whitmore to his Manhattan office, where they could hear her full story before making a decision.

On a bright autumn day in late November, Miller, Kaplan, and Mrs. Whitmore arrived at Reiben's book-cluttered office near Wall Street. Slim and of medium height, Reiben, who had just turned fifty, had the silver hair of middle age. As the result of an accident during his Army Air Force days with an anti-aircraft unit, he was hard of hearing and was compelled to wear two conspicuous hearing aids.

Mrs. Whitmore sat on the edge of her chair as she explained her plight to Reiben. He listened carefully, jotting notes on a pad. His policy was to hear anyone who came to him with a legal problem, even if he knew beforehand that it was not a matter he wanted to handle. If he felt unable to provide the best possible defense, he said "no" and never altered his decision.

For more than two hours, Mrs. Whitmore recited all the strong points of her son's defense. Above all, she was absolutely certain her son had been framed for the Wylie-Hoffert killings, because he had been in Wildwood during the entire summer of 1963, including the day of the murders. When she had finished, she burst into tears.

In his twenty years as a lawyer, Reiben had heard a hundred mothers go through similar sobbing litanies about the innocence of their sons. He might feel sorry for them, but few mothers ever believed their sons were guilty, regardless of the evidence. One factor in Whitmore's case, however, struck a quizzical chord in Reiben's mind. Even if Whitmore were guilty, he seemed to be receiving shabby judicial treatment. Reiben was suspicious of the District Attorneys for disposing of the attempted-rape case before clearing up the murder charges. He could see only one reason for their joint decision to hold the attempted-rape trial first: they wanted a sex-charge conviction to bolster the murder prosecutions because they had weak cases, or no cases at all, in the homicide accusations.

In describing her son's predicament, Mrs. Whitmore mentioned that a newspaper reporter for the *World-Telegram and The Sun* had uncovered evidence beneficial to Whitmore. Before making a decision, Reiben wanted to talk to the reporter and to Whitmore.

Information Reiben soon obtained from the newspaper increased his uneasiness about Whitmore. With all the irrefutable evidence the police said they had gathered against Whitmore in the Wylie-Hoffert case, the *World-Telegram* had been puzzled by his long confinement in Bellevue and the delaying of the two murder trials. Through its own inquiries, the newspaper verified Whitmore's claim that he had been in Wildwood during the summer of the Wylie-Hoffert murders. Dozens of Wildwood residents, although not sure of his exact whereabouts on August 28, 1963, recalled seeing him almost daily that summer. More important, the newspaper had located two witnesses who said Whitmore had been in Wildwood on August 28. That day was distinct in their minds because of the first civil rights march on Washington. The witnesses, Mrs. Jennie Montgomery and her fifteen-year-old daughter, Ludie, had been traced to Philadelphia, where they had moved. Ludie remembered seeing and talking to Whitmore at 2:00 or 3:00 P.M. on the afternoon of the murder, and her mother had spoken to him later in the afternoon. Their testimony, however, was not considered conclusive by the newspaper editors because it was conceivable Whitmore could have murdered Janice Wylie and Emily Hoffert in the morning and then sped back to Wildwood. The only way Whitmore could establish an invincible alibi was through a witness who could place him in Wildwood between 10:00 A.M. and 1:00 P.M., thereby eliminating the possibility of his having been in New York at the time the police said the murders had been committed. The newspaper told Reiben it was searching for such a witness.

The interviews with Mrs. Montgomery and her daughter also disclosed a major discrepancy in the police account of Whitmore's movements on the murder day. In his confession, he supposedly stated he returned to Brooklyn after the stabbings—not to Wildwood.

In addition to its skepticism about the Wylie-Hoffert case, the newspaper doubted that Whitmore had received a fair trial for attempted rape, with the shadow of a murder accusation clinging to him.

Because District Attorney Hogan declined to comment on the Montgomerys' statements, the *World-Telegram* was waiting for more solid evidence from its Wylie-Hoffert inquiries before publishing a story. The *World-Telegram* had offered investigative help to Leftow, but he felt it was unethical to accept such aid, which the court might consider interference from the press.

Reiben was now almost ready to commit himself. But, as a final test, he wanted to interview Whitmore.

Thick metal bars clanged behind Reiben as he walked into the lawyers' consultation room at Kings County Hospital prison ward. Whitmore was not surprised by the visit; his mother had told him a new lawyer might be undertaking his defense.

A few minutes of random conversation convinced Reiben that Whitmore would make a poor courtroom witness. He thought Whitmore spoke too softly, without forcefulness. But he had come to hear Whitmore's full story, and when the youth seemed ready to begin, Reiben said:

"George, I want you to tell me everything. Start with the morning you met the patrolman outside the laundry, and tell me every fact that you remember."

Whitmore recalled that his difficulties began on a Thursday morning. He had spent the night sleeping under a stairwell in a building on Amboy Street, after no one had answered his pounding on the door of his cousin's apartment across the street. His first thought was to get out of the building before anyone found him. He had no place to wash nor any money for breakfast. Brushing off his coat, which he had used as a blanket, he hurried to the intersection of Hopkinson and Sutter Avenues, where he had arranged to meet Shellie. The brothers had decided to look for work together that morning. A job, any kind of work, was what George wanted most of all.

It was 6:00 A.M. George was on time for the rendezvous, but Shellie was nowhere in sight. Whitmore stepped into the doorway of a laundry to escape the harsh wind; he was chilled and hungry.

Only a handful of people and cars moved on the streets. He saw a policeman walk by, look at him, and walk on. After going a few steps, the policeman suddenly turned around.

"What are you doing here?" the officer asked.

"I'm waiting for my brother to go to work," Whitmore replied.

The policeman looked him over. Asked to identify himself, Whitmore said he lived on Amboy Street with a cousin. He pulled out two letters he had received at his cousin's address, and his New Jersey driver's license.

"What was all that shooting about last night?" Whitmore said after the patrolman had examined his identification.

"What do you know about last night?"

"I was walking home on Sutter Avenue when I heard shots and this fellow ran into me. The fellow said: 'Hide me, hide me, the law's after me.' When I said there was nothing I could do, he ran into a building on Amboy Street." Whitmore thought the patrolman seemed interested in his information.

"What did this guy do?" Whitmore asked.

"He raped a woman."

"How low can you get?"

"Pretty low," the policeman answered. He ordered the youth to walk with him to a police callbox across the street from the laundry. On the phone, he asked that a sergeant be sent to the Oasis Launderette. "I got a possible witness to a rape," Whitmore heard him say.

In about five minutes, a green patrol car pulled up and a sergeant got out. Whitmore, after being warned by the sergeant about lying, repeated his story. He assured the policemen he could recognize the man he had seen running the night before.

As Whitmore was talking to the police, Shellie and two other young Negroes walked up to the patrol car. The police made no objection when Whitmore left with them.

The boys walked a half-mile to a salt-packaging plant where jobs might be available. The plant needed laborers, and everybody but George was hired; he lost the day's work because he did not have his Social Security card. Disappointed, he walked back alone to his cousin Lita Johnson's apartment, where the door had been locked the night before. This time George's younger brother Gerald answered his knock. Gerald, who had spent the night in the apartment, had been asleep when George tried to enter about 1:00 A.M. and had not heard him rapping on the door. The two brothers helped themselves to ham and eggs for breakfast. The food perked George up. As they ate, he talked.

"You know, the cops questioned me this morning about a rape case. I told them I heard shots and seen this guy running. They were sure interested in what I had to say."

"Watch out for the law," Gerald said. "I wouldn't mess with them."

"There's nothing to worry about. I didn't do anything."

After breakfast, George walked two blocks to the Paynes' apartment and spent the rest of the day there with Beverly. Neither George nor Beverly had money to go anywhere else. Beverly's mother was out working, and no one they knew would give or lend them money.

In the evening, Shellie came to the Payne apartment. He commiserated with George about not being able to get a job and urged him to find his Social Security card. Shellie, who was going to Manhattan for the evening, asked George to exchange coats with him.

"Why should I?" George asked.

"My coat's dirty. You got a good one and you're not going anywhere."

George shook his head.

"I'll throw in a dollar," Shellie pleaded. "Come on, it's only for one night."

The black trenchcoat Whitmore had bought for twenty-five dollars before coming to New York was still in good condition. He was reluctant to part with it, but the dollar was enough to break his resistance.

Shellie took the trenchcoat, handing George a dollar bill and his knee-length tan coat, which had an imitation-leather collar. The tan coat was grimy and lacked several buttons.

George left the apartment. After a few minutes, he came bounding up the stairs. "I got a feast for us tonight," he said triumphantly. With Shellie's dollar he had purchased two cans of spaghetti and meatballs, and a loaf of bread.

Beverly heated the canned food, and she, George, and Shellie sat down to eat it. Shellie left after the meal. George and Beverly watched television until 10:30 P.M., much later than he had intended. Again, he had spent too much time at the Paynes', for when he reached his cousin's apartment on Amboy Street his knocks on the door went unanswered. He could have shouted to awaken somebody, but that would have angered his cousin and the neighbors. Rather than cause trouble, he resigned himself to a second consecutive night in a hallway. He went to a building across the street, squeezed under the stairwell, and fell asleep.

The noise of people on the stairs above awakened Whitmore. From street sounds drifting into the hallway, he knew it must be daylight. He quickly arose and walked out of the building. Despite his attempt to look at ease, he was glad no one had seen him. Every time he slept under the stairs he feared someone would accidentally find him and tell the custodian of the building. He was sure that if this happened the custodian would look for him every night under the stairwell and, if he found him sleeping there, would either throw him out or have him arrested.

He had no plans that day; he had run out of places to look for work. It was about 8:00 A.M. of a clear, sunny morning as he walked toward Beverly's apartment. There, at least, he could wash and eat breakfast. Near the Oasis Launderette on Sutter Avenue, about one block from Beverly's apartment, he saw a gray car stop opposite him on the other side of the avenue. Two husky white men stepped out of the car and walked briskly toward him. One of them said: "I'm a detective. Are you the fellow who told this police officer yesterday that you had seen a man running from the police?"

Whitmore saw that the man held a small gold badge in his right hand. "Yes, I'm the one," he replied.

"We'd like to ask you some questions at the 73rd Precinct."

"Okay," Whitmore said.

Whitmore followed the detective across the street to the gray car. The young police officer who had questioned him the previous morning outside the laundry got into the rear seat with him. The detective slid behind the wheel. In a few minutes they were at the 73rd Precinct, which Whitmore had never seen before. He felt proud of the police interest in him, proud because he might become an important witness in a rape case. Even if he could not aid the police, he had nothing to lose; he had no place to go, nothing to do that day.

As soon as Whitmore entered the detectives' squad room, he discovered he was not to be treated as an honored guest. The detective said in a fierce voice: "Take off your coat and hat and empty your pockets."

Without a word of protest, he removed Shellie's tan coat and his own green hat. From his pockets he pulled out a pink-handled pocketknife, a wallet, and an address book.

After indifferently looking over Whitmore's possessions, the detective told him to lift his hands, and proceeded to search him. He led Whitmore to a strange-looking cell in the corner of the room and locked him inside. The younger police officer left the room. Whitmore was alone with the detective. He had never been involved with the New York police, but he realized he was in trouble now.

A few minutes later, he saw a short, fat woman enter the squad room with the young police officer, who took her into a side room and closed the door. Whitmore did not have to wait long for the next development. The detective opened the cell, motioning to him to come out.

"Stand here, next to me," the detective said, pointing to a spot in front of the closed door behind which the woman had disappeared. Whitmore did as he was told. He could see the brown door about ten feet away; the door had a tiny hole in it, a peephole.

He stood beside the detective for what seemed like five minutes without a sound penetrating the room. Finally, the door with the peephole opened. The young officer stepped out, pointed to Whitmore, and said:

"Say, 'Lady, I'm going to rape you. Lady, I'm going to kill you.' "

"Why should I say that?"

"Do it and don't ask any questions," the detective next to him said.

The other police officer stepped behind the closed door again, and Whitmore broke the silence, saying in a clear voice:

"Lady, I'm going to rape you. Lady, I'm going to kill you."

A minute after the two sentences were out of Whitmore's mouth, the young officer walked back into the room. He nodded at the detective. The woman also came out of the room and nodded.

"I'm placing you under arrest for attempting to rape a woman," the detective said. "She's just identified you as the guy."

"She's making a mistake. I saw the guy running away. I had nothing to do with it."

The two policemen shook their heads. "She's sure you're the guy," the detective said.

"Lady, you're making a mistake," Whitmore shouted at the woman as he was returned to the cell.

He squatted on the floor, wondering what to do. Looking up, he saw the detective opening the cell as the woman and the young officer left the main room. The detective took Whitmore into the side room the woman had been in, a small room containing a desk and several chairs.

"Are you ready to tell us the truth?" the detective began.

Whitmore repeated that he had been truthful. Again he went over his story of hearing shots and then having the brief conversation with the running man.

"You're lying," the detective said. "We know you tried to rape that woman."

The young officer now returned. Whitmore and the two policemen were the only people in the room. Whitmore watched the young officer rolling up his shirtsleeves as he advanced towards him.

Trying to anticipate their next move, Whitmore stood clutching the edge of the desk with his hands. The detective ordered him to stand in front of a chair. When he did, the detective moved in front of him, and the other officer got behind the chair.

Whitmore felt stinging pain simultaneously in his stomach, back, chest, and neck. The two policemen were slapping and punching him. He shielded his face with his hands, but they made no attempt to strike him in the face.

"Okay, did you rape that woman?" one of them said as the flurry of blows stopped.

"No, I didn't do anything," Whitmore said, trembling. "I was walking home from my girl friend's house when I heard a shot and saw that fellow running away."

A pair of hands knocked Whitmore into the chair. His back erupted in a flash of pain. Before he could cry out, he felt himself being lifted out of the chair onto his feet.

"We'll tell you what happened," a voice boomed at him. "You wanted a woman and you were prowling around when you saw a Puerto Rican woman near the subway station. You followed her, and you grabbed her around the neck. You pushed her into a hall and started feeling her up. You were going to rape her but she screamed and a cop almost caught you. That's right, isn't it?"

"No, those are lies. I never saw that Spanish woman before," Whitmore said, trying to sound convincing. He hoped his voice was loud enough to be heard by someone outside the room.

Again he was bombarded with punches, mostly in the stomach and back. He slipped, but as soon as he hit the floor, he was picked up by powerful hands and set on his feet.

"This is your last chance, George. Are you going to tell the truth?"

"I didn't do anything."

"Make it easy for yourself, George. We know you were hanging around the subway station at Livonia Avenue when you saw her. We know what you did."

The policemen hovered over him, interspersing slaps with questions. Whitmore was shaking when they sat him in the chair again. The burning pain in his back and chest refused to subside. His body quivered uncontrollably, despite his effort to regain command of his muscles. He was crying, and he knew of no way to fend off the blows or the questions.

"You wanted to rape that woman, didn't you, George?"

"Yes," Whitmore heard himself say. There was no other recourse. Maybe now they would let him alone. He saw the two policemen smile for the first time. The answer had pleased them, and the punches stopped.

The detective reached into a desk drawer and took out a large yellow writing tablet. "Okay, George, let's go over this once more," he said. While he wrote, the detective continued talking and asking questions.

"It was early Thursday morning, the morning of April 23. About midnight you left your girl friend's house and were walking around the streets. Right?"

Whitmore nodded.

"You were near the subway station when you saw a Puerto Rican woman. You followed her on Rockaway a few blocks until you reached Bristol Street, near Sutter Avenue. Then you grabbed her from behind with an arm lock and told her not to scream. Isn't that right?"

Again Whitmore nodded.

"You pulled her into an alley on Bristol Street and said: 'Lady, first I'm going to rape you, then I'm going to kill you.' You felt her pussy under her dress and had her against the wall when she started to scream and a cop came in. The cop chased you and shot after you, but you got away. Right?"

Whitmore stared back silently, nodding his head automatically.

"What'd you do the rest of the night, sleep in a hallway on Amboy Street?"

"Yes."

"Okay, see how easy that was, George. Now we can have some breakfast," the detective said as he stopped writing and looked up. Whitmore thought he looked extremely pleased.

The young police officer left the room as soon as the detective stopped writing. In five minutes, he returned with a paper bag filled with slices of buttered bread and containers of coffee.

Despite his nervousness, Whitmore was hungry. He bit into the bread and helped himself to a container of coffee. The detective offered him a cigarette, and he greedily inhaled on it. While he ate, the policemen asked him about Beverly Payne—where she lived and how often George stayed in her apartment.

Other men were coming into the room now, white men who looked stern and powerful. Occasionally, the detective would leave Whitmore's side and talk to one of them in whispers. Whitmore considered shouting to these newcomers for help, crying out what was happening to him and begging them to rescue him. "But they're probably cops, too," he reflected. "Why should they help a colored boy? I just don't want to be hit any more. As long as they don't do that to me."

He finished his bread and coffee and smoked his cigarette almost to the tip, trying to make the tobacco last as long as possible. When the waxed paper, crumbs, and empty coffee-containers had been cleared from the desk, the detective leaned back and asked casually:

"George, did you know a woman was stabbed on Chester Street last week?"

"No."

"Have you ever been on Chester Street?"

"I don't know, maybe."

"Come on, George, you know where Chester Street is. You must have been there lots of times. It's only a block away from Bristol Street, where you tried to rape the Puerto Rican woman."

"I don't know anything about that street."

"George, you tried to get another woman one night, a colored woman, as she walked home; and when she resisted you, you stabbed her. Isn't that so?"

"No, I never stabbed anyone."

"George, you like pussy, don't you? This colored woman wouldn't let you touch her. She screamed and you stabbed her."

"No, I don't know anything about that," Whitmore insisted.

The detective rose. Towering over Whitmore, he shouted: "If you don't tell us what we want to know in five seconds, I'm going to kick you in the balls. We don't want any more lies from you."

Sitting down beside Whitmore, the detective pulled out his yellow tablet. Again he talked and wrote:

"You were standing on Sutter Avenue on the morning of April 14, about 3:00 A.M. You were in a doorway across the street from the Junior High School when you saw a woman walking up Chester Street—isn't that so?

"You crossed the street after her, but she saw you and began walking fast. You ran after her, caught up with her, and put an arm lock around her. She screamed and said: 'What the fuck do you want?' You told her you wanted sex, and you tried to grab her, but she broke away and ran into an alley. You chased after her, caught her in the alley and, when she screamed again, you stabbed her. Isn't that right?"

"Yes," Whitmore said. "That's right."

The detective described the rape again. After a few sentences, he would stop and have Whitmore repeat what he had just told him. When they had gone over the rape several times, the detective talked about the stabbing. Whitmore would parrot what was told him until the detective seemed satisfied.

The room glowed with sunlight, but Whitmore had no idea of the time. His head ached from concentrating on what the detective explained to him. He was certain this was the best way to avoid any more punishment, and he would do anything to escape that.

"George, you realize you're in trouble," one of the policemen said. "And there's only one thing that will help you—the knife. Where's the knife you used?"

Whitmore looked blankly at the two officers. He groped for an explanation that might satisfy them, an answer that would spare him threats or punches.

"I think I lost it."

"Come on, George, don't lie. Tell us what you did with the knife."

"It's lost. I don't know where."

"Finding that knife is the only thing that's going to help clear you," one of the policemen said.

"I don't know. I guess I lost it."

To Whitmore's relief, the questioning stopped when another white man stepped into the room. The detective greeted the newcomer warmly and whispered excitedly to him. The two men walked over to Whitmore. The detective pointed to the new man, saying: "This is Detective ———" Whitmore could not grasp the name. The new detective was older than the first one, and he looked friendlier. The first detective stared at Whitmore with an expression of frozen hostility; the older detective was smiling. The questions started again.

"Now, George, we have to know where the knife is."

"Where'd you put the knife, George?"

"If you want to clear up this trouble, we have to know where the knife is."

Whitmore tried to think of an answer that would please them, but he could only continue to reply weakly: "I lost it somewhere."

The policemen—even the new detective—looked sullen and displeased by his answer. They whispered among themselves for a few minutes, and then the young policeman left the room. No questions were asked during his brief absence. When he returned, he marched quickly to the desk and slammed a knife down in front of Whitmore.

"Could this be the kind of knife you used?" a detective asked.

Whitmore looked at the weapon lying unopened before him. It had a black handle engraved with a silver panther.

"I don't know."

"We want an answer. Is it or isn't it?"

"I guess that's the same kind of knife."

The answer obviously pleased the three policemen.

"But where is the knife, George?"

"We have to know, George. It's for your own good."

Whitmore, convinced he could not continue to say it was lost, hit upon a new explanation:

"I hid it in the hallway on Amboy Street."

"Where on Amboy Street?" a detective shot back.

"I don't remember the number."

"Could you show us the building?"

"I guess so."

The two detectives talked quietly to each other, then walked out of the room together. Whitmore felt pitifully helpless. Regardless of what he said, they would drive and prod him until they heard what they wanted—not the truth but an answer that mysteriously satisfied them. He was caught in their trap and there was no escape for him.

The detectives returned. "Come on," one said. "We're going out for a while."

The three policemen and Whitmore got into the same gray car that had brought Whitmore to the precinct. A fourth white man was in the car; Whitmore assumed he was another detective. They drove to Sutter Avenue, only a block from where Whitmore had seen the man running. The car stopped near Junior High School 263 and everyone got out. One of the detectives began talking:

"You must have been standing in a doorway over there (he motioned with his right hand) when you saw the colored woman walking home."

Whitmore and the four men crossed the street as the detective continued:

"You followed her, running across the street to close in on her. You were here, right across the street from the school, when she started fighting with you and hollering at you. She got away from you over here and ran into the alley."

The group walked through the alley into the rear yard.

"This is where you stabbed her. Right, George?" Without waiting for an answer, the detective continued: "And this is how you got away by running out of this alley into the street."

As they walked along the street and through the alley, Whitmore, even without his glasses, could see faces pressed against windows, staring at him.

"Okay, George, now we'll go to Amboy Street and you show us the building where you hid the knife."

Whitmore was familiar with only one building on Amboy Street, Number 178, where his cousin had an apartment. As the car approached the building, he told the police to stop. They walked into the hallway.

"Where'd you leave the knife?"

"Under the stairway," Whitmore replied.

The younger detective got down on his knees and passed his hand through the thick dust under the stairwell. "There's nothing here," he said, getting to his feet. Addressing Whitmore, he added: "You'd better look and find it."

Whitmore, imitating the detective, dropped to his knees and went through the same act of running his hand into the dark corners under the stairwell. "It's not here," he said, straightening up.

"Let's get the janitor. Maybe he found it," a detective said.

The Negro building-superintendent and his son were politely asked if they had cleaned the hallway recently and, if so, whether they had found a knife. The janitor said it was cleaned frequently, but neither he nor his son had discovered a knife.

When the superintendent and his son had left, the detectives turned their attention to Whitmore.

"Did you leave the knife at your girl friend's house?" one of them barked.

"No, she doesn't know anything about this," Whitmore said. "You wouldn't believe me. I don't know where the knife is."

"Come on," a detective said, pushing Whitmore ahead of him out of the hallway. They climbed back into the car and drove to Hopkinson Avenue, where Beverly Payne and her family lived.

The police told Whitmore to lead the way, and they followed him up the four flights of stairs. Whitmore's knock brought Beverly to the door, but she kept the latch chain on. Puzzled by the appearance of George with so many white men, she asked what was wrong.

"Tell her it's okay," a detective said.

"You can let us in, Beverly; they're with me," Whitmore said reluctantly.

Once inside, the police identified themselves and brusquely searched the rooms. They asked Whitmore if he had any clothes in the apartment, and he showed them a closet that contained three pairs of his trousers and other garments belonging to Beverly's brother. The police pulled all the men's clothes off the racks.

The officers questioned Beverly in the kitchen.

"Did you ever wash blood off his clothes?"

"No."

"Watch out you don't lie to us. You're sure you never washed any bloodstains from his clothes?"

"Yes, I'm sure."

"Did he ever leave a knife here?"

"No, he never did. What'd you want from George? What'd he do?"

"Get your coat," a detective told her. "We want you to come along to the precinct."

With Beverly squeezed into the car, they returned to the station house.

The girl remained in the main squad room, and Whitmore was taken again to the interrogation room.

"You led us on a wild-goose chase for the knife," a detective said when Whitmore was seated at the desk. "You know if you get us mad we could get your girl sent to jail for being a delinquent minor."

"She had nothing to do with it."

"That's what you say."

"You're positive you don't know where the knife is?"

He shook his head. The room was silent. The detectives walked out, leaving him alone with the young patrolman.

Whitmore hoped they had finished with him. "Maybe they'll let me go now. Please, God, make them leave me alone," he prayed silently. The constant questioning and the trips to Chester Street, Amboy Street, and Beverly's apartment had left him exhausted. Even if he was still in a police station, it felt good to be let alone, to have a few minutes without the incessant questions, angry remarks, and icy stares of the policemen. The patrolman was not bothering him. Whitmore tried not to think about his problem. He concentrated on what he would do when they let him leave the station house. He decided he would stay close to Beverly and never go out alone on the streets at night. And he definitely would never talk to policemen.

He heard the door open. They were coming back.

"These pictures of white girls in your wallet, George, where'd you get them?" the older detective asked. He held up two photographs. They were snapshots Whitmore had found in a junkyard, pictures of white girls with which he tried to impress people. Some of his friends actually believed the white girls had given him their photographs, and George felt extremely important whenever someone believed this.

"I found them in a junkyard," Whitmore said.

"Where?"

"In Wildwood, New Jersey, where I was working."

"You didn't find them in an apartment on 88th Street, did you, George?"

"No. I got them in the junkyard."

The detectives shoved one of the snapshots toward Whitmore. It was a photograph of two white girls sitting in an open convertible. They were pretty girls, and Whitmore liked to look at the photograph.

"You're lying, George; we know it. Tell us where you got this picture."

It was starting again. His mind reeled as he tried to find an explanation that would satisfy them. There were more people in the room now, another white man or two, and their faces seemed to show hatred for him.

"I don't know what you mean. I found those pictures in a junkyard."

They laughed at his answer, and then the older detective said angrily: "Don't get us mad. We have more than one way of making you talk."

Whitmore could see it was futile to tell the truth; that was not the answer they wanted.

"A girl in Wildwood gave me that picture," he said.

"What's her name?"

"I don't remember, but her father had a riding academy and she gave me the picture as a present."

"George, you know you're lying. Didn't you find that picture in an apartment on 88th Street in Manhattan?"

"No, I got it in Wildwood. I don't know where 88th Street is."

"You're a liar, George, and we're going to get the truth from you."

Their faces grew red with mounting fury as they leaned over Whitmore to shout at him. They repeated the same question faster and faster: "Where'd you get the picture—wasn't it 88th Street?" He had no conception of what they were driving at. Why did they want him to say 88th Street? If he did, would they let him alone? Maybe this was the last question. If he said "yes" it might be all over and he could go home.

"Yes," he said, nodding. "It was 88th Street."

The policemen looked at each other and smiled. Whitmore was not sure who was in the room with him. All the men were white, but most of the faces were unfamiliar. The only ones he could recognize were the first detective who had picked him up that morning in the street, and the older detective, the one who smiled, who had come later to question him about the woman stabbed on Chester Street. People seemed to be coming in and out of the room constantly. There were too many faces to keep track of.

They were asking him how he got to 88th Street. Afraid of giving the wrong reply, he kept quiet, staring back at them. He knew they would eventually tell him the answer. One of the policemen was writing, just as the detective had done when they questioned him about the rape and the stabbing. The writer would not put a single word on the paper for several minutes; then, after they had gone over a point that the policemen kept telling him was important, the writer would move his pen quickly, even though no one was saying anything.

"You went to 88th Street by subway, didn't you, George?"

Whitmore nodded.

"Where'd you get off—at Times Square?"

He nodded.

"You know Times Square, don't you?"

"Yes, that's where I get the bus to Wildwood."

"Okay, that special day you went to Times Square. Then you didn't go to Wildwood. What'd you do that day—walk around?"

The questions muddled him, but he was afraid to do anything except nod his head.

You went into a building, didn't you, George?"

He nodded.

"Why'd you go into this building, George?"

They wanted something more than a "yes" answer, and he tried to find one. Before he could reply, a detective said:

"Maybe you like to look down from tall buildings, George. Maybe that's why you went inside."

"Yes, I wanted to look around."

"When you were walking up the stairs of the building, did you see an open door?"

"No, I didn't see anything," Whitmore said. He knew they were trying to get him into more trouble by making him say he went inside an apartment. He had to resist.

"Don't lie, George. We know you saw a door opened by a crack," a detective fired back at him. "You pushed the door open and walked right into an apartment, didn't you?"

"Yes."

"What was the first thing you saw when you walked inside?"

"A table?" Whitmore asked hesitantly.

"No, think again. Wasn't it a carton of empty soda bottles on the floor?"

Whitmore nodded. "Empty bottles, not a table." He was glad they did not ask him for too many complicated answers. He heard them describe his seeing a naked girl walking toward him, a blonde girl.

"What was she carrying in her hand, George? It was a bottle of some kind. Was it Vaseline or Noxzema you saw her carrying?"

"Vaseline?"

"No, George. Think again."

"Noxzema," he said, wondering what Noxzema was.

They told him that he had hit the girl over the head with one of the soda bottles, that he had dragged her into a bedroom and tied her up. They were making him lie; yet he was powerless to defy them.

"Now a second woman came into the apartment. Isn't that right, George?"

"Think, George, was there anything special about this woman? Was she wearing glasses?"

"Yes, she had glasses."

"You hit her over the head, too, and put her on the bed next to the other girl, right?"

"Yes."

"What happened then?"

"I don't know."

"All right. Remember, George, something got you angry and you stabbed the girls. You got the knives from the kitchen and stabbed them, right? Were you angry because you couldn't have sex with the girls?"

"Yes."

"You broke the knives, George, and it took a pretty strong fellow to do it. You're pretty strong, aren't you?"

He just stared back at the detectives.

"You probably broke the knives by putting them under your heel and snapping off the blades. Is that the way you did it?"

"Yes."

"Just keep cooperating, George, and everything will be over soon."

He was left in the room with only one detective. The other policemen looked excited as they left the room. He could hear their buzz of conversation outside. He knew now they would not let him alone; there would be more and more questions.

All conception of time was gone. The room filled again with white men. Now he was being told more details about the rape, the stabbing on Chester Street, and the stabbing of two girls on 88th Street.

First the police went over details of the attempted rape on Bristol Street. He was slowly told what had happened, and then asked to repeat what the police had just described to him. Not too many details were involved. He had been walking the streets when he saw a Spanish woman, followed her for several blocks, then grabbed her around the neck. Just as he pulled her into the alley, she started screaming and a cop almost caught him. That was all he had to remember.

The stabbing on Bristol Street was also easy. The police told him he had been standing in the doorway of a store when he saw a Negro woman walk by. He ran after her and tried to overcome her with an arm lock around the neck. She resisted, cursed him, and got away by slipping out of her coat. He chased her through an alley into a back yard. She fought once more; this time he got mad, pulled out a knife, and stabbed her. That same night he slept in the hallway on Amboy Street and hid the knife in the stairwell.

The police gave Whitmore a few minutes of rest before they started going over the details of what happened on 88th Street: how he had taken the subway to Manhattan and walked the streets until he aimlessly wandered into a building. When he found the door open, he walked in and eventually stabbed two girls. This was the story they went over with him more than once.

Several times the detectives interrupted their description to introduce him to men to whom they were extremely polite. One of the detectives said: "The big brass is here—they're the most important police officers in the city." All these men looked tall and old; many were gray-haired. They stared piercingly at him while he repeated parts of the story about 88th Street for them. Before anyone new came into the room, the detectives would rehearse him. Then they would say: "George, tell us how you got to Manhattan"; or, "George, what happened when you walked into the apartment? What did you see first?" Once, when he was slow in responding, a detective warned: "Don't get me mad—do we have to go through this all over again?"

Whitmore tried to repeat as best he could what had been told to him. Everyone seemed pleased by his words. The parade of listeners looked alike to him, vague faces that kept popping into the room to look at him.

Occasionally one of the detectives would leave the room for a few minutes and then come back to tell Whitmore something new about 88th Street. Once he was told he had used a razor blade to cut bedsheets into thin strips with which to bind the women. Another time, a detective asked him in a very serious tone why he had not raped the young blonde girl. When Whitmore could not think of an answer, the detective said:

"You wanted to rape her, but she had a Kotex, right?"

When Whitmore said "yes," he was told that he threw the Kotex under the bed. He repeated this several times, and then several of the "brass" came in and he told it to them.

His interrogators had different names for the two women on 88th Street.

"Remember the first girl you saw, the blonde who was wearing a towel? Her name is 'the young girl,' and the second woman you stabbed, the one with the glasses, call her 'the mother.' "

They also wanted Whitmore to write his name on pieces of paper and on the photographs. He did so. They would put a piece of paper in front of him and say: "Put your initials there," or, "Sign this, George."

The detectives grew happier and happier. When they took Whitmore into the main squad room to be fingerprinted, one of them said with a smile: "I got some good news for you, George. I just called the two girls on 88th Street and they're all right. They were kept in a hospital a short time. They're not mad at you."

Whitmore could not understand why the detective was so pleased at this remark, but he smiled as if he, too, appreciated the news.

While they were fingerprinting him, he looked around for Beverly, but no one he knew was in the squad room.

Some time that night—he had no idea of the time—they brought him a hamburger and a soft drink. He was not hungry, but he ate anyway. He wanted to regain his strength; he thought food would be good for him.

Later, he was asked to repeat each story once more: first, how he had tried to rape a woman; then how he had stabbed a Negro woman on Chester Street; finally, how he had sneaked into an apartment on 88th Street and stabbed two girls. Afterward, more people came into the room. The older detective who smiled a great deal told him they were going to take his confessions to the attempted rape and the stabbing of the Negro woman. The two detectives then brought in a man they said was from the District Attorney's office. Whitmore wondered if he should tell this man that the police had beaten him and made him lie. He decided against it. This man probably was a policeman, too. What good would it do to tell him? Everyone would probably shout at him and beat him again.

In the small room, the man from the District Attorney's office sat at a machine with long legs that looked something like a typewriter but did not make much noise. Whitmore had never seen such a machine before. The older detective asked him questions about 88th Street—again, the stabbing of the two women. All he had to do was say "yes" to the detective's questions. While the detective put the questions to him, the man from the District Attorney's office tapped the strange-looking machine. At last the questions ended.

They took Whitmore out of the small room and placed him in the cage. There was no room to sit down. He looked out at the detectives and waited for something else to happen to him. His body ached, but there was no way to rest in the cell. He could either stand upright or squat on his haunches in the tiny cubicle; there was not enough space to stretch out. His head and eyes throbbed. It was difficult to remember all that had happened; most of the past hours were a blur of faces and dim recollections about stabbings and following women, hiding knives, and hitting women over the head. None of it was clear to him any more.

More people seemed to be coming into the room. The police officers were waving the new people into a side room—the room from which the short fat woman had identified him through a peephole. He could see the new people sizing him up, running their eyes up and down, inspecting him. He stared back. What else could he do? He squatted and closed his eyes; at least he could rest his eyes and shut out the faces of people scrutinizing him. When his calves knotted with pain, he straightened up and looked out again at the squad room. The long night was over. The sun had burst into every corner of the room. Someone would look at him occasionally, but no one shouted at him any more or told him what he was supposed to remember. He could see some of the detectives getting ready to leave. They put on their suit jackets and came over to his cell.

"Okay, George, we have to go to court now."

They took him out and handcuffed his right wrist to one of the detectives. About twenty people stood outside the precinct when they got to the street. Some of the people had cameras and shouted: "Hold him. Let's get a shot of him"; and, "Give us a break—one more shot." The police quickly pushed Whitmore into a small green truck with wire screens and told him to sit on a bench along one side. In a minute they were moving. The detectives with him did not speak. It felt good to sit down, and Whitmore no longer cared where they took him or bothered to ask where he was going.

When the van stopped, the detectives led him into a large building. First they took photographs of him with a number under his face. He knew what this meant: just like in the movies they were going to put his face into the book with pictures of criminals. He was no criminal and he wanted to cry, but an inner pride prevented him. They pushed him into another room and told him to undress. "Take off everything." Perhaps he was in jail and they were going to give him a prison uniform. But when his clothes were off, a photographer entered the room carrying a huge camera and took pictures of his naked body, front, back, sides. He dressed again.

"Where do I go now?"

"You're going to court."

At the courthouse he sat for an hour in a small room with uniformed guards around him. Suddenly a door opened and he saw a courtroom and many people. He looked around and at last saw a friendly face. His brother Jerry was in the courtroom, and so were his uncle, his aunt, and several cousins. He smiled at them, and they waved back.

The police led him to a bench, and he heard his name called. He tried to pay attention. Maybe now he could tell someone what had happened to him, what the police had done to him. A voice—he had no idea whose—was saying: "George Whitmore, you are charged with murder. Do you have a lawyer to represent you?"

"That was when I found out they had accused me of murder. I didn't know till I got to court," Whitmore concluded.

Whitmore's story had contradicted almost every fact the police gave out about his arrest and detention. Yet Reiben believed the young Negro. His experience as a trial lawyer had convinced him that few guilty criminals, especially young ones, recant confessions. When caught, they are usually relieved to unburden their consciences. Only the hardened-convict type, the man who has spent a lifetime in the underworld, is crafty enough to try to wriggle out of a confession. And Whitmore scarcely seemed that type. Reiben felt it would not take much beating or brainwashing to frighten Whitmore into confessing to any crime. The inexperienced youth would be a perfect target for determined police officers who believed they had caught the right man.

Reiben spent another hour trying to find defects and contradictions in Whitmore's story. The youth freely conceded that Assistant District Attorney Lichtman had been able to confuse him and trip him up when he was on the witness stand during the attempted-rape trial.

Thirty years before, Reiben had grown up in Brownsville when it was a predominantly Jewish neighborhood. He knew the area well. The streets on which Whitmore supposedly murdered and tried to rape women were the streets Reiben had played on as a boy. He knew how tough it was to grow up in a ghetto, to feel you were friendless. But he had a warning for Whitmore:

"You may or may not be a victim of prejudice, I don't know yet. Nevertheless, what happens to you may be an important civil rights case for your people. I don't want you to let your people down, and I don't want you to let me down.

"I'm warning you now—I'm going to investigate everything you've told me, and if I find out you're lying, I'll pull the switch myself when they strap you in the electric chair."

Whitmore wet his lips before answering: "I'm telling the truth, Mr. Reibnens."

The lawyer laughed at the mispronunciation of his name. By this time,

Reiben believed Whitmore was not deceiving him. He had decided to represent him.

On December 2, 1964, while Whitmore was still in Kings County Hospital, Miller and Kaplan filed a motion in New York State Supreme Court in Brooklyn for court permission to take over Whitmore's defense. The lawyers cited a statement from Whitmore and his mother:

"My son and I are not satisfied with the manner in which Mr. Leftow has conducted the investigation and trial to date. We have been unable to agree with many of his decisions."

The move was a shock to Leftow. He had worked diligently and unsparingly for Whitmore. Although he was embarrassed at being fired without consultation by the Whitmore family, and without any explanation from them, he made no attempt to oppose the new legal team. With good grace, he wished the trio better luck than he had had.

Under the new arrangement, Reiben agreed to take the title of chief defense counsel; he would plan the defense strategy and argue in court. Miller and Kaplan would do the important legwork of finding evidence—providing that Whitmore was telling the truth, and that evidence existed.

12. *One Killer Too Many*

The first obstacle facing the new defense team was the conviction for attempted rape. Unless that guilty verdict was set aside, Whitmore would bear the stigma of a sex criminal when he went on trial for murder. Reiben prepared to appeal for a reversal of the conviction, but at the same time he thought ahead to the Wylie-Hoffert problem. This was the murder trial Reiben wanted first, since most of the prejudicial publicity surrounding Whitmore flowed from the double murder. District Attorney Hogan, however, refused to indicate when he would try Whitmore for these homicides.

The three lawyers dipped into their own pockets to carry out the search for new evidence. By declaring Whitmore indigent, they could have allowed the courts to appoint three lawyers, with total fees of up to $3,000, to defend him on each of the murder charges. But Reiben, because of his unpopularity with some judges, could not be certain that he would be designated as Whitmore's counsel.

One unexpected source of aid materialized for the defense. Newspapers besides the *World-Telegram* had become curious about the developments in the Whitmore case, and reporters volunteered their services to the lawyers.

Miller began the most important part of his legwork by trying to interview all the jurors who had voted guilty in the Borrero trial, and by visiting Wildwood to look into Whitmore's alibi. During the last days of 1964 the portly attorney puffed his way up and down Brooklyn stairways, seeking out the twelve jurors to determine if any extraneous matters had influenced their verdict. He also spent hours on the telephone, setting up appointments with possible witnesses in Wildwood.

He had little success with the first five jurors. Citing their legal rights, they flatly refused to discuss their reasons for having voted guilty; nor would they confirm or deny that some members of the jury had discussed the Wylie-Hoffert case during the Borrero proceedings. Each juror Miller spoke to maintained that knowledge of Whitmore's implication in the Manhattan double murder had not influenced his vote. One juror, Ernest E. Ricci, did give Miller hope. Ricci said he had been unaware of Whitmore's link to the Wylie-Hoffert case until this was implied by Lichtman during the empaneling of the jury. After hearing this, Miller determined to question the seven remaining jurors until he learned unequivocally whether the jury had been affected by the Wylie-Hoffert matter.

When Miller visited Wildwood, New Jersey, he learned that detectives from New York had been extremely busy in that area in recent months. The New Yorkers had asked the local police department for aid in finding a woman whose photograph they had shown the Wildwood policemen. Miller guessed what this signified: the New York police had traced the photograph found on Whitmore to Wildwood. Some Wildwood policemen who recalled Whitmore as "a nice kid, who kept out of trouble," provided Miller with a major clue. They told him the woman in the picture was Mrs. Arlene Franco, a pretty blonde who lived in a section known as Wildwood Crest. Mrs. Franco was generally cooperative with the lawyer, but she was disturbed by the possibility of becoming involved in a sensational murder case. All she could tell Miller was that two New York detectives, accompanied by a Wildwood policeman, had appeared at her home in late September or early October. They had shown her a small, faded snapshot that she had no trouble recognizing. She was the girl seated on the back seat of the convertible. To the best of her recollection the photograph had been taken in the summer of 1958, when she was a seventeen-year-old high school junior, at a school picnic in nearby Belleplain Park, a state forest preserve. A girl friend had kept the only print of the photograph that she knew of, and Mrs. Franco had no knowledge of what had happened to it. As for George Whitmore, Emily Hoffert, and Janice Wylie, she had never heard of any of these persons until the New York police told her about the murders.

Miller obtained the name of the woman who had kept the only print, and he hurried back to New York. He was convinced the photograph that had led the police to question Whitmore as a suspect in the Wylie-Hoffert murders was worthless as evidence. Most probably, just as Whitmore had claimed all along, he had found the snapshot in a rubbish heap in Wildwood.

As 1964 came to a close, Whitmore was discharged from Kings County Hospital. The psychiatrists there had spent a month examining him, and their report was similar to that made by the Bellevue psychiatrists: Whitmore was sane and capable of standing trial. There was no reference in the report to his being "a perpetual sex menace." Psychometric tests indicated he was of "low average intelligence," with a verbal I.Q. of 88, a performance I.Q. of 94, and a full-scale I.Q. of 90.

Early in January, Miller strengthened another part of Whitmore's defense by driving to Philadelphia and getting a first-hand account from Mrs. Montgomery and her daughter, Ludie, of their meetings with Whitmore on the day of the Wylie-Hoffert murders. Taking no chances of losing this crucial evidence, Miller wrote their statements in longhand, and then had each of them sign a separate affidavit.

In her statement, Ludie Montgomery said she clearly remembered the day of the Freedom March, having watched the demonstration on television in the Ivy Hotel in Wildwood. In the afternoon (she was uncertain of the exact time), she left the television set and entered the hotel restaurant.

"George was sitting as you go into the restaurant from the hotel, he was sitting at the second table on the left. He was sitting there alone. I walked over and sat down and said hello; he said hello and he said do you want to hear some records. He then played some records. He acted the same as he always did. Nothing seemed wrong or out of the ordinary. Clothing was not messed or anything unusual to call it to my attention."

Ludie remembered that the record Whitmore played on the juke box was *Down the Aisle*.

Later that afternoon, while the teen-agers were still sitting in the restaurant listening to the juke box, Mrs. Montgomery came to take Ludie home.

The New York police had asked Ludie the same questions Miller asked, and she had given them a similar statement in September or October, before Whitmore's trial for attempted rape. "About three or four months ago a Detective Lynch called me at my home and asked me about George on the day of the Freedom March," Ludie said. "I told him I did not remember. He said think about it and 'I will call you tomorrow.' I told my mother and she also told me to think, pray and be sure." The next day, Lynch, who described himself as a New York detective, telephoned her again. "After a while I did remember and told Mr. Lynch when he called," the girl said proudly.

Ludie assured Miller that, except for Lynch, no other person from the police had questioned her about Whitmore, and no one had suggested what she should say about August 28, 1963. "I saw it [about George] in the papers but did not connect it with the Freedom Day March," she added.

The Montgomerys told Miller that two weeks earlier, in late December, the New York police had asked them to come to District Attorney Hogan's office in Manhattan. They made the trip to New York on December 30. "I told the police [everything] and they showed me a bunch of pictures," Ludie said. "I picked out one of them and told them it was George. He did not have his glasses on in the picture. All the time I have ever seen George he was wearing his glasses. He had to squint when he had to take his glasses off."

The girl had one more bit of information for Miller. George, she said, "was always nice, never got fresh. . . . I never saw him drunk."

Mrs. Montgomery corroborated what her daughter said about seeing Whitmore that summer day in Wildwood. In addition, she had seen Whitmore in Wildwood on the night of August 28.

The lawyer had what he considered substantial proof that Whitmore had been one hundred twenty miles from Manhattan on the day of the Wylie-Hoffert murders. Since it would take at least three hours by auto or bus to journey from Wildwood to mid-Manhattan, Whitmore's alibi seemed solid. Ludie Montgomery had placed him in Wildwood in the afternoon; the murders had been committed on East 88th Street about noon. Ludie also gave Miller another lead. She was certain Whitmore had told her he had spent the morning of August 28 with a friend named Larry Wilson.

With reporters helping him find and interview jurors, Miller came across a strong scent of racial discrimination at the Borrero attempted-rape trial. One juror acknowledged having heard several of his colleagues discuss the Wylie-Hoffert case, despite admonishments from Judge Malbin and the jury foreman to exclude extraneous matters from their deliberations. More important to the defense, this juror said he had overheard another of the jurors twice make racial slurs against Whitmore. "What made me particularly mad," he told Miller, "was that on two separate occasions, once during lunchtime while we were deliberating and another time in the jury room [this juror] said: 'These fellows like their sex and they must get it some place—they screw like jackrabbits.' "

The juror who claimed to have overheard the racial slur refused to record his assertions in an affidavit. He maintained that Whitmore had still received a fair and true verdict, and that he himself would vote again for conviction.

The newly found evidence for Whitmore was not kept secret. Almost daily in December 1964 and January 1965, newspaper stories appeared about Whitmore's alibi; about the blonde in the snapshot being Arlene Franco, not Janice Wylie; and about the possible racial prejudice shown by the Borrero trial jurors. Reporters from the *Herald Tribune,* the *Daily News,* the *Post,* and the *World-Telegram* worked closely with Whitmore's lawyers to find the truth. For the first time stories favorable to Whitmore appeared. Hogan's office and the police seemed under indictment when headlines asserted: DOUBTS CLOUD WYLIE CASE; WHITMORE CLAIMS ALIBI AT TIME OF WYLIE KILLING; CASE FADES AWAY AGAINST YOUTH IN WYLIE GIRL KILLING; WHITMORE LAWYERS ACCUSE COPS, DA; WHITMORE JURORS ACCUSED OF BIAS; and THE PENDULUM SWINGING BACK FOR WHITMORE.

Almost every day, as more and more evidence apparently exonerating Whitmore was unveiled, reporters harassed Hogan's staff for explanations. Hogan's men resorted to a standard "No comment" in answer to all questions, refusing to indicate whether they, too, had doubts about Whitmore's guilt. Yet it was evident the lawyers had succeeded in one of their goals: they were bringing pressure on Hogan to try Whitmore for the Wylie-Hoffert murders or to drop the charge.

Near the end of January, any faint doubts the defense attorneys had about Whitmore's innocence vanished. Following Ludie Montgomery's advice, Miller located Larry Wilson, a seventeen-year-old high school student, still living in Wildwood. The Freedom March again played a coincidental but crucial role. Larry Wilson remembered talking to Whitmore about noon or 1:00 P.M. that day in the Ivy Hotel. That summer Wilson had worked as a dishwasher in the hotel, and he was certain he had been with Whitmore until noon or 1:00 P.M., when he reported for work in the hotel kitchen. He could reinforce Ludie's recollections of that vital day. During several breaks from his dishwashing chores, he noticed Ludie watching the civil rights rally on a television set in the hotel—exactly what she said she had been doing before her meeting with Whitmore.

Larry Wilson's affidavit, which Miller obtained in Wildwood on January 25, filled the remaining gap in Whitmore's alibi. If Wilson had seen him some time around noon, and the Montgomerys had spoken to Whitmore later in the afternoon, it virtually ruled out any possibility that he had made the three-hour journey to New York that morning or afternoon.

January 26 was a clear, pleasant, wintry Tuesday in New York. For Whitmore, it was another routine day in the Brooklyn House of Detention for Youth, with only a visit from Miller to interrupt the monotony of jail life. Miller explained the significance of Larry Wilson's affidavit, and Whitmore, who rarely smiled, seemed indifferent at the news. His hopes had been crushed too often in nine months of imprisonment for him to allow himself the luxury of optimism. Miller, a man who normally bubbled with enthusiasm, had no answer for Whitmore's incessant question: "When can I go home?"

"We're working as hard as we can, George," the lawyer said. "You've got to have faith in us. The thing to remember is even if nothing else happens in the Wylie-Hoffert case, you'll be getting a hearing soon on the Borrero conviction and, if all goes well, another trial."

Miller drove to his office in Brownsville, trying to concentrate on the traffic as he mulled over the myriad fragments of the jigsaw puzzle that was Whitmore's defense. Unknown to him, or to any of Whitmore's lawyers, almost at that moment another person was being arrested for the Wylie-Hoffert murders.

A few minutes before midnight, while Whitmore slept in his prison bunk, Assistant District Attorney Peter Koste, surrounded by reporters in the mildewed lobby of the 23rd Precinct in Manhattan, made a short announcement:

"I have directed the police to book Richard Robles for the double homicide of Janice Wylie and Emily Hoffert which occurred on August 28, 1963."

Neither Koste nor detectives would utter another word about Robles. This arrest, unlike Whitmore's, was accompanied by no news conference, no talk of statements or evidence. District Attorney Hogan had issued a "keep quiet" order to every police officer and official connected with the case.

That night, the man named Richard Robles was brought before a desk officer at the 23rd Precinct for booking. He stood with his wrists handcuffed behind his back as the officer asked him if he used narcotics.

"Yes, sir," Robles whispered. "About five bags of heroin a day."

"Five bags" meant a $15-a-day addiction.

From the precinct Robles was taken to New York's baroque police headquarters on Centre Street, where he got the nude-photograph treatment. Then he was whisked into a Manhattan prison known as the Tombs; there he was placed in a security wing, "Murderer's Row," where only homicide suspects are kept.

The police now had one man too many accused of the Wylie-Hoffert slayings. Before Whitmore's lawyers could make any legal move, the day after Robles's arrest Hogan offered his own motion in the State Supreme Court.

The District Attorney chose an obscure legal device to drop Whitmore as a suspect. Instead of automatically clearing him, Hogan had the Wylie-Hoffert indictment against Whitmore placed in limbo. He asked that Whitmore be "discharged on his own recognizance," which meant the indictment could be reinstated if fresh evidence were uncovered.

Much of the information dug up by the defense lawyers and newspaper reporters was at last confirmed by Hogan in his court papers. Hogan stated that Whitmore had been questioned about the Wylie-Hoffert slayings only because he had been carrying a photograph of a blonde who bore a "striking resemblance" to Janice Wylie. After police found that the photograph could not be connected with the Wylie-Hoffert apartment, Hogan said, his investigators checked out and confirmed what Whitmore originally had insisted—he had found the photograph in a Wildwood junkyard.

Robles's arrest did not unlock Whitmore's prison doors. A conviction for attempted rape was on Whitmore's record, and also an accusation of first-degree murder—sufficient grounds for keeping him in a cell, without bail.

Meanwhile, District Attorney Hogan was convinced that this time the Wylie-Hoffert killer had been captured.

13. *The Black Arts*

From a statistical viewpoint, police work is an undesirable, if not totally frustrating, profession in which all the odds favor the criminal. With the rate of crime having doubled in the United States since 1940, and with seventy-five per cent of serious offenses remaining unsolved each year, computers churn out mathematical projections that blend into an ugly picture of the underworld winning most encounters with the law.

These disheartening statistics have to be pounded into rookies at police academies and training schools to prepare them for the ordeal ahead—while at the same time the glories of artfully assembling irrefutable clues or capturing a criminal through the newest laboratory devices are described for the inspiration of fledgling patrolmen and state troopers. The modern police academy, however, cannot convey the true nature of the job. For not until a rookie puts on his blue uniform and discovers how impotent he and his colleagues can be when there are no clues or witnesses to a hideous strangling or a mugging, and not until he himself is imperiled for the first time, can he truly know the despair and hazards of his profession. Necessity quickly compels most policemen to substitute the high-principled theories of the classroom for the more practical tactics of the police black arts—informing, interrogating, and electronic spying.

Detectives and prosecutors are reluctant to boast about these methods, but if legwork fails to turn up a witness or a motive; if sifting through rogues'-gallery files for a likely suspect is unavailing; if microscopic examination of a crime scene discloses no fingerprint or tangible piece of evidence, always waiting in the wings are the informer, the police interrogator, and the electronic snooper.

The informer or squealer is an ancient ally of law enforcement. For money or another benefit, an underworld contact will lead the police to a suspect or an incriminating fact which otherwise would remain hidden. Every major police department has funds discreetly set aside to remunerate such informers. When the informer himself is in trouble, the bargain may be closed for a commodity more valuable than cash. Detectives or prosecutors, in exchange for extremely valuable tips or testimony, sometimes pay an informer by getting him a lighter sentence or a complete dismissal of a charge.

Interrogation, the second black art used in the modern police station, also has historic roots. Faced with a seemingly unsolvable puzzle, with no foreseeable way of tracking down the right man, the police often find a confession a tempting solution. Before he gets his badge, every detective is instructed in the art of asking questions. What he is not formally taught in the classroom he picks up by watching his more experienced colleagues in the back room. And, as an additional aid, there are training manuals that explain every facet of the art.

One celebrated and widely used text is *Criminal Interrogation and Confessions*. It outlines a framework of sympathy, cajolery, flattery, and trickery guaranteed to produce an incriminating statement from all but the most strong-willed of suspects. Written by Fred E. Inbau, former director of the Chicago Police Scientific Crime Detective Laboratory, and John E. Reid, a lie-detector expert, the book offers step-by-step strategies from the moment a suspect walks into the interrogation room until he eventually confesses. At the outset, Inbau and Reid caution that "patience and persistence" are mandatory requirements for an interrogator, because he must persuade someone into admitting not only that he has sinned but that he has also lied by not immediately acknowledging his guilt. Naturally, the decor of the interrogation room is of prime importance. The room should be in a quiet area removed from the ordinary hustle and bustle of a police station. Nothing in it should remind the suspect he is in custody and facing years or a lifetime in a penitentiary. Once the defendant is brought into this calm atmosphere, the interrogator should seat himself at eye level with the prisoner and, displaying an air of confidence, begin by remarking: "There's been a considerable amount of investigation in this case and it indicates that you haven't told the whole truth."

Next, Inbau and Reid advise hinting at what kind of evidence, if any, has been uncovered, and flipping through a large file of papers to convey the impression that a lengthy report has been compiled on the suspect. The presentation of a phony file is particularly effective against "a professional or business man who is himself accustomed to working with files and records," they note.

Inbau and Reid believe there are at least eight physical signs that imply lying: pulsation of the carotid artery; excessive activity of the Adam's apple; looking at the floor or ceiling rather than directly at the interrogator; foot-wiggling; wringing of hands; tapping fingers; picking fingernails; and frequent crossing of legs. In addition, interrogators are warned to be on the lookout for the suspect's remarking that he has a "peculiar feeling" inside him, or that his mouth feels dry. Other incriminating factors are the suspect's use of the phrase "I swear to God" to assert his innocence, or his claim to having a "spotless record" or of being a "religious man." These expressions are signals that the interrogator is close to bringing in the confession. When the suspect evades direct answers with "Not that I remember" replies, his remarks "should be treated as a veiled admission or half-truth."

Synthetic sympathy is a valuable weapon. "Sympathize with the subject by telling him that anyone else under similar conditions or circumstances might have done the same thing. . . . Reduce the subject's guilt feeling by minimizing the moral seriousness of his offense . . . . Suggest a less revolting and more morally acceptable motivation or reason for the offense than that which is known or presumed." A rape suspect might be comforted with a remark such as: "Joe, what happened? Did the girl go along with you at first, and then all of a sudden she let out a scream?" If necessary, the interrogator can ease the suspect's conscience by "condemning his victim, condemning his accomplice or condemning anyone else upon whom some degree of moral responsibility might conceivably be placed for the commission of the crime in question."

With particularly hard cases, the "friendly-unfriendly" act is suggested. In this tactic, one interrogator is verbally rough, seemingly on the edge of losing his temper, while his partner adopts a gentle, understanding attitude toward the suspect. Also known as the "Mutt and Jeff," "buddy," or "pal" act, it "serves to accentuate the friendly, sympathetic attitude" of one of the questioners and "thereby renders his approach more effective," the authors point out. Other general suggestions from these master interrogators include: get the subject to place himself at the scene of the crime or in some sort of contact with the victim; catch him in some kind of lie, because "once a subject has been caught in a lie . . . he loses a great deal of ground . . . this will bring him much nearer to the confession stage. . . ."; the uneducated and underprivileged person is "more vulnerable to flattery than the educated person. . . ."; point out the "futility of resistance to telling the truth . . . convince subject his guilt has been detected . . . capitalize on the fear his accomplice will talk."

Just in case the suspect wants to exercise his constitutional privilege of consulting a lawyer or friend, Inbau and Reid have an alternative: "The interrogator should respond by suggesting the subject first tell the truth to the interrogator himself rather than get anyone else involved in the matter. If the request is for an attorney, the interrogator may suggest that the subject save himself or his family the expense of any such professional service, particularly if he is innocent of the offense under investigation. The interrogator may also add, 'Joe, I'm only looking for the truth, and if you're telling the truth, that's it. You can handle this by yourself.' "

Another popular manual on the most effective ways of producing confessions is *Fundamentals of Criminal Investigation*, by Charles E. O'Hara, a former Federal investigator and a university lecturer in police science. O'Hara, who believes the back room should be a place where "the atmosphere suggests the invincibility of the forces of the law," provides this helpful summary:

"The investigator will, however, encounter many situations where the sheer weight of his personality will be the deciding factor. Where emotional appeals and tricks are employed to no avail, he must rely on an oppressive atmosphere of dogged persistence. He must interrogate steadily and without relent, leaving the subject no prospect of surcease. He must dominate his subject and overwhelm him with his inexorable will to obtain the truth. He should interrogate for a spell of several hours pausing only for the subject's necessities in acknowledgment of the need to avoid a charge of duress that can be technically substantiated. In a serious case, the interrogation may continue for days, with the required intervals for food and sleep, but with no respite from the atmosphere of domination. It is possible in this way to induce the subject to talk without resorting to duress or coercion. This method should be used only when the guilt of the subject appears highly probable."

One trick O'Hara proposes is the "Mutt and Jeff" act, which he graphically outlines: "In this technique, two agents are employed, Mutt, the relentless investigator, who knows the subject is guilty and is not going to waste any time. He's sent a dozen men away for this crime and he's going to send the subject away for the full term. Jeff, on the other hand, is obviously a kindhearted man. He has a family himself. He has a brother who was involved in a little scrape like this. He disapproves of Mutt and his tactics and will arrange to get him off the case if the subject will cooperate. He can't hold Mutt off for very long. The subject would be wise to make a quick decision. The technique is applied by having both investigators present while Mutt acts out his role. Jeff may stand by quietly and demur at some of Mutt's tactics. When Jeff makes his plea for cooperation, Mutt is not present in the room."

Fake identification is another stratagem offered by O'Hara. One way O'Hara has of doing this is to place the suspect in a line-up with others. "The witness or complainant (previously coached, if necessary) studies the line-up and confidently points out the subject as the guilty party." Then, O'Hara continues, the questioning resumes "as though there were now no doubt about the guilt of the subject." O'Hara's "reverse line-up" technique can also be applied when a confession is hard to obtain. It works this way: "The accused is placed in a line-up but this time he is identified by several fictitious witnesses or victims who associate him with different offenses. It is expected that the subject will become desperate and confess to the offense under investigation in order to escape from the false accusations."

There is no equivocation from Inbau and Reid or from O'Hara on the necessity of the back room. "Many criminal cases," Inbau and Reid declare, "even when investigated by the best qualified police departments are capable of solution only by means of an admission or confession from the guilty individual or upon the basis of information obtained from the questioning of other criminal suspects."

For centuries, informing and interrogating were the main police standbys. Recently, the contemporary marvel of electronic eavesdropping was added to the spectrum of the black arts. Wire tapping and planting of microphones (bugging) to overhear conversations have been utilized by police and federal officials for at least thirty years. But the Cold War brought a new standard of efficiency to spying gadgetry which increased its use in both large and small police departments. Miniature bugging equipment simplifies police work. Today a telephone is easier to tap than to install; an informer or police agent can be turned into a walking sound track by a recorder the size of a sugar cube; and no room or office is impregnable to the ear of a minute microphone.

The police must be careful in employing these ultramodern devices. The Supreme Court has outlawed the divulging of wiretap evidence in Federal courts, although some state courts permit it. The limitation on the use of bugging evidence in Federal courts is wrapped in a thick haze of conflicting court decisions, and Federal prosecutors are wary of presenting such evidence. In many states, however, the police—if they first obtain court sanction—tap phones, install bugs, and later present in court evidence thus obtained.

Despite the fuzziness of the electronic-eavesdropping laws and court interpretations, the police apparently are increasing their reliance on the latest black art. The Federal Bureau of Investigation and major police departments, like New York City's, are known to have extensive training programs for electronic specialists. For even if conversations secretly overheard are never brought before a judge or jury, spoken words can be useful to investigators. Information picked up through an illegal or judicially dubious telephone tap or microphone may still be used to batter down the resistance of a suspect—and can certainly be used to make him feel uneasy or betrayed. More important, illegal eavesdropping often provides the police with new avenues of investigation.

Few police officers consider these tactics reprehensible; the majority consider the black arts essential. The harsh truth is that most crimes today are not solved through scientifically established facts, through Sherlock Holmes sleuthing. More often, a murder, holdup, or rape is solved through the assistance of an informer, through a telephone tap, or through the work of a knowledgeable detective who has a talent for sniffing out a suspect and then getting him to specify the manner in which the crime was committed, who his accomplices were, where a piece of evidence can be found, and any other pertinent facts upon which a prosecutor can later construct a conviction.

In large cities, where the crime rate is highest and where police work is at the same time more difficult, the black arts are most popular. Unlike his comrades in small towns or suburban areas, the big-city cop is unaware of who is a stranger, unaware of who does have legitimate business or a home in his beat. In cities where the criminal can easily lose himself in the anonymous throng of a Times Square or a Loop, the black arts have become by-products of urban society.

It may be asking too much of policemen to expect them to be scrupulously respectful of the rights of a person they believe guilty, but against whom they have no concrete evidence. Every day it is the cops who see the broken, bloodied bodies of victims; every day it is the cops who are challenged by criminal minds, enemies who will never voluntarily incriminate themselves. Understandably, this makes for a tough police attitude. And this attitude is reinforced by a plethora of statistics proving that the war against crime is becoming more dangerous and that the policeman— just to hold his own—needs more, not fewer, weapons. Of every thousand men, women, and children in the United States, thirteen will be criminally victimized each year. With the crime rate inevitably climbing—it rose forty-six per cent from 1960 to 1965, to a total of 2,750,000 serious offenses, an average of five per minute—the police are constantly tempted to use the black arts, just as they eventually did in the Wylie-Hoffert case. To get George Whitmore Jr., interrogation was enough. To get Richard Robles, all the black arts were needed.

14. *"I Wouldn't Ice
Two Dames"*

Robles had been a suspect in the Manhattan murders long before Whitmore became enmeshed in the investigation. During the frenzied early days of the manhunt, one of the many probing rays emitted in the desperate search for the killer rested briefly on Robles before by-passing him as unworthy of attention.

Logically, the name of Richard "Ricky" Robles should have attracted the attention of detectives at the 23rd Precinct. Robles lived near the Wylie-Hoffert apartment; he had a record of burglary and assault; and he had a history of tying up his victims. In the first week of the investigation, detectives ploughing through thick files of criminals who used methods

185

similar to the killer's came across Robles's dossier; it made interesting reading even to a blasé cop.

Ricky Robles grew up in Yorkville, a neighborhood on the East Side of Manhattan extending from 80th Street north to 96th Street, with its other borders at the East River and Park Avenue. To Yorkville residents, Park Avenue is an important dividing line. Fabled Park Avenue and the numbered streets stretching westward from it to Central Park form a "Gold Coast" of ornate apartment buildings, expensive shops, and private schools —the section that was Janice Wylie's environment. East of Park Avenue is the other side of the tracks—where the middle class and poor of Yorkville live side by side in modest buildings or scarred tenements along First, Second, Third, and Lexington Avenues. Geographically, the "Gold Coast" and Yorkville are neighbors, but Park Avenue is a boundary that creates a perceptible financial and social barrier.

Although not a slum, Yorkville was a rough section for a teen-ager in the 1950's; a neighborhood where a youngster could easily get into trouble if his inclinations flared in that direction. Robles's homes in Yorkville were clean railroad flats in disintegrating buildings on 93rd Street between First and Second Avenues. Besides his parents, he had two older brothers, Michael and Robert, to look after him. Yet no childhood in a big city can be completely sheltered.

The first ominous shadow in Robles's adolescence materialized when he was thirteen. His mother, of French descent, and his father, of Spanish descent, were divorced. The Robles boys (who pronounced their name "Robe-els") remained with their mother and her second husband in the same section of Yorkville. Perhaps it was the divorce; perhaps it was a less fathomable reason; but soon after his parents split up, Robles made his first contacts with the midnight world of the junkie, the narcotics addict. He was a thirteen-year-old junior high school pupil when he became friendly with adult addicts who helped him take his first drag of a marijuana cigarette.

When he was fifteen, another family disaster shattered his life. In 1958, twenty-year-old Michael Robles, Ricky's older brother and idol, was killed in a parachute jump with the 101st Airborne Division while on maneuvers in Kentucky. Michael's death unloosed an inordinate emotional turmoil in Ricky. His first flow of despondent tears was followed by a solitary withdrawal from the rest of the mourning family. The boy would disappear for hours on long walks or into hideaways unknown to his family.

The boy's despondency gradually receded from the surface, but months later the family could see Ricky was still troubled. He would alternate between periods of unexplained joy and periods of sadness. His relatives, ascribing his changing moods to normal adolescence, were confident he would grow out of it. But they soon discovered his secret. Within a year after his brother's death, Robles had given up his occasional marijuana cigarette for something far more serious: heroin. His shocked family tried to help him before he got into deeper trouble. Although it imposed a financial hardship upon his mother and stepfather, the boy was sent to a psychiatrist. Robles had an I.Q. of 130, but the psychiatrist was unable, during a brief period of counseling, to halt the boy's growing reliance on narcotics. By the time Robles was a sixteen-year-old high school sophomore, he was "hooked" on a $20-a-day drug habit. And the only way for him to get that kind of money was through crime.

When the police caught up with Robles in February 1960, he was a seventeen-year-old baby-faced boy bandit who, with gangster-film bravado, boasted of burglaries and holdups committed during a six-month crime spree. Swaggering with pride, he rolled up the shirtsleeve on his left arm to exhibit to the police the needle punctures that marked him as a junkie.

How many burglaries Robles actually committed is uncertain. The police, who sometimes have a tendency to exaggerate the extent of a captured burglar's work as a convenient method of closing out otherwise unsolvable cases, claimed Robles had admitted one hundred burglaries, including one in which he had pistol-whipped a woman because she had no money in her apartment. In two burglaries he had supposedly tied up his victims, a man and a woman, before ransacking their apartments. He was indicted for nine burglaries but was never tried for any of them. Brought before a judge in Manhattan, he was permitted by the District Attorney's office to plead guilty to a charge of second-degree assault.

What happened to Robles is not unusual. Because of the crowded court calendars in New York City, it is an accepted practice for a District Attorney to accept a guilty plea on one charge, rather than go through several trials with a suspect who has been accused of multiple crimes.

In March 1960, at the age of seventeen years and two months, Ricky Robles became a con, sentenced to an indeterminate term of one day to five years at the Elmira Reception Center, a jail for males under the age of twenty-one.

Robles served thirty-eight months in Elmira, where he obtained a high school diploma and learned the machinist's trade. During all his time there he behaved with a rectitude admired by prison psychologists and guards. Even his fellow prisoners considered him a quiet, friendly con, not at all the troublesome "ape" type who is unable to adapt to prison environment.

On June 3, 1963, Robles was granted parole. The prison doors opened for him, and he returned to the only home he knew, his mother's apartment in Yorkville. Less than three months later, Janice Wylie and Emily Hoffert were found murdered in their apartment, a half-mile from where Robles was living. Not until twelve days later did detectives pick him up for questioning.

Robles had changed immensely in his three years at Elmira, so much that the detectives who had questioned the teen-aged burglar in 1960 barely recognized him now when he was brought into the 23rd Precinct. His taut, high-cheekboned features had mellowed, and the snarling brat had become a handsome—in fact, clean-cut—young man. Prison food and exercise had kept him a slim one hundred forty pounds, while thickening the shoulders and chest of his five-feet-eight-inch frame. He looked robust, wiry, and as though he had not a care in the world.

The police had more than twenty persons scheduled for interviews that day, some at the precinct, some at their homes, and some at their offices. Detectives still lacked any tangible clues, but the men directing the inquiry were optimistic that their methods would unmask the killer. Questioning Robles and other ex-cons was a routine part of the dragnet; he was a long shot, but any one of these former convicts might be the murderer or might know something about the killings. In any event, Robles was worth bringing in for a talk.

Martin Zinkand and John Lynch, the detective-partners who had responded to Max Wylie's distress call, handled Robles's interview in the second-floor squad room of the precinct. At that time, they knew as much about the investigation as any police officers in New York. Since the case technically was assigned to them, they read every report that eventually landed on the desks of superior officers in charge of the over-all inquiry. Lieutenant Francis M. Sullivan, commander of the Manhattan North Homicide Squad, who was spending most of his working days on the Wylie-Hoffert case and much of his time at the precinct, sat through the interview.

Robles had little to say. Of course he had heard about the double murder; but all he knew was what he had read in the newspapers. He assured the detectives that since his release from prison he had kept away from his old associates, concentrating on his job as a machinist, and doing his best to avoid trouble.

"I wouldn't ice two dames," he said.

"Okay, then where were you on August 28? Tell us where and how you spent the day," one detective said.

Yes, Robles recalled the day. The Bronx factory where he worked had been closed for the week. Since he was on vacation, he slept late—until noon—in his mother's apartment. After getting up, he puttered around the apartment most of the day, occasionally watching television. He was certain his mother could corroborate his statement.

There was no reason for holding him. His fingerprints had not been found in the apartment; no clues pointed to him. Still, his alibi had to be checked, and later that day Lynch and Zinkand drove to his family's ground-floor apartment on 93rd Street. Robles's mother, Mrs. Leontine Simon, was home. She indeed remembered the day of the murders, because it was the day of the civil rights rally in Washington, and she recalled having seen part of the demonstration on television. She was also certain of her son's movements. He had slept late, until about noon, spending the rest of the day in the apartment or outside on the street chatting with neighbors.

The two detectives were interested only in Robles's activities before noon. They questioned Mrs. Simon a second time, and she repeated: Ricky had been on vacation, and she even had trouble waking him at noon.

Like hundreds of ex-convicts in the police files, Robles had been examined and cleared of implication in the case. The only result of the interviews with Robles and his mother was another DD5 report, in triplicate, added to the bulging portfolio on the Wylie-Hoffert investigation. Sullivan and the other detectives assigned to the case forgot about Ricky Robles; he had an alibi.

The next entry in Robles's police record was made three months later. In December 1963, Robles went to his parole officer with the odd request that he be returned to prison. With unusual candor, Robles conceded that he was afraid of slipping back into drug addiction. The antiseptic harshness of prison—or "cold turkey" life—would prevent a narcotics relapse, he told his parole officer. Complying with his request, the parole board revoked his freedom, shipping him back to Elmira on December 19. His reentry into Elmira went unnoticed by the police officials then bogged down in the Wylie-Hoffert investigation. They had no reason to be interested in him; he was just another junkie in trouble with his parole officers.

Robles's second prison term lasted nine months. During that time, he read in newspapers that the Wylie-Hoffert killings had been solved through the arrest of Whitmore in April 1964. When Robles was paroled a second time in August 1964, Whitmore was in Bellevue Hospital undergoing psychiatric examination. In the summer of 1964, the Wylie-Hoffert case seemed closed—and certainly the police had no reason to bother Ricky Robles with a second round of questioning. A month after his release, Robles, who again had moved into his mother's Yorkville apartment, found a job in a Bronx machine shop. As far as the police were concerned, he was going straight. It would take another junkie and another murder to interest them once more in Richard Robles.

Late in the afternoon of October 8, 1964, Nathan Delaney, known to his friends as Jimmy, walked into a slum tenement on 100th Street in East Harlem. Delaney, a copper-skinned Negro, was thirty-five years old. He had a police record of thirteen arrests for armed robbery, burglary, and possession of narcotics, dating back to when he was thirteen years old. He was a junkie, spindly thin, with emaciated features; his wife, a white woman, was also a junkie. The Delaneys and their three children lived on income from their welfare checks, from the sale of narcotics, and from Mrs. Delaney's prostitution. Delaney was both an addict and a pusher, a peddler of narcotics, not an unusual trade for addicts in New York, who help support their expensive habit by selling any drugs or "goof balls" (barbiturates) they can lay their hands on.

That October day, Delaney was looking for Roberto Cruz Del Valle, a Puerto Rican pusher who conducted his illegal business dealings in the back alleys of 100th Street between First and Second Avenues. Shortly before 5:00 P.M., Delaney met Cruz in one of the tenement hallways. What happened then is unclear. The men quarreled; when the argument was over Cruz lay on the concrete floor, stabbed in the left temple with a dirk. He was dead by the time an ambulance arrived.

Cruz's murder fell within the jurisdiction of the 23rd Precinct. Detectives assigned to the case quickly learned from several witnesses that Jimmy Delaney was the man with whom Cruz had had his last quarrel. Three hours after the murder, the police traced Delaney to his six-room apartment on 84th Street in Yorkville.

At the apartment, a man identifying himself as Nathan Delaney blandly told two detectives that Jimmy Delaney was his brother. To show how cooperative he was, Nathan Delaney provided the detectives with a photograph of a man he said was Jimmy. The photograph was really a snapshot of Delaney's dead brother-in-law. With the picture in hand, the detectives left.

Later that day, at a friend's apartment, Delaney gleefully described to a gathering of companions, including Ricky Robles, the way he had outwitted the police. But his glee was short-lived. When Delaney returned home that night, the police were waiting for him; they had quickly discovered that he had tricked them. This time there was no way he could talk himself out of being arrested, even though he insisted he had stabbed Cruz in self-defense.

Delaney knew he was in serious trouble, even if the murder charge should be reduced to manslaughter. He was a three-time loser who had served a total of six years in prison. He had three times been convicted of felonies—once of attempted robbery and twice of selling narcotics—and he faced a possible life sentence in New York State if convicted of a fourth felony.

The police booked Delaney for murder at the 23rd Precinct on October 9, and placed him in the rear of a police van with Detective Patrick Lappin for the ride downtown to the Tombs. The drive took a half-hour, more than enough time for Delaney to startle Lappin with an extraordinary story.

"You guys got the wrong guy in the Wylie-Hoffert job—it isn't Whitmore," Delaney said.

"What do you mean?"

For the next few minutes Lappin listened with feigned indifference as Delaney explained that the real killer, a friend of his, had come to Delaney's apartment on the day of the murders and confessed he had just killed two women during a burglary. Delaney said the murderer was a narcotics addict, known to the police. The addict, Delaney said, told him he had slipped into an apartment to pull a burglary when he came across a nude blonde. After he had forced the blonde to commit a sexual perversion, another woman suddenly walked into the apartment. According to Delaney, the addict then tied up the women and stabbed them to death because he feared they might be able to identify him later.

Delaney told Detective Lappin this much—without, however, identifying the killer. Lappin had not been detailed to the Wylie-Hoffert investigation, and he had no way of judging whether his prisoner was speaking truthfully or was just concocting a tale in the frantic hope it might help him with his own murder accusation. After depositing Delaney with guards at the Tombs, Lappin returned uptown to fill out a report on the conversation for his immediate superior officer, Lieutenant Thomas J. Cavanagh, head of the 23rd Precinct detective squad, and Sergeant William Brent, second-in-command. They would know what to make of Delaney's bizarre boast.

To Cavanagh and Brent, Delaney's story was of exceptional interest. They were among a dozen police officials aware of the well-kept secret that the Wylie-Hoffert case was far from solved, that the evidence against Whitmore had disintegrated to the point where high officials in the police department and the Manhattan District Attorney's office seriously doubted his guilt. Cavanagh immediately forwarded Lappin's report to District Attorney Hogan's office, and there Delaney's story was studied with even more interest than it had commanded at the 23rd Precinct. Hogan and several of his aides knew in October 1964 that much of the purported evidence against Whitmore had crumbled under careful analysis, and that it was quite possible Whitmore had an alibi eliminating him as a suspect in the double murder.

Whitmore's confession did not make sense to the Manhattan detectives most familiar with the investigation and the evidence at the murder scene. Even allowing that Whitmore's low intelligence and faulty memory warped his recollection of the crime, they had become wary of his confession. They could not understand many essential parts of it: how Whitmore got onto the service stairway of the Wylie-Hoffert building through a lobby door always kept locked; how he first butchered the girls and then tied them up; how, with huge amounts of blood spilled, he avoided leaving a fingerprint. And they could not understand how Whitmore could have committed two savage murders without realizing that his victims were dead. These were only the major discrepancies in the confession. Many minor elements in the sixty-one page statement contradicted the evidence at the scene. In addition, the photograph that had prompted Bulger to question Whitmore was not a picture of Janice Wylie; and the snapshot itself could not be linked in any way to the Wylie-Hoffert apartment. More disappointing to the police and the prosecutor, Whitmore probably had found the picture where he originally said he had—in a garbage dump in Wildwood.

Manhattan detectives had doubted that the girl in the photograph was Janice Wylie as soon as they glimpsed the faded snapshot. When none of the victims' relatives or friends could remember having seen the picture in the girls' apartment, Hogan's office instructed detectives to work on the possibility that some former tenant in the apartment had left the photograph behind. In the summer of 1964, twenty former tenants of apartment 3C, mostly young bachelors, were traced and questioned in their homes in Maryland, Ohio, Texas, and Minnesota. None had any knowledge of the photograph, or could recall seeing it in the apartment.

When the photograph could not be tied in with the apartment, Hogan's office began concentrating on Wildwood, New Jersey. During September and October, New York detectives, working with the aid of Wildwood police, located Mrs. Franco, the girl in the photograph. On October 5, she was questioned at her home by men from Hogan's office, at which time she identified herself as the teen-ager in the photograph. As far as she knew, the only print of the snapshot had been kept by a friend, Barbara Ann Mitchell, who was a schoolteacher in Philadelphia. Several days later, Detective Arthur Connolly of the District Attorney's staff interviewed Miss Mitchell at the Gillespie Junior High School in Philadelphia, where she was teaching. Corroborating Mrs. Franco's statement, Miss Mitchell said a boy friend had used her camera to take the photograph of Mrs. Franco and herself at a 1956 school picnic (not in 1958, as Mrs. Franco recollected). The only print had been discarded with rubbish at her Wildwood home in 1961, two years before the murders. Like Mrs. Franco, she had never known either Janice Wylie or Emily Hoffert, and had never been to their apartment. Whitmore's story of having found the photograph in a Wildwood junkyard, not on 88th Street, suddenly began to ring true.

From Wildwood, the New York police traced Ludie Montgomery and her mother to Philadelphia, where the girl was questioned about seeing Whitmore on the murder day.

All this information, which reporters and Whitmore's lawyers later were to unearth by themselves, was in Hogan's office by early October.

Still other facts indicated that Whitmore might be innocent, facts almost impossible for a defense lawyer to discover. When misgivings about Whitmore's guilt began to multiply, Koste and another Assistant District Attorney, Melvin Glass, called in Detective Bulger from Brooklyn to review details of the confession. Neither Koste nor Glass was called upon in court to testify about that discussion with Bulger. Both A.D.A.'s, however, apparently were ready to swear that Bulger astonished them by claiming that he could always tell when a Negro was lying. A Negro's stomach, Bulger told the two assistant prosecutors, visibly quivered if he lied. Later, when Bulger was asked on the witness stand about having made this statement to Koste and Glass, he replied: "I don't remember saying it—I might have."

After this conversation with Bulger, there was another question in the minds of the A.D.A.'s: How reliable was the detective who had been chiefly responsible for obtaining Whitmore's confession to the double murder? And DiPrima, the other Brooklyn detective who questioned Whitmore, was not totally ignorant of the Wylie-Hoffert murder scene. In another of the weird coincidences that enveloped the investigation, DiPrima had been a patient of a physician on the ground floor of the building on 88th Street— and therefore had been familiar with the layout of the lobby when he was questioning Whitmore.

Delaney's story reached the ears of District Attorney Hogan himself on October 10. For eight days no move was made by anyone in Hogan's office to speak with Delaney. He remained in the Tombs, visited once by his wife, Marjorie, and his mother. Without forewarning, on the ninth day, October 19, at 3:00 P.M., Delaney was taken from his cell and escorted across the tenth-story "Bridge of Sighs" that connects the Tombs to the Criminal Courts Building, where Hogan and his staff have their offices. Two guards led Delaney into the sixth-floor office of Assistant District Attorney Peter Koste.

Waiting for him there were Koste and several men Delaney assumed were detectives. As soon as Delaney was seated, Koste got down to business; he wanted to hear Delaney's complete story about the Wylie-Hoffert slayings. The ex-convict, who was thirty-five but whose close-cropped gray hair and hollow cheeks made him appear ten years older than that, began talking in his customary whispery tone.

On the day of the murders, Delaney said, he was home with his wife in their Yorkville apartment. Two of their children, an eight-year-old boy and a nine-year-old girl, were at camp for the summer; their five-year-old daughter was spending that day with a relative. Delaney recalled that some time before noon the entrance bell rang. From the second-floor hallway outside his apartment, he could see a friend, a fellow junkie, standing behind the closed door on the ground level. Delaney rang a buzzer to open the vestibule door. His friend came upstairs and, as soon as he was inside the apartment, excitedly said he was in trouble. He told the Delaneys he had just killed two women.

"I asked him how, and he said in a burglary," Delaney told his listeners. "I noticed he had small quantities of blood on the front of his shirt—a white T-shirt—and his pants. I told him I didn't want to hear any more about it. Then I asked him if he came straight to my house. He said no, he had taken a couple of cabs first."

Delaney remembered his friend had been carrying a brown paper bag and a jacket on his arm. He said he needed a change of clothing, and Delaney gave him a pair of pants and a fresh shirt.

"I asked him if he found anything of value in the burglary, and he said: 'Only some money.' "

After changing into Delaney's trousers and shirt, the friend gave Delaney money to buy narcotics for the two of them and for Delaney's wife. Leaving his wife and his friend in the apartment, Delaney said, he went to 100th Street, returning within forty-five minutes with the "fixes." The trio then sat down and injected themselves with narcotics.

Before his friend left, Delaney said: "He asked me if the police could trace sperm in any of the girls' throats or stomachs. He said he had one of the girls give him a blow job. I told him in my opinion no, they couldn't trace it."

Delaney and his wife went uptown to visit his grandmother shortly after his friend's departure. About 9:00 or 10:00 P.M. that evening, the friend paid another visit to the Delaney apartment.

"He returned my clothes," Delaney said. "He had a couple of newspapers and we discussed the article about the murders. He said these were the two girls he was speaking about earlier in the day. These were the two girls he had stabbed to death."

The next day, Delaney learned more details about the killings from his friend. "He came over in the daytime. He had a paper with the pictures of the two girls. I told him one of the girls, Janice Wylie, looked rather attractive. Why did he have to kill the girls? When I pointed to Janice Wylie's picture, he said: 'She's not as attractive as the newspapers make her out to be.' "

A day or two later, Delaney said, he spoke again with his friend in the Delaney apartment. "I asked him how he got in and he said through a window. He surprised one of the girls in bed. She awoke just as he came in. I asked him: 'What about the other girl, was she there?' He said she came in later and, when he pulled off her eyeglasses, she said: 'I want to be able to identify you later.' He tied them up on the bed and he said he decided to kill them. He went into the kitchen and got two bottles and hit the girls on the head to knock them out so they wouldn't know he was killing them, so they wouldn't feel the pain, or something."

The friend even demonstrated for the Delaneys how he had struck the women with the soda bottles. He had crossed his arms and, in one scissors motion, simultaneously crashed the bottles against the victims' heads.

"They slipped off the bed in the struggle," Delaney said. "One girl died right away, but the other took a long time, and he had to stab her repeatedly in the stomach to get to her heart. He could see she was finally dead by her eyes. He also said the smell of the blood almost made him throw up."

The friend said he washed his hands and a knife in the bathroom after the murders, and then left the apartment. "He took two taxis, one downtown and one uptown to my house," Delaney added. "When I asked him why he had picked that building, he said he was walking down the street and decided to go in. He got in through the basement and a window. He said he got out the same way."

This was the story Delaney told his listeners. But there was one fact he was not ready to disclose immediately—the name of his friend.

He wanted to know what the District Attorney's office was willing to give him in exchange for the killer's name. Obviously, he wanted an assurance that in return for informing on the Wylie-Hoffert killer, the Cruz murder accusation against him would be dropped.

Reliving that interview later on the witness stand, Delaney said Koste left the room for several minutes and then came back to tell Delaney that he had conferred with his "boss" and in return for the name of the killer he could promise Delaney immunity from prosecution in the Cruz case. He also guaranteed that Delaney would not be held as an accessory after the fact in the Wylie-Hoffert homicide because of his failure to inform the police immediately. Delaney needed only a few seconds to consider Koste's *quid pro quo.*

"His name is Richard Robles—Ricky Robles."

At 8:00 that night, three hours after Delaney named Robles, Mrs. Delaney was driven from her home to the District Attorney's offices in an unmarked police car. In Koste's office, she was told her husband had informed on Robles; now the Assistant District Attorney wanted to hear her version of what Robles had supposedly told the couple.

The twenty-nine-year-old Marjorie Delaney had known Robles since he was thirteen years old. Not only were they good friends, but her aunt was Robles's girl friend. Koste knew she was informing on someone who was almost a member of her family; yet, in doing so, she was helping her husband. The petite woman, her auburn hair combed into a French twist, sat back and, with an air of resignation, described the way Robles had admitted the brutal crime to her.

She recalled that on the day of the murders she was home with her husband. "I was on my way to the kitchen to make coffee when the bell rang. I opened the kitchen door and looked down. I could see the vestibule. I saw Ricky down there," she said, her voice husky with tension. "I hollered back to my husband that it was Ricky. My husband was in the bathroom. And he came up the stairs hurriedly, two steps at a time. He asked me if Jimmy was home and he went straight to the living room. Ricky had a brown sport jacket and he had a brown paper bag in his hand.

"I said: 'Jimmy's in the bathroom.' When he got to the bathroom, he told Jimmy he was in trouble. He said he had just killed two girls. My husband looked up with an expression like 'Are you kidding?' My husband was washing up and I left.

"A few minutes later, my husband and Ricky came back to the living room and Ricky asked would he do him a favor and give him a change of clothes. I noticed he had blood on his left pants leg, a little above the knee.

My husband went to a chest and got out a shirt and pants. I saw Ricky taking things out of his pockets so I left the room.

"When I returned a few minutes later, Ricky had changed clothes. He asked my husband if he would go buy some drugs. He gave him a ten-dollar bill and a one-dollar bill. My husband said he wouldn't be gone long, he was going to 100th Street."

During her husband's absence, Mrs. Delaney said, she remained with Robles in the living room. She distinctly remembered he sat on the sofa, neatly folding the bloodstained clothing. When the clothes were folded, Robles asked her for a larger bag and she supplied him with a shopping bag. Curious, she watched him stuff into the bag the clothing he had taken off, a green sport shirt and dark trousers, as well as a pair of pink rubber gloves. Although she made no attempt to question him, Robles began a conversation about the murders.

"He said he was on vacation and needed extra money so he decided to do a burglary. I asked him how he got into the building, and he said through the service entrance. In the apartment there was a girl with a sheet wrapped around her. Then he said he thought he was a homosexual because he asked the girl to go down on him. He asked me did I think they could find out he made the girl do this to him.

"Just as he got through with the girl, he heard the front door and got up against the wall. The girl with the glasses came in. Just as she got in front of him, he tried to take her glasses. The girl said something like: 'Don't touch me, leave my glasses alone.' She wanted to get a good look at him. She repeated it a few times, about getting a good look at him. The other girl said: 'Do as he says and you won't get hurt.' He said he tied up the girls back-to-back on the bed, but he didn't know what to do. He thought it over for five minutes, and then decided to kill them. When he made up his mind, he said to himself: 'God forgive me.'

"He got soda bottles and butcher knives. He wanted to knock them out so it would be less painful. One went unconscious right away, the other didn't. He said he repeatedly had to stab one in the ribs to get to her heart. While he was doing this they slipped off the bed. The odor of blood was awful."

According to Mrs. Delaney, Robles said that after washing up in the apartment he left through the service door. Instead of going directly to the Delaneys', a ten-minute walk from the Wylie-Hoffert building, he had taken a taxicab downtown and crosstown to the West Side. After the first cab ride, he hailed another taxi for a trip back to the East Side. Robles, she said, told her he had stopped for a few minutes after the second ride, but she was not sure whether he told her he had spent the time buying handkerchiefs or making a telephone call. He had made the last part of the circuitous journey to the Delaney apartment in a third cab.

Mrs. Delaney recalled picking up the pink rubber gloves he had placed in the paper bag because she noticed they had ridges on the fingertips. "I thought the ridges might leave fingerprints, and I told him to press hard on a mirror. I looked and didn't see no fingerprints."

While Delaney was still out buying narcotics, Robles briefly left the apartment, which did not have a telephone, to make a call.

"My husband returned and we all took some narcotics, talked a little while longer, and then Ricky left and took his clothes in the shopping bag."

She remembered that at 8:30 or 9:00 that evening Robles, carrying several newspapers, appeared again at the apartment. "It's in the papers," he said. There was no need for him to explain what was in the newspapers. Together in the living room, the Delaneys and Robles read the stories about the murders.

"He was commenting on some things were right and some things were wrong in the papers. He made the remark that he was glad to see they didn't suspect it was a burglary."

The only other time she discussed the killings with Robles, Mrs. Delaney recalled, was the next night.

"He came with some newspapers again and we read the papers on the bed in the bedroom. He said he was glad to see that the police didn't know one of the girls was sexually attacked."

Koste now had oral statements from the Delaneys which seemingly matched in every important detail. There were differences in some areas of their stories, but the important fact was that both Delaneys had separately given almost identical descriptions of Robles's admission. He knew how rare it is for two persons to agree completely about incidents and conversations. The Delaneys' talks with Robles had occurred fourteen months earlier, sufficient time for their memories to have become hazy about such details as whether Robles had arrived at their apartment before or after noon, whether Delaney or his wife had buzzed him into the building, and exactly where they each had been at the moment he arrived. The vital parts of the two stories agreed enough to indicate that the Delaneys were truthful.

Mrs. Delaney and her hubsand had a hurried reunion for a minute in Koste's office. They kissed and she left for home. Koste and Delaney, however, were not finished yet. A detective had been dispatched to bring Robles in for a face-to-face confrontation with Delaney.

15. *Another Confession*

Close to midnight of Monday, October 19, 1964, two persons inside a flat on East 89th Street heard a not-too-gentle knock on the door. Richard Robles's girl friend answered the impatient pounding. At the door was Detective Zinkand of the 23rd Squad, who had been ordered by the District Attorney's office to find Robles. With his record, Robles knew the best policy was not to argue the absence of a warrant; he did not object to accompanying Zinkand "downtown," the police euphemism for a place of questioning.

The significance of his midnight summons was disclosed to Robles as soon as he stepped inside Koste's office. The Delaneys, he was told, had turned him in as the Wylie-Hoffert murderer. Nothing was said to Robles about the details the Delaneys volunteered about the slayings.

Robles made an angry denial. Couldn't the police see Delaney was lying? He had had nothing to do with the murders—hadn't the police checked him out a week after the crime? Didn't he have an alibi?

Delaney was silent, staring vacuously at Robles without any outward sign of emotion. Robles was adamant; he was innocent and he had no other statement except what he had given to the police in September of 1963.

When the confrontation broke up, Robles walked into the somber early-morning silence of lower Manhattan a free man, while Delaney returned over the Bridge of Sighs to his cell in the Tombs.

Hogan's aides and the police now evaluated the evidence against Robles. There was no need to caution any of them to be scrupulously careful in determining whether he was the right man. Whitmore was still under indictment for the double murder; the D.A. did not want a second man who would be found innocent after the prosecutor's office accused him of the crime.

There was a convincing sound to the Delaneys' charges. Delaney undoubtedly wanted the Cruz murder charge against him dropped, but he had implicated Robles in a crime that had been solved publicly with the arrest of Whitmore. The doubts about Whitmore's guilt had not been disclosed. Why should Delaney pick the Wylie-Hoffert case rather than one that was still seemingly unsolved?

The Delaneys' stories, however, were too incomplete and conflicting to become the sole basis of a murder indictment against Robles. They disagreed as to the time Robles said he had slipped into the Wylie-Hoffert apartment, and as to the exact manner of his entry. Neither of them recalled his having mentioned ransacking the apartment, smearing skin cream on Janice Wylie, or tying up the women with strips of bedding. Nor could they remember if he had told them that the victims had resisted or cried out for help.

Another factor to be considered was the value or credibility a jury would give the Delaneys' testimony once a defense counsel revealed—as he most certainly would—that they had informed only after Delaney himself had been arrested on an unrelated murder charge.

The District Attorney's men first had to convince themselves of the Delaneys' unquestioned reliability. The couple was asked to undergo lie-detector tests. The results would not be admissible courtroom evidence, but they would either undermine or strengthen the credibility of the Delaneys and help the police and District Attorney decide whether they were at last on the trail of the real Wylie-Hoffert killer.

The results of the tests were reassuring to the District Attorney's office. As far as the lie-detector experts were concerned, the husband and wife were telling the truth about Robles's confession. These findings gave the investigators a green light to begin gathering evidence against Robles.

Just as the police were prepared to initiate a full-scale investigation, Robles almost died. On October 27, he and a fellow narcotics addict collapsed from an overdose of barbiturates at a party in the apartment of Robles's girl friend. After one day on the danger list at Metropolitan Hospital, Robles and his pal both recovered. Some of their friends said the two stricken junkies had sworn a suicide pact, but neither of them would later discuss the matter.

On October 29, Delaney made another trip to Koste's office from his cell. This time his review of Robles's confession was recorded by a stenotypist. The next day, Delaney initialed every page of the twenty-three-page statement and put his signature at the bottom of the last page. On that same day, a grand jury acted on the evidence before it concerning Delaney's involvement in the Cruz murder. No true bill was handed up by the panel, which meant the evidence was insufficient to support an indictment against him. The District Attorney's office had quickly fulfilled its promise.

Although informers are an accepted part of police operations, making a deal with a murder suspect is still a rarity. In Delaney's case, Hogan's office saw no alternative. Even if they were to be criticized later for allowing one murderer to go free in exchange for another murderer, the District Attorney's men believed that closing the Wylie-Hoffert case was worth the price of a few brickbats.

Robles spent nine days in the hospital recovering from his escapade with death. During that time the police and District Attorney's aides studied his record and devised a strategy for trapping him. His mother was called in again for questioning, but she, too, reiterated her son's alibi; on the day of the murders, she said, Ricky had slept late, remaining in the apartment past noon.

The next step in the inquiry was the installation of microphones in places Robles frequented. After obtaining court orders, the police secretly planted miniature microphones in the Robles apartment, his girl friend's apartment, and the Delaney apartment. None of the occupants of these apartments was aware the police had surreptitiously installed bugs. Nevertheless, any conversations recorded could be used as evidence against Robles. Because of conflicting and confusing Federal court rulings, United

States agencies, such as the F.B.I., shy away from presenting electronic-eavesdropping evidence. But New York was one of five states that explicitly sanctioned such evidence if the police obtained permission from the occupant of the place where the equipment was installed, or if they had a court order specifying that the bugs were necessary for law enforcement.

Bugs sometimes have a way of backfiring against prosecutors. In the last decade the higher courts have increasingly thrown out convictions based on electronic evidence, for a variety of reasons, such as illegal trespassing or technical mistakes in court orders. Hogan's men were well aware of the possible pitfalls, but they wanted to back up the Delaneys' stories with the best possible evidence—incriminating statements from Robles.

Delaney and his wife agreed to cooperate in the investigation. Their part of the operation would be to draw details out of Robles through a deception; they were to convince him they had not revealed any of the intimate facts he had described to them. Part of the strategy called for the Delaneys to assure Robles that they had been compelled to inform on him as the only way of saving Delaney from a life sentence, and that now they were back on his side, helping him pass along misleading information to the police. This wrong information, they would explain, would either foul up the police investigation or convince the cops Robles was not the killer.

In arranging all this with the Delaneys, the police kept one secret from them. They did not tell the Delaneys that microphones had been hidden in their apartment.

An unanticipated problem, a troublesome one, arose for Hogan's office at this time. Someone from either the D.A.'s staff or the police gave newspaper reporters part of the story about Robles. This was the report of a new suspect which reached Leftow, Whitmore's lawyer. While Robles was still in the hospital, the lawyer tried to confirm the rumor. Hogan's aides refused to provide Leftow with any information, or any hope for his client. There had already been too much public discussion of a new suspect. Further publicity would only make Robles more wary, and the District Attorney's office was far from completion of its investigation.

Examining Robles's past, the police authorities assigned one more investigator to the case. He was David J. Downes, the detective who had arrested Robles for burglary and assault when he was seventeen years old. By being more sympathetic than other policemen involved in Robles's arrest, Downes had built up an unusually friendly relationship with the teen-ager four years earlier. Lieutenants Sullivan and Cavanagh thought Robles might be more talkative in the presence of Downes. In late October of 1964, Downes was transferred from a Queens precinct to the Wylie-Hoffert case. He quickly discovered that Robles's memory was sharp. Stepping into Robles's hospital room, he was greeted:

"Downsey, you son of a bitch, how are you? I thought you were working in Queens."

Robles had been following Downes's career in the newspapers. He knew the detective had been sent, several months before, to bring back a murder suspect from Paris; Robles asked him how he had liked France. Then he asked Downes what he was doing in the hospital.

"I'm here on an investigation. I want to speak to your girl."

"They're trying to frame me," Robles said forcefully. "I didn't kill anyone."

"We're trying to get the truth, nothing more; you know that, Ricky."

A week later, when Robles had left the hospital, Downes picked him up at his girl friend's apartment and took him to the District Attorney's office for another session of questions. Again Robles was friendly, joking with Downes about an old car the detective had owned the first time he arrested Robles. But that was the limit of Robles's camaraderie. He was offering no confession to Downes, to other detectives, to the District Attorney's men, or to anyone else.

Delaney was still in the Tombs when Robles was discharged from the hospital. Although fully aware that the Delaneys had accused him of the double murder, Robles, not knowing how much the Delaneys had told the police, continued to visit Mrs. Delaney at her home and to see her at his girl friend's apartment. Another factor brought him into frequent contact with her. During November of 1964, a police crackdown temporarily closed the heroin market in New York. Mrs. Delaney, who had methods of illegally obtaining goof balls, liberally dispensed the barbiturates to Robles and to other addict friends. Goof balls are a tame substitute for narcotics, but they can help take the edge off a junkie's discomfort. Despite her assistance, Robles was on his guard when he was with Mrs. Delaney. Before his first conversation with her, he inspected the six rooms of the Delaney apartment but found no signs of microphones. He had sound reasons for searching. Since his release from the hospital, he had discovered hidden microphones in his own and his girl friend's apartments. Almost with indifference, he had exhibited the electronic equipment, showing many friends the bugs the police had installed in various places in his girl friend's apartment. When his grandmother visited his apartment, he took her into the kitchen and beneath a window sill pointed out a small metal box that had been recently installed by two men claiming to be telephone-company mechanics. He shushed his grandmother with a finger over his lips and then proceeded to dismantle the metal box; out of it he pulled a miniature microphone.

The day before Thanksgiving, 1964, Delaney was released from the Tombs. He was a free man for the first time in more than a month, but he was also committed to obtaining incriminating evidence against Robles. As he headed uptown on the subway to his Yorkville apartment, he felt the strangeness of a metal instrument nestling against the skin of his waist. The District Attorney's office had provided him with a recording device. Three inches wide and five inches long, it was strapped under his shirt like a vest. He had instructions to turn on the recorder whenever he came into contact with Robles. The first night out of jail, he got a chance to use it.

Shortly before midnight, Robles appeared at the Delaney apartment. He had heard about Delaney's release and thought there might be matters for them to discuss, but he wanted to talk in the street. Before leaving the apartment, Delaney engirdled himself with the recorder and switched it on. He wore it that night and scores of other times when he was with Robles during the next month. But the vest-recorder proved worthless. Most of the times he was with Robles, Delaney was unable to operate the machine.

That November, when Whitmore was convicted of attempted rape, Robles kept seeing the Delaneys. He continued to get narcotics from Delaney, who was his connection, but he gave his pursuers no fresh lead or clue, even though on several occasions he discussed *Newsweek*'s $10,000 reward with Delaney. He visited the Delaney apartment frequently, and he and Delaney were questioned together several times at the 23rd Precinct. Robles could easily see that Delaney had influence with the authorities. Once while he, Delaney, and a third addict were strolling the streets of Yorkville, they were stopped for questioning by detectives who recognized them as junkies. Delaney stopped the questioning by asking the detectives to talk privately with him. After a brief exchange, one of the detectives went to a telephone booth and made a call. When he came back, the three junkies were released. Delaney proudly explained to his friends that he had given the police a private number in the District Attorney's office.

Eventually the Delaneys learned that they were not entirely in the confidence of the police and the District Attorney's office. On Christmas Eve, Mrs. Delaney was taking tree ornaments from a shelf in a living room closet when she came across a wire bored through a hole in the closet wall. She traced the course of the wire; it led to a miniature microphone embedded in a cornice above a window. Now the Delaneys knew their apartment, too, had been bugged.

Before the year ended, Delaney returned the vest-recorder to the District Attorney. He and his wife officially gave the District Attorney's office permission to install additional microphones in their apartment. During the first week of 1965, a microphone was placed above a living room window and another was hidden behind the refrigerator in the kitchen. Wires from these microphones ran through holes drilled in the walls to an adjacent apartment, where detectives and electronic specialists from the District Attorney's office took up round-the-clock posts. Any conversation in the Delaneys' living room or kitchen could be overheard and introduced as evidence in a New York court.

The detectives at the listening posts on the other side of the Delaneys' wall were kept busy during the month of January 1965. Robles, who had been working sporadically, visited the apartment almost daily, and the recording tapes whirled as the police listened through earphones to the conversations. A strict ritual governed the use of the tapes. Only an official in Hogan's office could issue fresh tapes. When each tape was returned to the District Attorney's office, another entry about the use of the tape was logged, and detectives would then sit down to hear the recording. A typewritten transcript of each recording was made for the District Attorney's aides before the tape was locked in a safe in the homicide bureau.

More than one hundred fifty tapes were collected in less than a month. In them, the Delaneys could be heard discussing with Robles personal matters about friends, children, jobs, and the problems of obtaining narcotics. Almost every time Robles visited, they tried to get him to talk about the murders. They warned him that detectives continued to call both of them in for questioning, demanding precise details about what Robles had told them in his admissions. There was talk by the Delaneys about their taking lie-detector tests, and discussions about whether or not Robles should take one. The Delaneys subtly but determinedly tried to draw out Robles, asking him for suggestions about ways in which they could mislead the police, at the same time trying to obtain answers that would betray him as the killer. Almost as if he knew he was engaged in macabre mental combat with the Delaneys and the police, Robles would reply with *double-entendres*. Sometimes he would ignore an obviously dangerous question with a grunt, an "um hum," or a laugh. Late in the evening of January 14, 1965, the Delaneys returned to their apartment with Robles, and that night, the investigators believed, Robles became careless.

Detective Frank Lyons of the Manhattan North Homicide squad had the 6:00 P.M. to 2:00 A.M. assignment of sitting in apartment 2E (East) next to the Delaneys' 2W (West), on Thursday night and Friday morning,

January 14 and 15. Since Robles had not been in the apartment that night, there had been no work for Lyons or the other two men assigned to the listening post. At 11:45, Lyons heard the door of the Delaney apartment open. He immediately turned on one of the two recording machines. Familiar with the voices of the Delaneys and Robles, Lyons listened as the three of them sat talking at a kitchen table.

They were discussing the best way of sharing a supply of narcotics among themselves. It was obvious that each of them was getting a fix that very moment. There was a surrealistic tinge to these three-way dialogues in the Delaneys' home. The language was the argot of the junkie, hippie world, replete with profanity and the cryptic nuances of addicts ecstatically coasting on the wings of heroin. Their voices sounded tired, and Robles mentioned he had left his job before quitting time that day because he had been ill. Mrs. Delaney soon switched the conversation to a topic of interest to Lyons. She told Robles detectives from the District Attorney's office were coming for her the next day for another interview downtown. She wanted his advice on what answers to give them when she was interrogated about the murders. The first problem, she said, was whether she should change the time Robles had arrived at the Delaney apartment on the day of the murders.

"No, I don't think you should change the time," Robles said.

"You think I should stay on the time, the same time?"

"Stick with it."

Mrs. Delaney continued: Eventually she and her husband would have to offer a reason why they had lied and tried to frame Robles for the murders. Lyons then heard the following.

Robles: "And this is the reason. . . . Some day I'm getting me something to save my ass, you know."

Delaney: "Yeah."

Robles: "And like, eh, you know about this story and how you read it in the newspaper, everything, you know."

Mrs. Delaney: "See, I won't fit in."

Robles: "Right, and you figured some day you might need it. You understand. And, er, then that's when you told the truth. Of course I wasn't here and you made the story, you made the story up once so you, you know, go along with it."

Mrs. Delaney: "Yeah."

Robles: "You dig it, knowing that some day you might need it."

Delaney: "At the time, at the time."

Robles: "But wait, what?"

Delaney: "Wait, at the time."

Robles: "Yeah."

Delaney: "I used it, in other words, say the ace in the hole."

Robles: "Yeah."

Delaney: "This, er, er, case, this Emily Hoffert and Janice Wylie case is supposedly, er, finished, a finished product, see."

Robles: "Yeah, they mentioned that to me."

Delaney: "They had a guy. They had a guy for it. So why?"

Robles: "Yeah."

Delaney: "How come I still use it?"

Robles: "Yeah. Here, here's how. Er, it was your last opportunity, you understand that, like a . . ."

Delaney: "You know that's not true 'cause they had picked up this guy?"

Robles: "No, no, no, no you didn't. Like you were so down and out you said fuck it, I'll try it anyway. You understand, you dig it. You were so up tight you said, well, I'll try it anyway, you dig. And like you hadn't talked to Margie about it for some time and that's why you got your stories a little different, you know."

Robles suggested the Delaneys tell the police that shortly after the Wylie-Hoffert murders they had invented a tale about Robles committing the slayings. The Delaneys' reason for framing Robles would be a desperate attempt to help themselves in case they got in trouble with the police again.

"This is gonna save me, man, if I'm caught," Robles explained.

Later, Mrs. Delaney started talking about Robles's trip to the Delaneys' apartment after the murders. The police wanted more precise information about this subject.

Mrs. Delaney: ". . . remember when you told me you got the cab. You went west, then downtown, then you went east."

Robles: "And east and north, right."

Mrs. Delaney: "And stopped first and went into a store, drug store or something, to either make a phone call or buy some handkerchiefs, and then, in other words, to lose a few more minutes before you caught us here in the next cab."

Robles: "You told them that?"

Mrs. Delaney: "No."

Robles: "Oh, well, then don't tell them that."

The three of them soon began talking about lie-detector tests and possible methods of deceiving the machine. Robles urged both Delaneys to undergo the tests and convince the authorities he really was innocent. But Delaney said:

"Yeah, you can refuse it. If we take that test, Ricky, it's, it's just gonna hang you."

Delaney suggested that Robles take the lie-detector test instead: "But this is, this is square business. What you want to do is put into your mind, any kind of way you can about this deal and take that test."

Robles answered: "If I could only plant in my mind that you made this up and it really didn't happen, like I would take that test."

The trio was still talking at 1:00 A.M. when the first recording spool ran out of tape. Lyons hurriedly placed another spool in the machine; only ten seconds of conversation were lost.

Mrs. Delaney raised the question of what she should tell the District Attorney's office about Robles's entry into the Wylie-Hoffert apartment.

Mrs. Delaney: "Later on, since we had talked, you understand, you said you had, you know, told me, remember the time we were talking about open windows? You said you got in through the window."

Robles: "Hmm."

Mrs. Delaney: "Now what should I eliminate? I have to eliminate the right way that you got in. Which I believe is better for you."

Robles: "Well, what did you tell them?"

Mrs. Delaney: "You understand, now I said that you either . . ."

Robles: "Stick with what you said."

Mrs. Delaney: "You don't understand."

Robles: "Oh, you said what?"

Mrs. Delaney: "Now this is what I'm trying to explain."

Robles: "Yeah."

Mrs. Delaney: "Now, I've got to eliminate one of them because they were harping on this, you understand. I want to eliminate the right one, you understand?"

Robles: "Okay, well, say then that I said I got in through the service entrance door."

Mrs. Delaney: "Instead of the window?"

Robles: "No, say I got in through the window."

Mrs. Delaney: "Through the window?"

Robles: "Yeah, say I got in through the window."

She had a final topic of interest—Emily Hoffert's glasses.

Mrs. Delaney: "Now the glasses part. I didn't tell them that, er, you got the glasses off of her."

Robles: "Hmm."

Mrs. Delaney: "You understand. I told them that."

Delaney: "Did you get the glasses off of her?"

Robles: "Hum."

Delaney: "Huh?"

Robles: "Um hum."

Delaney: "Oh, you did."

Mrs. Delaney: "Yeah."

Delaney: "I thought you said you didn't get the glasses off of her."

Robles: "Eventually I did. Now look, Jimmy."

Mrs. Delaney: "Well, I need this. I need it so that you didn't get the glasses off the way I said it originally."

Robles: "Yeah, everything originally. When it comes down to the . . ."

Delaney: "Did they come off of her?"

Robles: "Huh?"

Delaney: "Did you take them off of her?"

Robles: "Yeah, but she gave them to me."

The rest of the conversation focused on Mrs. Delaney's question as to what she should say about Robles's exit from the building.

Robles: "Well, say, say the service."

Mrs. Delaney: "Huh?"

Robles: "Say the service."

Mrs. Delaney: "Say the service?"

Robles: "Yeah."

Mrs. Delaney: "But that's the way you came out, man."

Robles: "So what?"

At 1:18 A.M., Robles left the apartment and Lyons switched off the recording machine. Later that morning, investigators in Hogan's office, listening to the one-hour-and-twenty-three-minute conversation, believed they possessed for the record a dozen self-incriminating remarks by Robles. The most important were his comments on what would save him if he were "caught" and on the method of entering and leaving the Wylie-Hoffert apartment; his instructions to the Delaneys to forget about the details of the cab ride from the death scene to their apartment; and, possibly most damaging of all, his admission that he had "eventually" taken Emily Hoffert's glasses.

Despite the apparent evidence contained in the two tapes, and despite the incessant newspaper stories questioning the evidence against Whitmore, the District Attorney was not ready to arrest Robles. More abundant evidence might still be obtained as Robles continued to make his visits to the Delaney apartment.

On the afternoon of Sunday, January 24, Robles sat at a kitchen table in the Delaney apartment discussing sarcastically a newspaper story that said the evidence against Whitmore was disintegrating while the police concentrated on a new suspect, a young narcotics addict. In the next apartment, Detective Thomas Lyons was on duty at the recording machine. Lyons heard a twenty-six-minute conversation between the Delaneys and Robles, sometimes mingled with the voices of the three Delaney children as they cavorted in the apartment. Part of the conversation dealt with a sexual perversion, fellatio, committed on Janice Wylie before the murders. It was the final tape heard by detectives. The investigators now believed they had enough evidence to implicate Robles. Two days after that conversation was recorded, Lieutenant Cavanagh ordered Robles arrested.

The time was 12:45 P.M. on January 26, 1965—nearly seventeen months after the Wylie-Hoffert murders. Almost from the moment the bodies had been found, Detective Martin Zinkand had spent most of every working hour thinking about the deaths of Janice Wylie and Emily Hoffert. He had been one of the first detectives from the 23rd Precinct to reach the murder scene, and he was still assigned to the investigation. Zinkand, a stocky man in his mid-forties with a placid expression and steel-gray hair, looked like a salesman making his rounds of grocery or drug stores in Yorkville. Leaning against the brick wall of a tenement at the corner of Third Avenue and East 89th Street, he kept his eyes on the hallway of a building in the middle of 89th Street between Third and Second avenues. Across the street from him, a taxicab was parked at the intersection with a driver seated at the wheel and a man in the rear seat. The taxi was a police vehicle used for undercover purposes, and the two men in it were detectives assigned to the same surveillance as Zinkand—who now stiffened to attention as a lean-looking man in his twenties emerged from the building with a teen-aged girl. Zinkand recognized Robles and his girl friend's daughter, leaving the building where the girl and her mother lived. Together, they walked into an adjacent apartment building. Within ten minutes, Robles came out and turned west toward Third Avenue. As he neared the corner, Zinkand walked over to him.

"I have to take you," he said. "You're under arrest." There was no need for an introduction or an explanation; Robles knew why he was being arrested.

With his close-cropped brown hair, knee-length black raincoat, blue sweater, and tight-fitting khaki pants, Robles resembled a student informally dressed for college classes. He was, in fact, one day short of his twenty-second birthday when Zinkand led him to the parked police car where two other detectives waited. In the back seat, while Zinkand patted his clothes for weapons, Robles asked that someone call his lawyer.

"You'll have enough time. Nobody will prevent you from speaking to your lawyer," Zinkand said.

One of the detectives drove the taxicab north, or uptown, on Third Avenue. Four blocks from where they had arrested Robles, they stopped to pick up Detective Lynch. They drove past the 23rd Precinct to a dead end at the Franklin D. Roosevelt Drive and 106th Street, where Lynch got out to telephone Lieutenant Cavanagh. Cavanagh directed Lynch to have the cab meet him in a half-hour at the corner of Third Avenue and 93rd Street. Precisely at the agreed time, the cab pulled up at the corner. Cavanagh and Sergeant Brent got into the rear seat beside Robles as Lynch and another detective gave up their seats.

"This is D-Day, Ricky. It's all over," Cavanagh greeted Robles.

Robles pulled out a card bearing the name and telephone number of his lawyer, Jack S. Hoffinger. "I want to get in touch with my lawyer," he said.

None of the policemen replied. Instead, they drove downtown on a five-minute trip to the Delaney apartment. In the apartment adjacent to the Delaneys', Assistant District Attorneys Koste and Glass and several policemen were at the listening post when Robles arrived.

In the Delaneys' home, the apartment Robles knew so well, the police immediately informed him of a fact they were sure would surprise him: the Delaneys had been working with them to trap Robles. To show Robles how neatly he had been tricked, Cavanagh unveiled the microphones hidden in the kitchen and living room. Robles now knew that all of his talks with the Delaneys had been overheard by the police.

Robles was kept in the apartment for almost four hours, the police later testified. During that time Robles's guards confidently asserted they had amassed sufficient evidence to convict him of the double murder, regardless of what defense his lawyer would use in court. Only a statement indicating remorse would help him when he came to trial, the police said, shaking their heads in unison.

Robles refused to confess or make a statement. Once more, while Koste and Glass listened in surreptitiously, he asked that his lawyer be notified of his arrest.

Twice Robles requested a fix. Cavanagh offered to summon a private physician or a city-hospital doctor to provide a narcotics injection, but Robles said these doctors would not give him a strong enough shot; he needed the quantity of heroin he normally took. Cavanagh, observing none of the symptoms an addict usually displays during the painful withdrawal period, such as abdominal cramps, nausea, or a running nose, declined to obtain an illegal fix for him.

At 6:30 P.M., Robles was taken for a brief drive through the now-dark streets to the precinct at East 104th Street. He was led one flight upstairs, taken through the swinging gate of the squad room, and locked in the cage.

A half-hour later, still in the detention pen, Robles asked to see Assistant District Attorney Glass, whom he had noticed at the precinct. Glass, a man in his late twenties, heavy-set with an oval face, possessed of a perpetually calm demeanor, walked slowly to the cage. Later, at a closed court hearing Glass recalled the conversation:

"I understand you want to speak to me. . . . What's on your mind?"

"What can you do for me?" Robles asked.

"It's not what I can do for you, it's what you do for yourself. You've obviously been living with this thing for a long time, so you might as well get it off your chest. I understand that you've asked for a lawyer. So until you see a lawyer, anything you say can't be used against you."

"What about psychiatric help?"

"It appears to me that you panicked in that apartment."

"It wasn't panic. Something went wrong."

"Want to tell me the whole story?"

"I'd rather speak to my lawyer first," Robles said, ending the talk.

At 7:30 P.M. his lawyer arrived. Hoffinger had been informed of the arrest by Robles's mother, not the police. The daughter of Robles's girl friend had seen him arrested and put into the taxi. The girl told her mother, and she immediately telephoned Robles's mother, who relayed the news to Hoffinger's office. The lanky, six-foot-tall lawyer had defended Robles in his first arrest, almost five years before. Robles had sought him out again for legal help after the police had confronted him with Delaney's accusation. Hoffinger, a former Assistant District Attorney under Hogan, knew that if Robles had been arrested for the double murder he would be booked at the 23rd Precinct.

The police permitted Hoffinger to confer in private with Robles for thirty minutes in the clerical office of the detective squad. When the lawyer left the room, Detective Downes was stationed outside as a guard.

"Will you watch him?" Hoffinger said to Downes. "I want to talk to someone."

During the next hour, Downes and four other police officers walked in and out of the tiny clerical room. This hour was a critical one in Robles's life, but he has never publicly described it. Of what occurred during those sixty minutes, only one account is available—the police version as told on the witness stand in court.

Robles was seated, his hands folded in his lap, in a chair alongside the one desk in the room when Downes strode in.

"Hello, Ricky, how are you?" the detective asked, perching on the edge of the desk.

"As well as can be expected."

"Do you need a shot?"

"Yeah, I'm overdue. I haven't had a fix since 2:00 A.M."

The door opened and Detective Lynch entered, carrying a cardboard box containing sandwiches and containers of coffee. He offered Robles and Downes a choice of cheese or corned beef sandwiches. Robles took a corned beef sandwich and coffee, and Downes helped himself to coffee. Pouring a liberal quantity of sugar into his coffee, Robles stirred it while taking two bites of his sandwich. He chewed for a minute or two before suddenly turning around and spitting bits of meat and bread into a wastebasket.

"This food is making me sick," he said, pushing away the remainder of the sandwich.

Without prompting from Downes, Robles started to reminisce, recalling that the last time he and Downes had had a long conversation was five years earlier in the precinct. He remembered it clearly because the next day would be his twenty-second birthday, and he had been arrested the first time in January 1960, a few days before his seventeenth birthday.

"You sure made a mess of your life in that time," Downes interjected. "What really happened?"

"I don't know, Downes. I went to pull a lousy burglary and wound up killing two girls."

"You mean Janice Wylie and Emily Hoffert?"

"Yeah," Robles replied with a half-sigh.

"How'd you get in?"

"I grabbed the window sill from the stairway window below and lifted myself into the kitchen window." Robles rose to demonstrate how he had climbed into the Wylie-Hoffert apartment. With his back to the detective, he pressed his face against the wall. To slip into the apartment, he said, he had clambered onto the window sill of a service-stairway window and reached up with his left hand to grab the kitchen window sill of the Wylie-Hoffert apartment.

"Like this," Robles said as he stretched out his left hand toward a section of molding on the wall. Finishing his performance, he sat down.

"Then what happened?" the detective asked.

"I picked up two knives in the kitchen and started to walk through the apartment. All of a sudden, this girl sat up in bed. She was nude and she pulled the sheet around her. She asked me not to hurt her. I think she said: 'Take anything you want.'

"I decided to hump her. She had the rag on and she pulled it out, or I did, I'm not sure. She asked me not to hurt her, and I walked her into another room to get some Noxzema. I tried to fuck her in the ass but she complained it hurt her, so I made her put it in her mouth."

"Were you on a bed?"

"Yeah, it was on a bed."

"What about the knives? She wasn't doing this voluntarily."

"No, I kept the knife on her."

"When did the other girl come in?"

"All of a sudden she started to scream 'Rape! Rape!' Another girl was in the doorway of the bedroom. Janice must have seen her first. Emily said: 'What's going on? I see what's going on!' I jumped off the bed and ran after her. I grabbed her by the hair. I caught her just before she got to the door.

"I tied them up with pieces of sheet and I was gonna leave but something told me I had to kill them. I got two soda bottles and knocked out Janice and only stunned Emily. I just kept stabbing them. The knife broke in Emily's back; I think I must have hit a rib."

"How'd you leave?" Downes asked.

"I went out the service door, down the stairs, and through the building. Then I hailed a cab and went to the Delaneys' apartment. I changed my shirt there and I think my undershirt, too."

"Then the Delaneys' story is true?"

"Yeah."

"What happened to the shirt?"

"I threw it into the East River."

"Did you take anything from the apartment?"

"Thirty or forty dollars from Emily's pocketbook. Closer to thirty."

"Before or after you stabbed them?"

"Before."

Realizing that Robles was finally in a talkative frame of mind, Downes continued to ask questions, and he got important answers. Robles said he had bought rubber gloves before the burglary and had worn them when he climbed into the apartment. The gloves were to prevent his leaving fingerprints. He had tossed them, along with his shirt, into the East River.

"Was that your first burglary after getting out of jail?"

"The first and last," Robles replied, with a lame smile.

"Does your lawyer know all of this?"

"I just told him for the first time."

Lieutenant Cavanagh walked in at that point. Downes was still perched on top of the desk, with Robles seated alongside of him. Observing the partly eaten sandwich, Cavanagh asked: "What's the matter? Aren't you hungry?"

"No, I'm not hungry," Robles said. "I don't feel well."

Without attempting to determine if Robles had become more amenable to questioning, Cavanagh tried a new approach.

"One thing's been puzzling me. Did you know Janice Wylie?"

"No, I'd never been there before."

"How about your friends?"

"I think some of them shot up in the cellar, but I was never there before."

"How'd you get in?"

"Through the window."

The answer surprised Cavanagh because he knew there was no fire escape leading into the apartment. He allowed Robles to continue.

"When I hit the kitchen I grabbed a couple of knives. She must have heard me and jumped out of bed."

"Why'd you take her into Emily Hoffert's bedroom?"

"That was the first one we came to."

Robles repeated for Cavanagh what he had told Downes about his sexual assault on Janice Wylie, the arrival of Emily Hoffert, and the stabbings.

"Did the girls holler when you left them alone?" Cavanagh asked.

"No, when I left the room to get the bottles they probably thought I was leaving the apartment."

Cavanagh had heard enough. He went outside to tell the others that Robles had talked.

Lieutenant Sullivan quickly entered the clerical room. He began his questioning by asking Robles how he had entered the apartment. Once more Robles said it was through the kitchen window, but this time he added that from the stairway landing he could see the kitchen window was open.

Sergeant Brent joined the group just as Robles described how he had got into the apartment through the window. Knowing the window was thirty feet above a concrete yard, Brent said:

"You must have taken quite a chance going through the back window."

"He's a cat burglar," Downes said, explaining Robles's agility.

Sullivan resumed the questioning:

"Where'd you first see Janice?"

"I believe it was in the hallway of the apartment. She was naked."

Robles's chin drooped on his chest. He kept his eyes away from the three detectives as he continued his narrative. The admission he gave was substantially what he had told Downes the first time, but he added more details, such as having forced Janice Wylie at knifepoint to walk with him into the bathroom where he found a jar of skin cream which he smeared over her, and having purchased the rubber gloves for twenty-nine or thirty-nine cents in a Yorkville Woolworth's. In this version, he told the police he had taken twenty or thirty dollars, not thirty or forty as he had earlier told Downes. He said that the strips of cloth he had used to tie the women came from a sheet in one of the bedrooms, but he was not certain which room. His voice quivered as he described the last minutes before the murders.

"Where were the bodies when you left the room?" Sullivan asked.

The question unnerved Robles and he burst into a string of sobs. "Please," he pleaded. "I'm trying to erase it from my mind. I don't want to think about it."

When he regained his composure a minute or two later, Brent asked him how he had felt when he read about Whitmore's being arrested for the two murders.

"I felt relieved. They had him for two other jobs anyway in Brooklyn."

Brent offered a favor: "Ricky, I promised if you told me the truth I'd try to explain this situation to your mother and girl friend."

"Just tell them to forgive me."

Hoffinger then entered the room and the interrogation ended abruptly.

In that one hour, the police said, Robles told them what they had been unable to obtain by trailing him for three months, repeatedly questioning him, and secretly recording his conversations. After resisting them for seven hours that day, Robles voluntarily supplied them with a confession in his own words.

16. *Trial and Conviction*

Robles's trial for murder took place eight months after his arrest, in the summer-scented days of October and the raw, rainy days of November 1965. He appeared in court dressed like a college graduate seeking his first job, his blue suit offset by a white shirt and a properly conservative striped tie, his black shoes gleaming, his hair neatly trimmed. In the dimly lit courtroom, he watched and listened without a flicker of emotion on his prison-paled features as witnesses testified and lawyers argued. The trial lasted seven weeks; the jury of seven men and five women required only six hours of deliberation to convict him of the murders of Janice Wylie and Emily Hoffert.

The prosecutor's strategy rested on Robles's purported oral admissions to Nathan and Marjorie Delaney and to four police officers, and on those parts of his taped conversations with the Delaneys which the prosecution chose to replay in the courtroom.

On the surface, the confessions with the background accompaniment of conspiratorial-sounding recordings produced a strong argument for conviction. The argument, however, rested on circumstantial evidence that became less sturdy under close scrutiny.

One of the most difficult puzzles of the Wylie-Hoffert investigation was the way the killer managed to get into the apartment. The original police theories, or guesses, focused on the most logical methods: one of the victims had opened the front door or the kitchen service door and let the murderer in; the killer had had a key to the front door; or he had so skillfully picked one of the locks that experts could uncover no sign of forced entry on either of the doors.

Until Robles came along, the police believed the doors were the only possible routes into the third-floor apartment. Lieutenant Cavanagh and other officers involved in the investigation acknowledged in court their astonishment when Robles supposedly informed them he had clambered into the apartment through the kitchen window, a route the police had initially dismissed. In the first hours of the investigation, before the bodies had been removed from the apartment, a police photographer took scores of photographs of the five rooms and the two doors. The kitchen window was not deemed important enough to photograph to show whether it had been open or closed when the first detectives arrived. Two years after the murders, at Robles's trial, Lieutenant Sullivan searched his memory to recall that when he arrived at the apartment he noticed the kitchen window was open eighteen inches from the bottom. Detective Lynch remembered it was open eight to twelve inches, while Inspector Coyle, one of the highest-ranking officers at the murder scene, believed it was closed.

Possibly the most accurate testimony about the window came from Patricia Tolles, the first known person in the apartment after the slayings. She said that she was uncertain whether the window had been open when she left in the morning and when she returned at dusk, although she said that during the three August weeks the women had shared the apartment the window normally was open on warm days, because there was no air conditioning in any of the five rooms.

Even if the window had been open wide enough for Robles to slip through, the crucial question is whether Robles could have entered that way. Downes testified that Robles described to him the way he had perched on a hallway-landing window between the second and third floors, grabbed

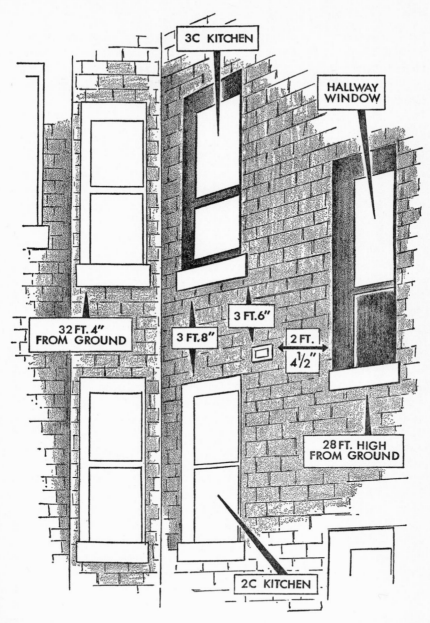

3C KITCHEN

HALLWAY WINDOW

32 FT. 4″ FROM GROUND

3 FT. 8″

3 FT. 6″

2 FT. 4½″

28 FT. HIGH FROM GROUND

2C KITCHEN

3C is the kitchen window of the Wylie-Hoffert apartment. Was Richard Robles an acrobat?

the sill of the kitchen window on his left, and then lifted himself into the apartment, a feat worthy of an acrobat.

The hallway window is twenty-eight feet above a concrete rear court-yard, and the kitchen window is thirty-two feet four inches above the ground. The closest distance from the hallway window sill to the kitchen window sill is five feet one inch. At the trial, the prosecutor was careful to point out that an aluminum ventilation duct protruded from the building wall only two feet four and one-half inches from the hallway window, and that this duct was a mere three feet six inches below the kitchen window. Although he never spelled it out for the jury, his implication was obvious: Robles stepped onto the hallway window sill, stretched out his left foot to the ventilation duct, parallel to the hallway window sill, and then reached up to hoist himself in through the kitchen window. On the witness stand, Downes noted that Robles was a cat burglar, and the prosecutor in his summation described Robles as a healthy young man who was not a "midget" or physically deformed.

Robles, five feet eight inches tall and weighing one hundred forty pounds, was thin and wiry-looking. There was, however, no evidence of his having been a cat burglar or of having accomplished any adroit climbs during his teen-age crime career. The one burglary for which he was convicted had been achieved by forcing his way into an apartment through the front door, not through any extraordinary human-fly techniques.

What Robles's defense lawyers tried to emphasize at the trial, and what the prosecution ignored, were the difficulties Robles would have met in bridging the gap between the hallway and kitchen windows.

First, he would have had to get into the basement of the building without being seen by any of the three employees on duty at the time. He would then have had to take the self-service passenger elevator or the manually operated freight elevator from the basement to one of the floors above the lobby. Either elevator would have given him easy access to the service stairway on any floor above the lobby.

His next problem would have been leaning far enough out of the forty-two-inch-wide hallway window between the second and third floors to determine if the Wylie-Hoffert kitchen window above him was open. This author and two employees of the Wylie-Hoffert building, each of us taller than Robles, were unable by craning out of the hallway window to see if the kitchen window was open or closed. One person able to get a good look in this manner at the Wylie-Hoffert kitchen window was a reporter who was six feet four inches tall, eight inches taller than Robles.

Just getting onto the window sill is a gymnastic achievement: whereas the bottom portion of the hallway window can be raised vertically twenty-nine inches, there is barely room for a grown man to crawl out onto the sill. A horizontal metal bar extending from frame to frame on the inside of the window allows nineteen inches of opening through which to squeeze from the hallway onto the outside sill.

After maneuvering his body through the narrow opening, Robles would have been confronted by another difficulty—the absence of molding on the outside of the window and on the brick wall to grasp for balance while standing on the sill. The prosecution implied Robles's confessions indicated that, once he was on the sill, he used the ventilation duct as a foothold. The duct, however, is not so helpful as it sounds. It extends along the brick wall for eight and one-half inches, less than the length of an average man's foot, and it protrudes only three-quarters of an inch—about the width of a man's finger—at a downward slant from the brickwork.

In addition to these hazards, the climb would have occurred in daylight in a courtyard where Robles could have been observed from at least thirty-one of eighty-one apartment windows.

Why, if he had been bent on burglary, would Robles have defied these obvious obstacles—in addition to the risk that someone might have been in the apartment when he came lurching through the window—rather than simply wandering through the building in the hope of finding an open rear door or a bolt easy to unclasp? In his summation to the jury, John F. Keenan, the prosecutor, maintained that the police knew only as much as Robles was willing to admit. But he neglected to explain why the police had waited until after Robles's arrest in January 1965 to investigate the window theory, instead of doing it in October 1964, when the Delaneys supposedly provided them with the first tip about the window.

To anyone skeptical about Robles's chances of entering through the window, there is a greater ring of truth to one of the first police speculations about the way the killer penetrated the apartment. Since there was no sign of forced entry, and Patricia Tolles believed both doors were locked when she left, the police originally felt Janice Wylie or Emily Hoffert might have unsuspectingly opened the door for the killer, admitting someone known to one of them. Robles did not fit into this theory. There was no evidence that either of the victims knew him or would have opened the door for him. Even if Janice Wylie was not ordinarily cautious about opening doors to strangers, she presumably would have put on a bathrobe before doing so, and there was no evidence of her wearing a bathrobe when the killer appeared. If Robles could not have walked in, police logic left only one other possible method of entry—through a window thirty-two feet four inches above the ground.

Several indisputable facts permit at least some reconstruction of events on the morning of the murders. The medical examiner's expert opinion was that the women died before noon. Janice Wylie received a telephone call that morning to report to work at 11:00 A.M. When Patricia Tolles left at 9:30 A.M., Janice was alone, sleeping nude in her bed. Emily Hoffert was in The Bronx, nine miles from the apartment, at 10:45 A.M. The rest of the events that morning can only be conjectured.

Drawing upon the Delaneys' testimony, the prosecution portrayed Robles committing the murders some time in the morning and then going to the Delaney apartment. Exactly when he showed up at the Delaney home is a mammoth question mark. Delaney testified that Robles came to confess before noon, possibly as early as 11:00 A.M. Mrs. Delaney believed Robles made his dramatic entry "around noon." There is one flaw in the Delaneys' description: according to Robles's confession to them, it would have been almost impossible for him to have killed the women and reached their apartment by noon.

Since Emily Hoffert did not leave The Bronx until at least 10:45, it is reasonable to assume that, even with ideal driving and parking conditions, the earliest she could have returned to her Manhattan apartment would have been a half-hour later. Therefore, if Robles is the killer and his confessions are valid, within forty-five minutes, between 11:15 and noon, he had to: subdue Emily Hoffert; cut strips of bedding, carefully tie the women separately, and then bind them together; ransack the two bedrooms; think "for five minutes" about what to do with the women; commit the murders; wash himself; halfheartedly rinse one of the murder knives; leave the apartment; and take two or three cabs downtown, crosstown, and back uptown to the Delaneys', with one stopover either to buy handkerchiefs or to make a telephone call. To have arrived at the Delaneys' around noon, as Mrs. Delaney testified, Robles would have had to have been fast afoot as well as extremely lucky in hailing taxicabs.

The discrepancies in the Delaneys' testimony about the time of Robles's arrival at their apartment and who opened the door for him were explained away by the prosecution as an understandable confusion in time, since they were not the type of people who paid attention to the clock; and furthermore, if they had wanted to concoct a story, the simplest item to agree upon would have been the precise hour Robles came to confess. Nevertheless, if the Delaneys slipped up or lied about such significant evidence as the time he arrived, then their complete story is jeopardized and open to suspicion.

There is yet one more note of mystery about the time: could the murderer have been in the apartment as late as 3:30 P.M. that afternoon, more than three hours after Robles supposedly left?

On August 28, 1963, John Lane, a slight, thirty-five-year-old former seaman who supported his wife and three children through janitorial jobs when not at sea, was employed at the Wylie-Hoffert building as a doorman-porter. Lane spoke to Patricia Tolles that morning, when he delivered a package of towels to apartment 3C at 8:45 A.M. He observed her leaving for work about forty-five minutes later, but he did not see Janice Wylie or Emily Hoffert any time that morning.

One of Lane's chores was to collect garbage twice a day in the building. Tenants placed their refuse in receptacles on the landing outside their kitchen doors. Lane would ride the freight elevator to each floor and dump the tenants' garbage into a huge can in the elevator. On August 28, he made his first rounds, as usual, between 10:00 and 11:00 A.M. He noticed nothing amiss outside the kitchen door of 3C when he picked up and emptied the plastic garbage pail left there earlier by Patricia Tolles. He clearly recalled that his second collection was made between 3:00 and 3:30 P.M. This time, he found garbage cans outside 3B's kitchen door, five feet across the hallway from 3C. The pail from 3C was empty. Lane did notice something curious about apartment 3C. At Robles's trial he testified:

"While I was picking up garbage from 3B, I heard sounds in 3C like the shuffling of feet; water was running; someone was moving around in the kitchen. I stopped and listened and went about my business. . . ."

The kitchen door was open, he said, "not in the sense you could see through it . . . but cracked like."

If it is accurate, Lane's testimony completely destroys the prosecution's version of the crime, because it places an intruder in the apartment three hours after the murders.

Prosecutor Keenan tried to discredit Lane's testimony by describing him as unreliable. The prosecutor noted that after leaving work that day at 4:00 P.M., Lane spent three or four hours in a nearby bar, and that he could not positively affirm on the witness stand that he had told detectives about the open door when he was questioned on the night of the murders.

Lane pointed out that he was unable to recall all of the hundreds of questions put to him by police after the slayings. Under the sternest cross-examination, he stuck to his story of hearing noises and seeing the door open "a crack" at 3:30 P.M. on the day of the murders. Oddly, a single line in Whitmore's confession buttresses Lane's testimony that he probably had told the police about the door in the early stages of the investigation. Whitmore's police interrogators undoubtedly had access to Lane's statements; and, in Whitmore's false confession, he said the reason he had entered the women's apartment was that "I saw the door cracked," almost the same description used by Lane.

A piece of circumstantial evidence adds still more credence to Lane's account. When Patricia Tolles came home at 6:45 P.M., she found the kitchen door not open by a crack but ajar about two feet. If Robles had left through the kitchen door before noon, when he assertedly did, the door should have been wide open when Lane came by at 3:30 P.M., as it was when Miss Tolles arrived. Unless Lane lied, someone left the apartment between 3:30 and 6:45 P.M.

Lane's testimony cast a giant cloud of confusion over the police version of the crime, and Keenan was well aware of it. In trying to discredit the value of Lane's testimony, the prosecutor suggested that Lane might have been mistaken, or that he had a macabre desire to play a key role in an important murder case. Yet Lane did not seek out the defense lawyers. Robles's attorneys came across him in the middle of the trial, when the District Attorney passed along to them the names of witnesses questioned during the investigation. At the trial, Lane's memory appeared sharp; he even recalled which apartments in the building had been vacant two years earlier on the very day of the murders.

The simplest way of establishing innocence is through an alibi, proof that the defendant was elsewhere when the crime occurred. In Robles's case there was an alibi—vital evidence that the jury never heard.

The one person who might have vouched for Robles's innocence was hospitalized, in the last stages of cancer, when Robles's trial began, and died before the verdict was reached. The alibi witness was Robles's mother, Mrs. Leontine Simon, the woman whose statement the police apparently had believed the week after the murders were committed.

One month before Robles's trial, two defense lawyers, the prosecutor, and presiding Judge Irwin D. Davidson attempted to obtain testimony from the mother at her hospital bedside. She lapsed into a coma before any questions could be put to her. A week later, Mrs. Simon rallied briefly, and this time her bedside testimony, through direct examination by defense lawyers and cross-examination by Keenan, was recorded in the judge's presence. After reviewing the statement, Robles's lawyers decided against having it read to the jury, even though Mrs. Simon had sworn that her son had spent the morning of the murder day sleeping in her apartment.

Hoffinger, the chief defense counsel, feared her testimony might backfire against the defense. He believed Mrs. Simon had been incoherent because of her illness and confused about the number of the building where she had lived in August 1963. She had also referred to her son's criminal record, which Hoffinger and his co-counsel, Frederick H. Block, believed could adversely influence the jury. After several days of indecision, the two counsels gambled by withholding the statement. They felt the mother's statement was less convincing on paper than it would have been coming from her own lips on the witness stand.

One other person—Robles's maternal grandmother—might have corroborated his alibi, but her testimony was hearsay, inadmissible in a courtroom. Nevertheless, Mrs. Leontine Brochard, the grandmother, an alert widow in her early sixties, holds an interesting piece of the puzzle.

On the day of the double murder, Mrs. Brochard was employed as a clerk in a Bronx branch of the New York State Division of Employment. A woman accustomed to a meticulous daily schedule, she always left her desk for a morning break between 10:30 and 11:00 A.M. She had brunch during that time in a restaurant across the street from her office which served a fifty-five-cent breakfast of eggs, rolls, and coffee until 11:00 A.M. Mrs. Brochard made sure she arrived before 11:00, because afterward the same meal would cost her eighty-five cents. One other rule she observed each morning was to call her daughter, Mrs. Simon, before leaving for her snack. Mrs. Brochard had good reasons for remembering the murder day. Many of the Negro employees in her office had taken the day off to attend the civil rights rally in Washington. With almost half the normal staff away, Mrs. Brochard and the other employees there that day were temporarily overworked.

On Monday, two days earlier, the grandmother had made her customary morning telephone call at about 10:30 A.M. The ringing telephone had awakened Robles, who was sleeping late on the first day of his vacation. To insure that Robles's morning sleep would be undisturbed by the telephone bell, Mrs. Simon had arranged to call Mrs. Brochard from her home every morning about 10:30 A.M.

At 10:30 A.M. of Wednesday, August 28, 1963, Mrs. Brochard was waiting impatiently for her daughter to telephone. Because Robles had been out of prison only three months, she did not want to miss the call, which usually assured her he was not in trouble. At about 10:45 A.M., her telephone rang, and she picked it up and spoke to her daughter.

"We had the same dull conversation we usually had," Mrs. Brochard recalled. "Everything was all right with my daughter, and everything was all right with me. I asked her if that demon, Ricky, was still sleeping, and she said he was still in bed and she might have to blast him with dynamite because she wanted to wash the windows in his room and there was no sign out of him that he was getting up.

"I knew it was getting close to 11:00, and since we were so short-staffed I wanted to get back to the office as soon as I could. So I said to her: 'I'll have to cut this conversation short because many of our colored people are in Washington, and I'll call you tonight.'

"When I hung up it might have been fifteen minutes or ten minutes of eleven, and I know she said Ricky was still in bed."

Alibi testimony from a mother or grandmother is always questionable. But it is interesting to bear in mind that the police believed Mrs. Simon at the time they first questioned her, twelve days after the murders, when she was still healthy and mentally unimpaired. Mrs. Brochard's recollections are inadmissible because she herself did not see Robles in her daughter's apartment, yet the petty details she connects with the morning telephone call add to the impression of truthfulness. Hearing from her daughter at 10:30 A.M. would be an important ritual for her; getting to the restaurant before 11:00 A.M. obviously was important for her budget; and the matter of the excess work load on the day of the civil rights march is the type of problem that would linger in her mind.

If Mrs. Brochard's memory is accurate, Robles may have been in his own bed, a half-mile from the Wylie-Hoffert apartment, shortly before 11:00 A.M. By that time, the killer should have been in the apartment, since Janice Wylie had not even begun dressing for her 11:00 A.M. work assignment when the prelude to the murders began.

All the evidence against Robles was derived from the alleged confessions and from three recordings made of conversations in the Delaney apartment. The District Attorney's office was wary of using the Delaneys' testimony—the testimony of narcotics addicts who informed only after Delaney was promised a concession in his own murder case—as the main foundation for convicting Robles. After the Delaneys had implicated Robles, the District Attorney's office and police went to inordinate lengths in the next three months to gather more evidence against him; the results were meager, however.

Hours after Delaney first spoke to Koste about the murders, Robles, without any warning, was pulled out of his girl friend's apartment and taken to the District Attorney's office, where he received the chilling news that two of his best friends had accused him of double murder. In the next three months, Robles was questioned a half-dozen times by the police and the D.A.'s aides. On the day of his arrest he was interrogated for more than five hours, both in the street and in the Delaney apartment with the recording machines spinning next door. In all this time he refused to confess.

The evidence the District Attorney needed to convict him, the vital corroboration of the Delaneys' accusations, unexpectedly burst forth from Robles during one hour in which he was alone with four police officers in the clerical room at the 23rd Precinct. The confession flowed from Robles at the last opportunity the police would have to question him before he was booked and arraigned for the murders, and passed out of their hands. When Robles went into his one talkative period, there were no recording machines or stenographers present. In fact, none of the four policemen took any notes while he talked. Detective Downes and Lieutenant Sullivan said they wrote out versions of the confession three hours after listening to Robles; Sergeant Brent waited until the next day to record his recollections on paper; and Lieutenant Cavanagh allowed six months to pass before jotting down a word about this important confession. These investigators said note-taking might have deterred Robles from his sudden streak of cooperativeness. Whitmore's questioners supposedly recorded quantities of notes in his presence without fear of stopping his tongue, whereas Robles's interrogators were certain the mere sight of pencil and paper was the surest way of stopping a killer from confessing.

As soon as the police questioners left Robles's side at the precinct, he again lapsed into his familiar posture of innocence. Despite his obvious craving for narcotics, despite an uncomfortable withdrawal period, Robles volunteered no admissions when Assistant District Attorney Koste questioned him two hours after the detectives claimed he had confessed to them.

Probably the most irrational aspect of Robles's arrest was his short-lived loquacity with Downes, Cavanagh, Sullivan, and Brent. If he was ready to bear the mantle of guilt, if he had finally cracked under the pressure of a relentless investigation, why did he revert to protestations of innocence when Koste came for an official "Q and A" confession?

Without a written version of Robles's various descriptions of the crime, the prosecutor had to present confession testimony by the Delaneys and four police officers. In this testimony the Delaneys disagreed as to what time Robles had arrived at their apartment and who had let him in. And in this testimony veteran detectives acknowledged having neglected to ask Robles such vital questions as: Did he ransack the apartment? Why did he leave the jewelry behind? Did he gag the women? Why had he disemboweled Janice Wylie if she put up no resistance?

The tapes were the second salient part of the presentation against Robles. They were recorded conversations that Keenan labeled as evidence "unmistakably, clearly and incontrovertibly" stamping Robles as the killer of Janice Wylie and Emily Hoffert.

Lieutenant Cavanagh and Sergeant Brent were convinced Robles had been unaware the Delaneys' place was wired for sound. They remembered his surprised look when the microphones were thrust at him on the day of his arrest. But it is difficult to believe that Robles would be this naive about the possibility of the police bugging the Delaney apartment. He had found clandestinely installed recording equipment in his own home and in the apartment of his girl friend. Yet one brief search of the Delaney apartment before Delaney was released from jail presumably convinced him it was safe to talk there—with the two people who had pinned a murder charge on him.

To understand Robles, one should not forget his overriding weakness— narcotics. He needed the Delaneys; they were his connection, a safe, inexpensive source of drugs at a time when he knew he was being watched by the police, and at a time when he had little money and for several weeks was unemployed. Even if he had avoided the Delaneys, the information they had given the District Attorney would not have changed. In the pre-arrest questioning sessions, he repeatedly told the police the Delaneys were trying to frame him. The police, however, knew he had to return to his friends for narcotics. If Robles was innocent, what did he have to lose by finding out from the Delaneys what they had told the police about him? By visiting them, he got narcotics inexpensively and, at the same time, learned what they had said about him.

Robles's defense consisted of cross-examination of the prosecution witnesses, Lane's testimony, testimony from George Whitmore Jr. about his confession to the double murder and finally, testimony from the detectives who had obtained Whitmore's confessions. The major part of the defense's strategy was a double-edged concept: either Whitmore was guilty as the police had originally charged, or his confession spotlighted the untrustworthiness of the police in their desperate attempt to solve the Wylie-Hoffert murders.

Hoffinger and Block decided against putting Robles on the witness stand. Without his mother's corroborative testimony he could contribute little to his own defense, and on the witness stand he would have to admit much about his criminal past and narcotics background. Quite possibly the jury would accept his denial that he had confessed to the Delaneys, but would the jurors believe his lone contradiction of four police officers who said he had admitted the crime to them? The defense lawyers must have realized the hopelessness of trying to rebut multiple police testimony solely through Robles. Under cross-examination, Robles would probably be questioned fully about his past as a juvenile burglar, and the resultant testimony would make a jury less likely to release him. And Robles faced one other danger as a witness. Narcotics addicts, especially after several months' imprisonment without drugs, can be poor witnesses. Too often they are hyperemotional, excited, and jittery, possibly exposing unstable personalities. Thus Robles's explanation, if he had any, of what had brought him to trial for double murder remained locked up inside him.

Robles's attorneys, without an alibi and without witnesses to contradict directly the witnesses who said Robles confessed, obviously were looking beyond the verdict toward an appeal and a possible new trial—in which, perhaps, the tape recordings or the police testimony about alleged admissions would be thrown out as evidence. The verdict of the jurors was not surprising, especially after they had examined three blood-crusted murder knives; viewed the horrifying photographs of the dead women; heard recorded conversations in which Robles talked calmly about murder and perversions; and got glimpses of the sleazy, immoral underworld life he had led.

Despite the verdict, doubts in the Wylie-Hoffert case remain. Many of these stem from the methods employed to solve the murders, especially the tactics used against Robles and Whitmore by District Attorney Hogan's office and the police. Early in the investigation, the police had the opportunity to examine Robles, and at that time, after superficial soundings, they dismissed him as a suspect. They accepted the word of his mother, the kind of alibi police normally distrust. No attempt was made to contradict his original statement by questioning neighbors to determine if anyone had seen him outside his apartment on the morning of the murder, or if anyone had noticed him coming into the building in the afternoon. None of Robles's friends, many of whom were known to the police, was interviewed about his behavior following the murders.

Fourteen months later, the District Attorney's office and the police entered a phase of the investigation which bordered on the amateurish. The initial action taken by the authorities probably was the least desirable development. Before the Delaneys' accusations were fully evaluated, before a complete campaign was organized to determine if Robles was the killer, the District Attorney's aides informed Robles that the Delaneys had turned him in, and asked if he was ready to confess. When the easy way out—a confession—failed, the District Attorney's office then botched the task of secretly planting microphones in the places he frequented. The police were watching everything Robles did—but he probably knew it.

The biggest blunder the police made occurred nine months before Robles's arrest, when Whitmore was brainwashed into confessing and producing a sixty-one-page concoction that Brooklyn detectives tried to pass off as the solution to the crime. During the first week after Whitmore's arrest, this enormous mistake was compounded when accurate and in-accurate details of the slayings were disclosed to the press—and thus became available for everyone, including the Delaneys, to read and to remember.

The flagrant inconsistencies in Whitmore's "Q and A" confession should have created grave doubts about his guilt as soon as his statement was analyzed in Hogan's office. There were too many warning signals that could not be lightly dismissed as inconsequential errors of Whitmore's low intelligence. There were too many incomprehensible mistakes in his de-scription of the murders. Hogan or someone in his office should have been suspicious as soon as he read that Whitmore walked aimlessly for fifty blocks from a Times Square subway station to the Wylie-Hoffert building and, after the murders, without any signs of blood on him, retraced his long route; that Whitmore brazenly strolled into the building lobby and onto the service stairway through a door that was always kept locked; that Whitmore described twenty-three-year-old Emily Hoffert as "the mother"; that Whitmore attributed foul language to her when she found him in the apartment; that Whitmore forgot he had stabbed Janice Wylie in the stomach, although her abdomen had been torn apart; that Whitmore stabbed the women and then tied them; that Whitmore rolled down Miss Hoffert's panties, although the police knew her underclothes had been undisturbed; that Whitmore found the carving knives in a kitchen table, although there was no table in the kitchen and the murder weapons came from a wall cabinet; that Whitmore was confused about the time he committed the murders, and corrected himself only after being aided by questioners. And the giant flaw in the confession was: how could Whitmore have been unaware, as he obviously was from his confession, that the women were dead?

The inconsistencies in Whitmore's "Q and A" were at first pushed aside. After his arrest, no attempt was made to verify his alibi, while the District Attorney's office devoted five months to a search for someone who could connect Whitmore's photograph with the Wylie-Hoffert apartment.

When Whitmore was arrested, the District Attorney's men knew all too well that only a confession would solve the murders, and his statement, absurd as it sounded, was still considered worthy of acceptance. His alibi, which should have been investigated at the first stage of the inquiry, not only to protect him but also to safeguard the public interest, was checked out only in one of the last phases of the investigation. By unjustly accusing Whitmore and then delaying his exoneration, Hogan's office contaminated any future confession in the case. Keenan, while prosecuting Robles, accused the Brooklyn detectives of providing Robles with a built-in defense. An equal measure of the shame emanating from Whitmore's counterfeit confession clings to the District Attorney's office; Hogan and his aides remained silent much too long to be absolved of complicity.

And, after what happened to Whitmore, how much unquestioned faith can be placed on assurances by the District Attorney and the police that Robles's admissions were voluntary or valid?

17. *The Wrong Men*

In most aspects of their work, the police are excellent record-keepers. They keep precise count of every kind of crime committed in their jurisdiction, the age groups of criminals, whether each type of crime is increasing or diminishing, and their success in closing out cases. But the police decline to keep statistics for one category—the number of coerced confessions. No police official or prosecutor likes to discuss this subject publicly.

Privately, among themselves or with friends, detectives who have conducted interrogations stress one contention: an innocent man will not confess falsely, despite physical or mental pressure. The core of this interrogation philosophy is that only the guilty crack. But, if the confession

233

is to remain a part of our legal system, new procedures must be introduced to protect the rights of suspects and, at the same time, permit the police rightfully to obtain voluntary admissions. The police, with their long record of reluctance to surrender any back-room prerogative, rarely initiate safeguards. Reforms usually must be imposed on the interrogators. The Miranda Ruling helped the balance of justice in the back room, but more improvements are needed to guarantee against future "wrong man" confessions.

George Whitmore Jr. became known as a classic "wrong man" only for extraordinary reasons. After his "confessions" the depravity and hideousness of the Wylie-Hoffert murders attracted only notoriety and scorn to Whitmore. But the extraordinary public interest in the double murder eventually brought him the attention and legal help he needed. Other victims of the back room have been less fortunate. They have dissolved into lost statistics of the confession system. Rarely is the thick door screening the confession room belatedly opened so that outsiders can glimpse the procedures used to squeeze admissions out of suspects. Not just in New York but in other parts of the country as well, in the back rooms of precincts in Illinois, Alabama, and Florida, other proven cases of false confessions have occurred. Police techniques for obtaining these worthless confessions differed, but there was a remarkable similarity in the way the police defended themselves. Each time, the police and prosecutor were certain they had bagged the right man and were acting in the best interests of justice.

In many ways Earl Heywood Pugh was very much like George Whitmore. Both were teen-aged Negroes, unaware of their legal rights when they got into trouble. Pugh's difficulties began on a 1936 September night in Chicago. A slim nineteen-year-old from Tennessee, Pugh had been living in Chicago for several months and was short of money and friends. One of the few persons he knew was Walter Fowler, an older Negro who lived near him on the South Side, and with whom he occasionally walked and chatted. On an Indian Summer evening, Pugh was strolling on the South Side with Fowler when the seemingly insignificant incident that would mar their lives occurred.

A drunk stopped Pugh and challenged him to a fight. It was obvious the drunk, swaying from side to side, was in no condition for a serious brawl, and Pugh began sparring with him, laughingly sidestepping his wild lunges. No blows had landed in the mock bout when a police patrol car pulled up. Suddenly, the drunk screamed that Pugh and Fowler had tried to rob him, and within minutes Pugh and Fowler found themselves under arrest at the Maxwell Street police station. It was Pugh's first encounter with the law; but, unknown to him, Fowler had served time in Ohio and Michigan for robbery.

Three hours later, Pugh was in a small basement room in the precinct with two detectives. They gravely informed him that the accusation was not robbery but the fatal stabbing of a white man two weeks earlier during a holdup in a park. In 1936, few Chicago police were concerned about extending constitutional privileges to Negroes, and Pugh would later recall that one of the detectives candidly explained: "We've got a killing on our hands, and you're going to have to take the rap for it." When Pugh insisted he knew nothing about the crime, his ordeal began. It was to last six days. Besides being questioned almost round the clock, he was denied the right to call a lawyer or a friend and was given virtually no food or water. Each time he refused to confess, he was punched, beaten with night sticks, or pistol-whipped. When two days of beatings failed, the police tried a different technique. Pugh was placed against a basement wall and used as a target by detectives who competed in firing bullets close to but not into his head. The police also tried the Mutt and Jeff system. After a particularly cruel beating on the fourth day, a detective whispered into Pugh's ear in a friendly tone: "Don't worry, I'm going to protect you. Go ahead and sign the confession." The trick failed. With blood trickling from his lips, Pugh continued to mutter his innocence. Exasperated by his steadfastness, the second detective knocked Pugh to the floor, nuzzled a gun against his temple, and angrily shouted: "I should shoot this son of a bitch!"

On the sixth day, with his left arm broken and his aching body covered with bruises and welts, Pugh still defied his interrogators. Now he was brought into a basement room at the station house for a meeting with Fowler. Fowler, who had confessed quickly, advised Pugh: "Man, you'd better sign that confession 'cause these people are going to kill you." At last Pugh's resistance crumbled. He, too, signed a piece of paper.

Although Pugh and Fowler recanted their confessions at a joint murder trial, both men were convicted solely on the strength of their having signed admissions. There was no corroborative evidence to link either of them to the murder. The jury did not require any. The detectives testified that Pugh and Fowler had confessed voluntarily; Fowler's lengthy police record indicated his criminal temperament; and the two men had been arrested in a street brawl while trying to rob a drunk—that was enough evidence. Nevertheless, the jurors were lenient; they recommended life imprisonment instead of the electric chair, and the judge accepted their advice. In

January 1937, Pugh and Fowler began serving life sentences in Joliet Prison.

For Fowler, the prison term lasted twelve years. He died and was buried in the prison cemetery in 1949. But Pugh, who showed his physical and mental stamina during those six days in the Maxwell Street station house, never stopped trying to get out of Joliet. He wrote endlessly to relatives, lawyers, and state officials, describing what had befallen him and begging for rescue. Even after sixteen years of vainly trying to interest someone on the outside, he refused to concede the hopelessness of his predicament. During the seventeenth year of his sentence, he at last found a receptive ear: George Leighton, a Negro lawyer partly influenced by the ceaseless campaign of Pugh and his relatives to reopen the investigation. Within six months, Leighton disinterred a remarkable piece of evidence which the police had entombed for seventeen years. At a hearing in 1955, the lawyer revealed that the prosecution in the 1936 trial had suppressed information that would have exonerated Pugh and Fowler. Two eye-witnesses had seen the killer, a white man, stab and chase his victim in the park. Both witnesses had given statements to the police, but neither of them had been called by the prosecution; nor had their evidence been turned over to the defense at the trial. As a result of these disclosures, Pugh's conviction was set aside, and the Cook County prosecutor decided against retrying him for murder.

Pugh and Fowler had been framed by a brutal confession system, and the state of Illinois made amends. It was, of course, too late for Fowler, but Illinois paid some of its debt to Pugh. He was awarded a settlement of $51,000—$3,000 for each year behind bars, or eight dollars a day—as solace for having been forced to sign a confession.

No one beat a confession out of Stanford Ellis Fewell. A more subtle approach than the fist or club was used by the Jefferson County, Alabama, police to pry a phony admission out of him for the 1949 sex-murder of his nine-year-old second cousin in a rural community near Birmingham. Fewell's ordeal started in 1952, after the gruesome murder had remained unsolved for three years. The ruggedly handsome farmer, a Korean War veteran, was brought in for questioning when two young girls complained he had made sexual overtures to them. Recalling the murder of Fewell's cousin, the police questioned him about that crime. He denied being implicated. But the police, although they had no clues linking Fewell to the crime, were a patient lot. Through fabled police intuition, they became convinced he was the killer, and they had no intention of letting him slip away. They were so certain of his guilt that they questioned him for two weeks without letting him see a lawyer or a relative. During this time, Fewell remained adamant about his innocence. On the fifteenth day, the interrogators won the mental war with one clever ruse. Unless he confessed immediately, Fewell was told, his mother would be arrested for complicity in the murder. This is how Fewell explains his capitulation: "My mother, she was in pretty bad health at the time, and they told me that if I didn't make a statement to the fact that I was guilty, then they would put her in jail. So I did and I made the statement."

Whatever facts Fewell needed for his admission were indirectly supplied to him by the police. "They questioned me in such a way that by the time I made the statement, I knew how the crime was committed. They were asking me: Didn't I steal a car in front of a movie? And didn't I go and pick the girl up and take her out, close to the lake? And while I was out there, didn't I hit her in the mouth? And what time I got home, didn't I get home at a certain hour of the morning? And didn't I go to see people at a certain time of the day? And did I hit her with a hammer? And by the time I came to make the statement, I knew in my mind, I had just about every detail available as to how it was committed and how it was went about, and so I just made the statement."

The confession resulted in a conviction and a thirty-year prison sentence. Clancy Lake, former city editor of the Birmingham *News*, had doubts about Fewell's guilt. While Fewell was in jail, Lake and Fred J. Bodeker, a Birmingham private detective, took a close look at the evidence compiled against Fewell. Except for the confession, they discovered, there was no case. More important, their volunteer sleuthing turned up evidence that unmistakably confirmed Fewell's innocence. Although the police had never exerted themselves to investigate Fewell's alibi, Lake and Bodeker did. They located four witnesses who had moved from the area shortly after the 1949 murder and had been unaware of Fewell's conviction three years later. These witnesses belatedly backed up Fewell's contention that at the time of the slaying he was with them and his mother in the Fewell farmhouse, thirty miles from the murder site. The new evidence was sufficient to convince the Alabama Parole Board that a mistake had been made. On May 4, 1959, Fewell walked out of Kirby Prison in Montgomery, a free man for the first time in seven years.

About the time Fewell was getting out of prison, Joseph Frank Shea was walking into a confession trap in Florida. It was a trap that Shea willingly sprung on himself, and it almost proved fatal for him.

February 23, 1959, was a perfect day for the Florida tourist industry; the temperature was in the low eighties, the skies were clear, the seas were calm. Mrs. Mary Meslener, a pretty twenty-three-year-old from New York City, a newcomer to Florida, was at her job as an airline reservation clerk at Miami International Airport. After a routine eight-hour shift, she tidied up, said good night to her co-workers, and started walking toward her car in a nearby parking lot. She was never seen alive again. Two days later, her bullet-mutilated body was found on the bank of the Miami River, three miles from the airport. Her bloodstained car was recovered two weeks later, two hundred fifty miles away in Tampa.

Mrs. Meslener's murder was not a standard homicide case; quite the opposite, it was a tough one for the Dade County Homicide Bureau. They had neither the murder weapon, fingerprints, nor a single good clue. As for suspects, every one of Mrs. Meslener's relatives and friends had an alibi, and the crime appeared motiveless. More than a month of detective work had been fruitless when Shea, who was stationed at the West Palm Beach Air Force Base, entangled himself in the investigation. The twenty-year-old airman, who looked closer to thirty because of his thick mustache, stuttered out a vague story to a sergeant about having injured a baby. He was unable to remember exactly what he had done, but he was positive he had committed a crime. In addition, he was unable to explain why a blood-stained shirt was among his belongings.

Shea's superior officers were skeptical of his story and of his complaints of mental blackouts. They had long since labeled him a shirker, a man trying to feign mental illness in order to be discharged from the service. Nevertheless, they checked his bizarre story as best they could. All nearby police departments were notified of Shea's tale of having possibly injured a baby, and the airman was kept under surveillance at the base. None of the police departments had any open cases involving children, but the Dade County Homicide Bureau chose to question Shea about the Meslener murder. Philip Thibedeau, the detective in charge of the inquiry, visited Shea at an Air Force hospital where he had been ordered for psychiatric tests. Thibedeau found nothing linking Shea to the crime. A week later, however, when laboratory tests on Shea's shirt indicated that the stains were human blood, two detectives began a second round of interrogation with Shea. This time, Shea offered rambling, incoherent reviews of gang warfare during his youth in Queens, New York, and repeated: "I almost stole a baby in Miami." Again, he failed to mention the Meslener murder.

At the conclusion of this interview, the detectives left Shea alone in a consultation room as they stepped outside to talk with two Military Police officers. The walls were thin enough for Shea to overhear the conversation that ensued. For the next fifteen minutes, the Miami detectives described their theory about the way the murder was committed and divulged several essential facts about the crime. When the civilian police stepped back into the consultation room, Shea's memory had unexpectedly improved. Although earlier he had been unable to provide a single detail of the Meslener murder, he now confessed, repeating almost entirely to the police what they had just told the M.P.'s on the other side of the wall. Shea said that on the night of the murder he had been on leave from his post. He was rifling Mrs. Meslener's car in the airport parking lot when she surprised him. Before she could cry out for help, he knocked her out, pulled her into the car, and drove off. When she regained consciousness, he shot her, finally dumping the body in a clump of bushes by the riverside. The detectives accepted the confession as a rational account.

That same day, an Air Force psychiatrist was less satisfied with Shea's mental state. Several hours before confessing, Shea had undergone a mental examination at the hospital. The psychiatrist described him as "agitated, depressed, anxious . . . he has difficulty making coordinated movements (involuntary jerks and starts, eyes blinking)."

Shea was still in a talkative mood the next day. He repeated his confession almost word for word to an Air Force psychiatrist. But two days later, when detectives booked him for murder, he denied the charge. The police were not finished with him. Within a week of his arrest, they obtained a second admission, this one volunteered by Shea after he was told that his fingerprints had been lifted from the dead woman's car, that a lie-detector test had proved he was guilty, that eyewitnesses could place him in Miami on the night of the murder and, finally, that the blood on his shirt was the same type as Mrs. Meslener's. The police lied to Shea. None of his fingerprints was in the car, the lie-detector tests indicated that he was innocent, there were no eyewitnesses, and the blood on his shirt was his own type, not Mrs. Meslener's type.

No corroborating evidence was required to convict Shea. A jury accepted the detectives' version of the confession and, in 1959, Shea was sentenced to life imprisonment. He might still be a lifer in Raiford Penitentiary if not for the zeal of three men: Philip Thibedeau, the detective who believed Shea was innocent and who worked in his behalf after quitting the Dade County Sheriff's office; Warren D. Holmes, a lie-detector expert who had tested Shea at the time of his arrest; and Gene Miller, a reporter for the Miami *Herald*. This trio conducted an investigation and uncovered evidence that Shea had been on duty at the Air Force base, eighty miles from Miami, on the night of the murder. In 1966, six

years after the case had been marked "closed," Shea was retried. This time
he was acquitted, despite the use of the confession once more as evidence
against him, and despite the prosecutor's plea:

"They fooled him a little, maybe a lot, but wouldn't you want the police
to do what they can within the limits of the law to apprehend a murderer?"

Harry W. Prebish, the lawyer who took over Shea's defense in 1965, is
convinced the police asked Shea enough leading and informative questions
to fill out his admission and make it sound logical. At the time he was
subjected to police interrogation, Shea was depressed because of an
unhappy love affair during a tour of duty in the Philippines. His mistress,
refusing to marry him, had run off with their baby. The bloody shirt and
the story of harming a child were Shea's own inventions. He smeared blood
on the shirt as part of a plan to feign amnesia and a mental breakdown.
After many sessions with Shea, Prebish felt he understood why Shea twice
confessed to a crime of which he had no knowledge: "Why did he confess?
I think he was trying to destroy himself. It was almost a mania with him at
that time. He was convinced he had done something wrong."

A photograph involved George Whitmore in the double-murder case.
Similarly, a photograph almost sent Santos Sanchez to the death house in
New York. Sanchez, a Puerto Rican, was forty-five years old and married,
with six children, and led an ordinary life. This all changed dramatically
one day in November 1964. Two detectives appeared at Sanchez's place of
work and took him away for questioning. They were investigating the
murder of one of Sanchez's cousins, who had been stabbed and strangled in
her Bronx apartment two weeks earlier. Searching the apartment, the
detectives came across a photograph of Sanchez—sufficient reason, they
thought, to bring him in for questioning. Before he could notify his wife,
Sanchez was driven to a station house in The Bronx. On the way, he
proclaimed both his innocence and his ignorance of the murder. In fact, he
told the police in broken English, he hardly knew the dead woman.

At the precinct, he was taken upstairs to the back room and handcuffed
to a chair, his hands behind him. No charge had been made against him,
but Sanchez saw he was not being treated like a witness. The only questions
the police asked him were about the murder and the way he had committed
it. As best he could in his limited English, Sanchez denied again and again
any knowledge of the slaying. After several minutes of this, Sanchez said,
the police began slugging him systematically in the face and stomach.

"Four or five cops took turns beating me," he said later. "I was hit in
the face and punched in the ribs. I don't even remember signing the
confession."

The next day, Sanchez was brought into court for arraignment. Again he protested his innocence, begging the judge to look at his bruises. A physical examination was ordered, and Sanchez was sent to a prison hospital for treatment of internal injuries and damaged ribs.

Sanchez's lawyer, Oscar Gonzalez-Suarez, who found three witnesses to corroborate Sanchez's alibi that he could not possibly have been at the scene of the murder, pressed for a speedy trial. When the Bronx District Attorney refused to move the case ahead of others on the court calendar, Gonzalez-Suarez made the D.A. an unusual offer. His client would take a lie-detector test and offer the findings, whether harmful or beneficial to the defense, as evidence in court. The D.A. agreed. The test results were overwhelmingly in Sanchez's favor. Faced with the lie-detector data, plus the uncomfortable possibility that Sanchez's lawyer was ready with three alibi witnesses, the District Attorney's office dropped the charge. Finally, without standing trial, Sanchez was released. Since a homicide charge in New York is automatically a non-bailable offense, Sanchez had been confined for one year in jail before his lawyer's persistent motions and appeals to the judiciary overcame the power of a confession.

18. *Where the Prosecution Begins*

Police and prosecutors everywhere in the United States, in crime-besieged big cities and in placid backwater areas, dismiss Whitmore, Fewell, Shea, Sanchez, and other confession injustices as freak exceptions or guilty men who escaped with the help of crafty lawyers and technicalities. They deny that reliance on admissions is a prop for inefficient investigators or a flaw in the legal system. Yet the plight of unknown and known victims of the confession system must have been in the minds of the Supreme Court majority that eventually ordained drastic changes in the back room.

The first significant sign of the Court's concern came in 1964, when the Escobedo Ruling slightly shocked "business as usual" police complacency.

In 1960, Danny Escobedo, a thin, diminutive drifter with a record of several arrests on various charges, a "Mex" well known to the police, was picked up by Chicago detectives for questioning following the murder of his sister's husband. Escobedo denied complicity in the murder and was released after fourteen hours of interrogation. Ten days later, the police brought him in again. A lawyer, alerted by Escobedo's relatives, hurried to the precinct and exchanged brief glances with his client through a half-open door. The police, however, refused to permit him to meet with Escobedo. During the interrogation that followed, none of the detectives informed Escobedo of his right to advice of counsel (an attorney who was standing outside the door of the interrogation room), or of his right to remain silent. Instead, the detectives apparently lured Escobedo into a well-constructed trap by telling him he had been identified by a friend as the murderer. Brought face-to-face with the alleged squealer, Escobedo blurted out: "You did it!" Whether Escobedo had known anything about the murder or was totally innocent, his words indirectly implicated him, and he knew it. After several more hours with police interrogators, he allegedly admitted paying $500 to a friend—the same man the police said had accused him of firing the fatal shot—to execute his brother-in-law. At his trial, Escobedo recanted, insisting he had been cajoled into confessing by a promise that the police would release him. The police denied tricking him, and the jury believed them. Found guilty of being an accomplice to the murder, Escobedo was sentenced to life imprisonment.

For three years Escobedo's lawyers argued his case relentlessly up the judicial ladder of appeals, until it reached the Supreme Court. In 1964, by a five-to-four vote, the Court reversed the conviction because Escobedo's lawyer had been prevented from consulting with him in the police station. Though the Court was specific in Escobedo's case, stating that his lawyer should have been permitted to speak to him when he arrived at the precinct, the decision was vague about the more decisive issue of whether the police were required in all interrogations to inform a suspect of his constitutional rights at the time of questioning. Basically, nothing in the prevailing system of interrogation had changed.

Two years later, the change came. The Miranda Ruling altered the confession system by stating explicitly that a suspect's right to remain silent and to have counsel begins the same time the prosecution begins—in the station house, not in the courtroom. As forewords to their revision of American law, the justices used four obscure confessions made by Ernesto Miranda, convicted of rape and kidnapping in Phoenix; by Roy Allen Steward, convicted of murder in Los Angeles; by Michael Vignera, con-

CHAPTER EIGHTEEN • 245

victed of robbery in New York; and by Charles Calvin Westover, convicted of bank robbery in Sacramento. Each of these men had confessed without being advised of his constitutional rights.

The five justices who composed the new rules for the back room had additional reasons for doing so. In their decision, they plucked out the Whitmore case—which they knew about but which had not reached the Supreme Court—as an example of the way the interrogation process "trades on the weakness of individuals." Various tricks and tactics recommended in police manuals for eliciting confessions also were recounted by the Court in explaining the background factors contributing to the ruling. Somberly delivering the landmark decision, Chief Justice Earl Warren said:

"This atmosphere [the back room] carries its own badge of intimidation. . . . The current practice of incommunicado interrogation is at odds with one of our Nation's most cherished principles—that the individual may not be compelled to incriminate himself. Unless adequate protective devices are employed to dispel the compulsion inherent in custodial surroundings, no statement obtained from the defendant can truly be the product of his free choice. . . .

"The warning of the right to remain silent must be accompanied by the explanation that anything said can and will be used against the individual in court. This warning is needed in order to make him aware not only of the privilege, but also of the consequences of foregoing it. It is only through an awareness of these consequences that there can be any assurance of real understanding and intelligent exercise of the privilege. Moreover, this warning may serve to make the individual more acutely aware that he is faced with a phase of the adversary system—that he is not in the presence of persons acting solely in his interest."

Obviously foreseeing the outcry that would follow, Warren asserted that the ruling was not an obituary for confessions:

"In dealing with statements obtained through interrogation, we do not purport to find all confessions inadmissible. Confessions remain a proper element in law enforcement. Any statement given freely and voluntarily without any compelling influences is, of course, admissible in evidence. . . . There is no requirement that police stop a person who enters a police station and states that he wishes to confess to a crime, or a person who calls the police to offer a confession or any other statement he desires to make. Volunteered statements of any kind are not barred by the Fifth Amendment and their admissibility is not affected by our holding today."

The acrimonious reaction was swift in coming. It came that same day, from the same bench in the Supreme Court building. In a fist-pounding rebuttal, Justice John M. Harlan warned: "This doctrine . . . has no sanction, no sanction. . . . It's obviously going to mean a gradual disappearance of confessions as a legitimate tool of law enforcement."

Justice Harlan, in his written dissent, further declared:

"What the Court largely ignores is that its rules impair, if they will not eventually serve wholly to frustrate, an instrument of law enforcement that has long and quite reasonably been thought worth the price paid for it. There can be little doubt that the Court's new code would markedly decrease the number of confessions. To warn the suspect that he may remain silent and remind him that his confession may be used in court are minor obstructions. To require also an express waiver by the suspect and an end to questioning whenever he demurs must heavily handicap questioning. And to suggest or provide counsel for the suspect simply invites the end of the interrogation.

". . . We do know that some crimes cannot be solved without confessions, that ample expert testimony attests to their importance in crime control, and that the Court is taking a real risk with society's welfare in imposing its new regime on the country. The social costs of crime are too great to call the new rules anything but a hazardous experimentation."

Continuing the unusual display of rancor within the Court, another dissenter, Justice Byron M. White, prophesied:

"In some unknown number of cases the Court's rule will return a killer, a rapist or other criminal to the streets and to the environment which produced him, to repeat his crime whenever it pleases him. As a consequence, there will not be a gain, but a loss, in human dignity. The real concern is not the unfortunate consequences of this new decision on the criminal law as an abstract, disembodied series of authoritative proscriptions, but the impact on those who rely on the public authority for protection and who without it can only engage in violent self-help with guns, knives and the help of their neighbors similarly inclined. There is, of course, a saving factor: the next victims are uncertain, unnamed and unrepresented in this case."

Most of the nation's police and prosecutors lined up with the minority group of justices. Publicly and privately, they were almost unanimous in a torrent of protest, in a cascade of warnings that the Supreme Court had finally "shackled," "handcuffed," and "strait-jacketed" lawmen whose only desire was to serve and safeguard society.

There was a familiar sound to these jeremiads. At the turn of the century, during the Roaring Twenties, and continually since World War II, with every perceptible increase in crime statistics the cry has reverberated that the nation is imperiled by a "crime crisis," that "criminals are being coddled," or that the courts are more considerate of the rights of criminals than of the rights of the public. When the police had virtually unlimited powers to obtain confessions, long before the Escobedo and Miranda Rulings, they continually issued the same gloomy appraisals. Naturally, after decades of dependence on the confession, they can be expected to overstate the indispensability of such evidence and accuse the Supreme Court of misapplying the eighteenth-century principle of non-self-incrimination to a twentieth-century milieu that has little similarity to the conditions prevailing in Colonial America. In the view of many police and prosecution officials, the Fifth Amendment has been outdated by modern crime methods. But here, too, the evidence seems to be against these confession advocates. Arthur E. Sutherland, Jr., Bussey Professor of Law at Harvard Law School, compared crime problems of the 1780's and the 1960's in a 1965 article in the *Harvard Law Review*—and found more similarities than differences between the two periods:

Sometimes the suggestion is made that today's statistics on crime demonstrate that criminological conditions in late eighteenth century America were so different from those today that constitutional principles then proclaimed are unsuited to modern cities. The incidence of crime in the 1780's and 1790's, when the Federal Bill of Rights of 1791 and the state bills of rights with similar provisions were being formulated and adopted, is even harder to ascertain than useful statistics in 1965. One can derive some idea of the commonest crimes from the scattered reports of decisions, from the few available texts, and from the notes of law teachers and students of that time. There were of course no great cities like those of the twentieth century and congestion is one factor in crime. But the available data suggest that the characteristic crimes of the late eighteenth century were the same offenses that today cause outcry against constitutional immunities. Little public emotion stirs today because of such late-vintage crimes as Food, Drug, and Cosmetic Act violations, or ingenious offenses under the Securities Exchange Act. People, quite understandably, get angered and alarmed at robbery, rape, and murder. Our forefathers committed these same crimes of bodily violence and depredation. The Bill of Rights of 1791 and state constitutions and statutes, adopted and enacted and reenacted from that time to our time, were devised precisely to make prosecution and conviction of these and other crimes more difficult. Our predecessors . . . distrusted arbitrary executive government, and chose to allow some guilty men to escape punishment rather than to subject themselves to unrestricted arbitrary power of officers, characteristic of what we now call a "police state."

Police reluctance to change their back-room manners is understandable, since the confession has become an ally for them in their daily tasks. Most detectives are not frozen in their jobs by protective civil service classifications. To remain out of an ordinary blue uniform, to keep his detective's badge and the extra pay, fringe benefits, promotions, and prestige it brings, a detective has to make arrests and make sure these arrests result in convictions. After years and years of misuse, the confession has become an easy and safe tool. "Grilling" has to some extent replaced the digging and investigation that the public assumes is the method used to catch most criminals. Too often, detective work consists of nothing more than finding a pliant and talkative suspect; then the evidence, if any exists, is collected.

Confessions are deemed so valuable that, even when there is tangible incriminating evidence, the police still like to "nail down" a suspect by using a confession as a hammer. Ironically, in each of the four cases of the Miranda Ruling there was either an eyewitness or other valuable evidence against the defendant; yet detectives were not satisfied until an admission was added to the record. Indeed, Ernesto Miranda was subsequently retried for rape and kidnapping, and without the confession as evidence he was convicted and sentenced to a minimum of twenty years in prison.

The back room has not only spawned unjust convictions, but as a factor in reducing crime—the very reason why, according to the police, it should be preserved—it probably has little value. The veteran or recidivist criminal (F.B.I. statistics reveal that seventy-six per cent of crime in the U.S. is committed by repeaters) probably suffers least from this American Inquisition. He is usually cognizant of all of his rights, and is less apt to be pressured into a statement. It is the person confronted for the first time with the terror of the back room who is more likely to confess falsely or make incriminating statements, even if innocent. Embedded in the confession system is a subtle discrimination against the poor and against the legal illiterates—the Whitmore species of suspect—who are either unaware of their rights or lack the means for quickly obtaining legal help. In a 1964 article, "An Historical Argument for the Right to Counsel During Police Interrogation," the editors of *The Yale Law Journal* denounced this double standard of justice in these terms:

> . . . The police speak continually of the dangers of organized crime when they seek to have their powers extended; yet the overwhelming majority of confession cases which have been before the

Supreme Court in recent years have involved either private crimes of passion or property crimes committed by sociopaths in the lower economic brackets. Thus there is a strong suspicion that it is only the weak and the first offenders who confess under police pressure while the hardened criminal knows of his right to keep silent and refuses to talk to the police, unless it is to his advantage in striking a "plea bargain.". . . The basic danger with interrogation is that use of it in many cases undercuts a basic premise of our system of justice; we do not feel that a man should be made against his will to condemn himself out of his own mouth.

Despite the Miranda Ruling, the suspect still has more to fear in the back room than the interrogator. Methods the police have relied upon for decades will not be discarded overnight. Oddly enough, Justice Harlan, in his Miranda dissent, touched upon this problem by predicting that police "who use third-degree tactics and deny them in court are equally able and destined to lie as skillfully about warnings and waivers. . . . The rules do not serve due process interests in preventing blatant coercion . . . they do nothing to contain the policeman who is prepared to lie from the start."

The universal police dismay at the ruling creates a mammoth doubt as to how willingly and scrupulously they will comply with it. Then, too, there is a hidden weakness in the Miranda Ruling: how will the courts determine if a suspect has waived his rights, even though the burden of proof must be borne by the interrogators? This weakness could lead to an endless series of debating matches in which a phalanx of detectives insist that the suspect confessed after being told of his rights, while a single defendant swears he did not. In the past, judges and juries, usually of middle-class background and temperament, have overwhelmingly trusted the testimony of the authorities when a disputed confession was the key issue. There is no reason to suspect that this trend will change overnight in favor of the accused. The reluctance of judges and juries to accept the word of one defendant when it is weighed against the evidence of detectives is an accepted fact of the judicial system. George Whitmore's history offers a prime example of what a defendant must overcome in a confession case. His trial for the murder of Mrs. Minnie Edmonds ended unresolved in a hung jury, although the only piece of evidence against him was a recanted confession. Even with an alibi and with the fraudulent Wylie-Hoffert confession to reinforce his argument, Whitmore was unable to convince a judge and four jurors that he had been forced into confessing falsely to the Edmonds slaying.

19. *The Thirteenth Juror*

Welcome mats for the public have never been part of the furnishings of police stations. Labeling themselves semimilitary, the police have made city precincts and rural barracks "off limits" to anyone they wish to exclude, and have operated in these places with whatever privacy they want. This secrecy undermines the Supreme Court's desire to bring the Constitution into the interrogation room. If a defense lawyer is not present during a confession—and this is certain to occur frequently—what test or what person will later confirm that a suspect waived his rights and voluntarily implicated himself? Whenever an admission is obtained in the absence of a defense counsel, a battle over a recanted confession probably will flare up

251

in a courtroom, thereby returning the confession controversy to the same cloudy realm it occupied before the Miranda Ruling.

In the aftermath of the Miranda Ruling, several police departments have begun groping for a foolproof system of verifying that they have complied with the new rules. New York City is planning an experiment with sound tapes and closed-circuit television to record the warnings given to suspects, and to record their actual statements. A similar pilot program, using television to monitor interrogation sessions, has been under way since August of 1966 in the detective bureau at the New Orleans police headquarters. Police officials in Detroit and Miami also are tinkering with the idea of using television tape as the best method of proving that they have met the court requirements. Reliance on television, however, presents one drawback. There is no way of establishing what happened off-camera before the question-and-answer interrogation began, and no way of establishing whether any coercion or coaching was employed prior to turning on the TV camera.

A simple way of fulfilling the goals of the Miranda Ruling, a practical method of verifying the legality of every confession, would be to introduce into the back room an impartial observer—the public's representative, the Thirteenth Juror.

The Thirteenth Juror would inform a suspect of his rights; and if the suspect confessed voluntarily without consulting an attorney, the Thirteenth Juror could later attest to this in court. With a Thirteenth Juror stationed in a precinct house, no question about the validity of a confession would arise, since he would hold the conclusive evidence of whether or not the police acted properly and the defendant intelligently waived his constitutional protections.

Formal legal training would not be necessary for the Thirteenth Juror. All he would have to know about criminal law is the essence of the Miranda Ruling: that every suspect has a right to remain silent; that he has a right to counsel, even if the police have to obtain a lawyer for him; and that the police can exert no pressure whatever on a suspect during interrogation. As soon as the police are ready to question a possible defendant at a station house—even before booking him—the Thirteenth Juror would have to be called in to inform him of his constitutional guarantees. If the suspect indicated his willingness to talk without consulting a lawyer, the Thirteenth Juror would remain in the interrogation room during the questioning. If the suspect requested an attorney, the Thirteenth Juror's responsibility would end as soon as the lawyer presented himself.

In most parts of the country, especially in large cities, there would be little difficulty in establishing a corps of impartial witnesses as eyes and ears of the public. State legislatures could empower the courts, the police, and bar associations to agree upon minimum qualifications for service. These standards should not preclude the participation of lower-income persons. A Thirteenth Juror need only have a background free of criminal taint, a high school education or its equivalent, and the ability to understand and fulfill his role in the back room.

Brief training courses given by bar associations or civil rights groups could teach laymen how to conduct themselves in the station house. The competence of each Thirteenth Juror could be certified by the local bar association or civic groups authorized by the judiciary.

A typical assignment for a Thirteenth Juror might develop in this manner: Upon entering a precinct, he signs in, specifying the time he arrived. In the interrogation room, he advises the suspect of his constitutional protections, explaining them and ascertaining that the suspect understands what they mean. If the suspect requests a lawyer, the Thirteenth Juror remains in the interrogation room as long as the suspect is kept there. As soon as a lawyer arrives, the Thirteenth Juror withdraws. If, however, the suspect declines any legal consultation, the Thirteenth Juror remains in the room until the interrogation is over. He is there to observe and listen—not to interfere in the questioning, offer suggestions, or advise the suspect in any manner. He notes the time the questioning begins, and the time it ends. If the result is an unchallenged confession, the Thirteenth Juror's job is finished. He would be called upon to testify only if the confession were recanted.

The expense of recruiting and administering these public witnesses would hardly be burdensome in comparison with the multimillion-dollar yearly cost of maintaining police departments, courts, prosecution staffs, and prisons. If many Thirteenth Jurors served without pay, the over-all cost would be insignificant. And quite possibly retired judges and lawyers, as well as law students eager for previews of police-station procedures, would agree to volunteer duty. Others without formal legal training probably would sign up with the same enthusiasm that is displayed by the thousands of persons who devote their free time to service as auxiliary policemen, volunteer firemen, or unpaid charity workers. Only big-city "combat precincts," which compile numerous confessions, would have to be staffed full-time by Thirteenth Jurors. Most station houses do not get confession cases very often, and they could be served adequately by Thirteenth Jurors "on call," who could be summoned when the police brought in a suspect for questioning.

The program would be feasible even in New York, which has more "combat precincts" than any city in the country. No more than fifty of New York's seventy-nine precincts are in neighborhoods with high crime rates. On any given day, a maximum of one hundred and fifty volunteers would be required to cover three eight-hour shifts at the fifty station houses. Eleven hundred volunteers—in a city of eight million—each putting in no more than one eight-hour tour of duty during the week, could cover all of New York's busiest precincts. And in smaller communities that have a single precinct or police barracks, communities where confessions are rarer than in big cities, the program would be simpler to maintain.

If the number of volunteers is inadequate, recruitment might be spurred by offering qualified trial jurors the alternative of serving as Thirteenth Jurors with the same token remuneration paid for courtroom duty. Their services possibly could save money for communities by preventing unnecessary trials. With a civilian looking on, the police would be restrained from resorting to threats or tricks. And a suspect who had waived his rights and confessed freely in the presence of an impartial witness would have second thoughts about lying to a jury. Everyone—the suspect, the police, and the public—would benefit from the Thirteenth Juror's confirmation of what happened in the back room. The suspect would be assured of being briefed on his rights, the public would have its fears about possible coercion allayed, and the police would be protected against fictitious charges of brutality or brainwashing.

The police can be expected to argue that the presence of an outsider in their midst, especially in the interrogation room, will further impede their crime-fighting efforts—which, many of them assert, already have been compromised by the Miranda Ruling. But there is no reason why a police station should be inviolate to public scrutiny. Moreover, the Thirteenth Juror would have no authority to examine confidential files or material evidence; he would not be privy to any strategy sessions among the police; and he would not be allowed to interview or observe the questioning of witnesses. His sphere would be the interrogation room and what occurred there.

Some may argue that the police might overcome the Thirteenth Jurors by frightening or brainwashing suspects into saying, untruthfully, that they want to confess; or that the Thirteenth Jurors might be manipulated into becoming part of the police establishment, convenient tools for fake confessions. But Thirteenth Jurors, instead of being converted into accomplices for false confessions, would through their watchdog presence be a deterrent against both subtle police coercion and harsh brutality. They would provide the strongest possible protection against infringements of constitutional rights in the back room. The police would have no control over the assignment of Thirteenth Jurors; and, more important, few police officers would jeopardize their jobs and pensions by asking a civilian— someone they may have never seen before—to join a conspiracy.

Without some such institution as the Thirteenth Juror, the vulnerabilities of the Miranda Ruling will transform this intended reform into an impotent document. Whenever a defense lawyer is missing from the interrogation room, the ruling becomes worthless, undermined by the same system that existed when Whitmore "confessed," two years before the decision was written. And Whitmore's plight spotlights weaknesses that remain as a legacy of the confession system.

The police officers who obtained Whitmore's confession insisted they had repeatedly informed him of his privilege to remain silent. They testified that Whitmore objected to having any relative or friend alerted to his arrest, or to calling anyone for help. In contrast, Whitmore later steadfastly denied that such offers were made. Under the terms of the Miranda Ruling, these same policemen could swear on the witness stand that Whitmore had been apprised of his constitutional rights, had been offered a lawyer, and had confessed anyway. Whom would a jury believe—the detectives or Whitmore?

The eventual appearance of Postal, an Assistant District Attorney from Brooklyn, and Koste, his counterpart from Manhattan, made little difference for Whitmore. At court hearings and trials, Whitmore could not recall having been questioned by either of the A.D.A.'s, although they undoubtedly interviewed him, Koste for more than two hours. Whitmore could have lied—and sounded more truthful—by claiming he confessed to the A.D.A.'s because he had been brainwashed or was too frightened to proclaim his innocence to them. His failure to remember Postal and Koste indicates how relentlessly the police machinery bore down on him; and, when viewed against the total background of events in the 73rd Precinct, his statement seems logical. By the time the assistant prosecutors arrived, Whitmore was in a miasma of bewilderment, exhaustion, and fear. Sixteen hours in the back room had transformed him into a robot capable of parroting a sixty-one-page confession to a double murder he could not have committed. Koste's casual advice, "You don't have to tell me anything," came much too late to do Whitmore any good.

Whitmore's confessions to the Borrero attack and the Edmonds murder also are full of puzzles. They contain numerous errors, such as his following Mrs. Borrero on wrong streets, and his identifying Mrs.

Edmonds, a forty-six-year-old Negro woman, as twenty-nine years old, white, and "Spanish." In the Borrero "Q and A," he omitted the climax of the crime—that a police officer came to Mrs. Borrero's rescue and chased and shot at him. In the Edmonds confession, he was confused about the identification of the murder weapon, and said he had washed the blood off his pants "the same night" of the murder, not the next morning as the detectives maintained he had previously told them.

The language used by Whitmore was untypical of his normal speech. He repeatedly used such strained-sounding phrases as "I tried to have relationship" or "intercourse," expressions commonly associated with police euphemisms in courtroom testimony. Whitmore's memory was further aided by leading questions and the "yes" and "no" answers that made up sixty per cent of each confession. The discrepancies, ambiguities, and mistakes in the confessions to the murder of Mrs. Edmonds and the attempted rape of Mrs. Borrero should have marked these statements as worthless—just as worthless as the Wylie-Hoffert confession. Yet neither of these supposed admissions was discarded under the old system, nor would they automatically be disallowed in a courtroom today.

What happened to Whitmore and Robles could happen again, any-where, any time a suspect is alone with the police. Until a sound system of verifying confessions is established, until more light is allowed to shine into the back room, there will be no way of forestalling the kind of inconclusive and questionable confessions that have made it virtually impossible to determine who killed Janice Wylie and Emily Hoffert.

Afterword

In the spring of 1967, four years after the Wylie-Hoffert murders, the concluding judicial word remains to be written for both Richard Robles and George Whitmore Jr.

Robles was sentenced to life imprisonment for the murders of Janice Wylie and Emily Hoffert. If his conviction is ultimately upheld, he will have to serve at least twenty-six years, until 1991, before becoming eligible for parole. While Robles attends to his chores at Clinton Prison in Dannemora, New York, his lawyers have put into motion slow-moving legal machinery that is intended to win him a new trial. The central points of Robles's plea for a second trial are that his constitutional rights were violated by the use of presumably illicit methods to obtain his alleged oral confession, and that the tape recordings of conversations in the Delaneys' apartment were inadmissible evidence. One vital element in Robles's appeal is the contention that he was deprived of his right to counsel by the police and two Assistant District Attorneys, who disregarded his frequent requests to see his lawyer.

If the tapes and the disputed confession are thrown out by the higher courts, the only remaining evidence against Robles will be the Delaneys' testimony. Under these circumstances, Robles's lawyers would probably put him on the witness stand, confident he could refute the Delaneys and leave the court a free man.

Whitmore, after being exonerated of the Wylie-Hoffert murders, went through two lengthy hearings and two trials in Brooklyn. In March 1965, two months after Robles's arrest, Whitmore's conviction for the attempted rape of Mrs. Elba Borrero was set aside because of racial slurs made by jury members during the trial. Ordering a new trial, Brooklyn Supreme Court Judge David L. Malbin declared: ". . . Whitmore was the victim of injustice . . . sufficient proof was produced to raise grave doubt whether the accused received a fair and impartial trial."

Whitmore was then tried for the murder of Mrs. Minnie Edmonds. That nineteen-day trial, which took place during April of 1965, culminated in a deadlocked jury. The jurors later told reporters that at one point in their deliberations, the vote was ten to two for acquittal. The only evidence against Whitmore was his alleged confession, and he had an alibi for his whereabouts at the time of the slaying. (Laboratory analysis of Whitmore's undershirt and trousers, once said to have been soaked with Mrs. Edmonds's blood, had proved inconclusive.) During the trial, he was still "discharged on his own recognizance" on the Wylie-Hoffert accusation, which meant that this indictment could be reinstated against him. Several jurors who voted for conviction were confused about whether he had really been cleared of the double murder.

Following the no-verdict Edmonds trial, Whitmore returned to the courtroom in March 1966, to stand trial again on the Borrero charge. His legal problems became further entangled during this trial. Because the presiding judge refused to permit the fictitious Wylie-Hoffert confession to be introduced as evidence, Stanley Reiben presented a mute defense, refusing to call a single witness or to deliver a summation to the jury. He maintained that the discredited confession was vital, because it reflected upon the testimony of Detectives Aidala and DiPrima, who had helped to obtain the Wylie-Hoffert, as well as the Borrero, confession. Without hearing defense testimony, the jury brought in a "guilty" verdict. Whitmore, thus convicted a second time of attempted rape and assault, was sentenced to five-to-ten years in prison.

The Supreme Court's Miranda Ruling did provide some help to Whitmore. Because he had not consulted a lawyer during his questioning at the 73rd Precinct, his confession to the Edmonds murder could not be introduced as evidence in a new trial. Brooklyn District Attorney Aaron E. Koota finally dropped the Edmonds accusation against him, in June of 1966. And on July 13, 1966, after twenty-six months in jail, Whitmore was freed in $5,000 bond while the second Borrero conviction was appealed.

Whitmore's lawyers arranged for him to live and work near Wildwood, New Jersey. Two months after his release, a young woman in Greenwich Village assertedly picked Whitmore's photograph out of the rogues' gallery, identifying him as a possible purse-snatcher. Two detectives drove her to

Wildwood. No charges were pressed when it was learned Whitmore had been in Wildwood on the day of the theft, which took place in New York. His lawyers, wondering how his photograph had conveniently appeared, accused the police of harassment.

The Whitmore family was seriously involved with the police again in February of 1967, while Whitmore was visiting his family in Brooklyn. Following a street brawl between Negroes and Puerto Ricans, Whitmore's younger brother, Gerald, was accused of murdering a man by stabbing him with a broken billiard stick. The charge was dropped by the Brooklyn District Attorney when an autopsy disclosed that the victim had not died from a wound inflicted by a billiard cue.

About this same time, a long-smoldering dispute erupted between lawyers Reiben and Arthur Miller over defense strategy at the second Borrero trial. Miller, as Whitmore's lawyer of record, announced that Reiben was no longer representing Whitmore, whereas Reiben maintained that he was still active in Whitmore's behalf. An appeal of the second Borrero conviction was filed by Miller and Osmond K. Fraenkel, a legal expert on civil rights. Their contention that the Wylie-Hoffert confession is an integral part of Whitmore's defense and should have been admissible evidence was upheld unanimously by a New York State appellate court which ordered a third trial for Whitmore on the charge of attempted rape and assault.

Thus, a jury may, for the first time, hear the full story of the Borrero case including: the complete circumstances of Whitmore's interrogation; a surprise witness who contradicts part of Mrs. Borrero's testimony; and an F.B.I. report that was not disclosed to the jury at the first trial. At that trial the prosecutor, in his summation, referred to the apparent incriminating link between the button Mrs. Borrero tore from the coat of her assailant and Whitmore's tan coat, which lacked three buttons. The prosecution, however, withheld as "inconclusive" evidence the findings of an F.B.I. laboratory analysis of the button and coat. This report, requested by the Brooklyn District Attorney's office, states: "The [button offered in evidence] and the buttons remaining on the coat are different in size, design and construction. Sewing thread attached to the [evidence] button is different from the sewing thread remaining on the coat in color, diameter and degree of twist. It was not possible to determine whether or not the . . . button had been attached to the . . . coat."

The police photographs taken of Whitmore after his arrest may also become a controversial issue. Although Lichtman, the prosecutor, declared, without being challenged, at the first trial that the photographs proved

Whitmore was uninjured, Reiben insists that a close examination reveals welts and bruises on Whitmore's back and shoulders.

In retrospect, police zealousness undoubtedly was a factor in saving Whitmore from a murder conviction. If he had been accused only of the Brooklyn crimes, these obscure cases would have received little notoriety. He probably would have been defended by a court-appointed lawyer, would have pleaded guilty to the Edmonds murder charge, and would now be a Sing-Sing cipher, serving a life sentence. The Wylie-Hoffert accusation put Whitmore in the spotlight, where someone had to notice him. Ironically, the notoriety attached to the Wylie-Hoffert "confession" helped to bring about a virtual end to capital punishment in New York State. The unjust accusation against Whitmore was cited by sponsors of the 1965 legislation.

Detectives Bulger and DiPrima, who were primarily responsible for obtaining Whitmore's admission to the double murder, have retired. Except for Captain Frank E. Weldon, who has died, the other police officers and prosecution officials involved in the lengthy interrogation at the 73rd Precinct remain at their jobs. The day after Robles's arrest for the Wylie-Hoffert murders, Michael J. Murphy, the New York Police Commissioner, ordered an investigation to determine who was responsible for Whitmore's discredited confession. Police officials have so far declined to reveal their findings because, they contend, these facts could prejudice Whitmore's remaining trial. Therefore, the results of that inquiry remain a secret.